The Books of Job

The Books of Job

By

Maurice J. O'Sullivan

CAMBRIDGE SCHOLARS PUBLISHING

The Books of Job, by Maurice J. O'Sullivan

This book first published 2007 by

Cambridge Scholars Publishing

15 Angerton Gardens, Newcastle, NE5 2JA, UK

British Library Cataloguing in Publication Data
A catalogue record for this book is available from the British Library

ISBN 1-84718-120-1; ISBN 13: 9781847181206

CONTENTS

Introduction 1

A Job Primer 9

Part One: Translation As Colloquy 17

Chapter One: Oh That My Words Were Now Written! Oh That They Were Printed in a Book! 19

Chapter Two: Knowest Thou The Ordinaces of Heaven? Canst Thou Set The Dominion There of on Earth? 37

Chapter Three: And Now Am I Their Song 61

Chapter Four: Hast Thou Perceived the Breadth of the Earth? 85

Works Cited 120

Part Two: The Books of Job 131

Chapter One: The Early Wycliffe Bible (c1382) 133

Chapter Two: John Purvey (The Later Wycliffe Bible, c1388) 134

Septuagint Addition (Charles Thomson,1808) 135

Chapter Three: Miles Coverdale (1535) 135

Chapter Four: The Matthews Bible (John Rogers, 1537) 136

Chapter Five: Richard Taverner (1539) 137

Chapter Six: The Great Bible (1539) 138

Chapter Seven: The Geneva Bible (1560) 140

Chapter Eight: The Bishops Bible (1568) 141

Chapter Nine: The Doway Bible (1609) 142

Richard Challoner's Revision (1750) 144

Chapter Ten: Hugh Broughton (1610) 145

The King James Version (1611) 147

Chapter Eleven: Joshua Sylvester (1614) 148

Chapter Twelve: Francis Quarles (1624) 149

Chapter Thirteen: George Sandys (1638) 150

Chapter Fourteen: Thomas Manley (1652) 152

Chapter Fifteen: Arthur Brett (1661) 154

Chapter Sixteen: Symon Patrick (1679) 157

Charles Garden (1796) 159

Chapter Seventeen: Richard Blackmore (1700) 161

Chapter Eighteen: Thomas Heath (1756) 164

Elizabeth Smith (1810) 164
Chapter Nineteen: William Langhorne (1760) 166
Chapter Twenty: Anthony Purver (1764) 167
John Fry (1827) 169
Chapter Twenty-One: Thomas Scott (1771) 171
Chapter Twenty-Two: Thomas Wemyss (1839) 173
Chapter Twenty-Three: George Hunt (1825) 175
Henry Tattam (1846) 176
Chapter Twenty-Four: John Hamilton Gray (1836, 37) 177
Chapter Twenty-Five: Isaac Leeser (1853) 178
Chapter Twenty-Six: The Earl of Winchilsea (1860) 179
Chapter Twenty-Seven: J.M. Rodwell (1864) 180
Chapter Twenty-Eight: Francis Bolton (1866) 182
Chapter Twenty-Nine: John Noble Coleman (1869) 183
Chapter Thirty: William Meikle (1869) 186
Chapter Thirty-One: Rossiter W. Raymond (1878) 188
Chapter Thirty-Two: Henry John Marten (1869) 191
Chapter Thirty-Three: William Kelly (1879) 193
Chapter Thirty-Four: Henry James Clarke (1880) 195
Chapter Thirty-Five: Samuel Cox (1880) 197
Chapter Thirty-Six: G.H. Bateson Wright (1883) 198
Chapter Thirty-Seven: Henry Frederick Gibbons and William M. Thompson (1889) 200
Chapter Thirty-Eight: Anonymous (1779) 203
Chapter Thirty-Nine: George H. Gilbert (1889) 210
Chapter Forty: Otis Cary (1898) 212
Chapter Forty-One: William Thompson (1726) 213
Farrar Fenton (1898) 215
Chapter Forty-Two: Ralph Sadler (1897) 216
Coptic Addendum: Henry Tattam (1846) 218
Testament of Job: Kaufmann Kohler (1897) 219

Part Three: A Job Bibliography of Translations 221

Index 241

INTRODUCTION

> Ye have heard of the patience of Job, and have seen the end of the Lord; that the Lord is very pitiful and of tender mercies.
>
> *The General Epistle of James*, 5:11

During the spring and summer of 2003, Jerome Saibil and Eli Batalion toured the American and Canadian fringe theater circuit with *JOB: The Hip-Hop Musical.* Performing as MC Abel and MC Cain, the two young Canadian composer/performers presented their experimental rap story of the trials of a successful young professional couple. This surprisingly effective contemporary interpretation of *The Book of Job* is simply one of the most recent attempts to reinterpret one of our culture's most enduring stories for a new audience.

A generation earlier, the opening scene of *Tender Mercies*, Bruce Beresford's 1983 film about loss and redemption, had Robert Duvall first appear on screen as a shadowy figure fighting an unidentified roommate for a last drink. Living frugally in a run-down motel on the edge of a nondescript Texas town, this broke and broken Country and Western singer and composer must cautiously piece together relationships with his family, his community, and his God as he confronts the Lord's tender mercies.

With his country gentleness and puzzled patience, Duvall's character differs radically from Muriel Spark's elegantly ineffective Harvey Gotham, the wealthy reclusive protagonist of her 1984 novel *The Only Problem.* In this sparely witty comedy of morals, the urbane Gotham has withdrawn to France to prepare a monograph examining how God could inflict so much suffering on Job, the only problem which he finds worth contemplating and the one which permeates his conversation and correspondence. Like *JOB: The Hip-Hop Musical*, the appearance of these two works in consecutive years, especially during a decade often dismissed for its emphasis on material values, reflects our continuing fascination with the story of Job.

That fascination can be traced throughout the literature of the last century. Just as H.G. Wells turned to Job as he puzzled over the legacy of the Great War in *The Undying Fire* (1919), Archibald MacLeish found him the perfect model for questioning the heritage of its successor in his Pulitzer Prize winning *J.B.* (1958). Where Robert Frost found a parallel to his own bleak, spare vision in *A Masque of Reason* (1945), Richard Wright could discover a prototype for his confused rebel Bigger Thomas in *Native Son* (1940) and Robert Heinlein a model for his comic science fiction voyager in *Job, A Comedy of Justice* (1984). *Job* has spoken equally effectively outside fiction. William Safire, the New York *Times*' resident iconoclast and language czar, sees its hero as an early pattern for Richard Nixon and other political outsiders in *The First Dissident: The Book of Job in Today's Politics* (1992), while David Penchansky imagines a neo-Marxist, postmodernist Job inspired by Frederic Jameson in *The Betrayal of God* (1990). Of course, this has not been an uniquely Anglo-American phenomenom during the twentieth century. Franz Kafka recreated Job's *Trial* in 1914; Oskar Kokoschka provided an expressionist vision of his crisis in his 1917 *Job*; Carl Jung offered his own *Answer to Job* in 1952; Elie Wiesel imagined the story in Eastern Europe as *The Trial of God* in 1979; and the noted Peruvian theologian Gustavo Gutiérrez found the book a source for liberation theology in *On Job: God-Talk and the Suffering of the Innocent* (1986).

This instinct not only to read *Job* but to re-imagine it echoes throughout Western history. Geoffrey Chaucer and Henry Fielding explored the book's comic possibilities; John Milton and Alexander Pope attempted to emulate it; and John Donne and Thomas Carlyle found it a rich mine for moral and aesthetic reflection. Its many translators have shared this imaginative process, engaging, as in all translations, in a dialogue of homage, commentary, and critique with the original. Each new reader has reinscribed *Job*; each new translator recreated it; and each new poet, novelist, or playwright reimagined it. The history of *Job* explains the title of this work, for there is no single *Book of Job*, rather a series of books of Job.

My purpose in the following sections is to concentrate on one aspect of one component of that history: English translations of *Job* through the end of the nineteenth century. I have chosen to focus on the period from Aelfric through 1900 for one major reason. For over two and a half centuries--from the middle of the seventeenth until the end of the nineteenth--a single work, the King James Bible, has shaped not only all English translations but the very ways in which English speakers conceived of Scripture and, arguably, of their very language. When the complete Revised Version appeared in 1885 and the American Standard Version in 1901, however, that hegemony collapsed. Despite the continuing popularity of the King James, it no longer occupies quite the same role. In all honesty, it could not. With an increasing interest in alternative versions legitimated by revisions of the King James and fueled by the improved global access to original texts, with the geometric growth of research universities, with an anomalous increase in both skepticism and fundamentalism, and with the great migrations which brought a rich tradition of Eastern European Jewish scholarship into more direct contact with England and the United States as their communities fled west, new translations inevitably arose to challenge the elegantly archaic language and occasionally questionable interpretations of the Authorized Version.

The twentieth century may well prove the most fertile and exciting period for biblical translation since the Renaissance. In addition to the American Standard Version in 1901, the *Twentieth Century New Testament: A New Translation into Modern English from the Original Greek*, Richard Francis Weymouth's *The New Testament in Modern Speech*, and Farrar Fenton's *Holy Bible in English* appeared soon after. During the Twenties versions by James Moffatt[1] in England and Edgar J. Goodspeed in America continued the movement to provide contemporary voices for scripture. Ronald Knox's Roman Catholic translations in 1944 and 1949 effectively replaced the Douai-Rheims Version, while the *Revised Standard Version* (1952) and *The Jerusalem Bible* (1966) achieved broad popularity. During the 1970s the *New English Bible*, the *New American Bible*, the *New American Standard Bible*, and the complete version of the *Living Bible* appeared, although the last work encountered broad scholarly opposition for its extensive paraphrasing before going on to sell some forty million copies in next quarter century. Other popular versions have been the *Anchor Bible* (1966-), the *Good News Bible* (1976), the *New International Version* (1978), the *New King James* (1982), and the Jewish Publication Society's *Tanakh* (1985).

By the end of the century, most of these works had appeared in revised editions: *The New International Version* (1985); *The New Jerusalem Bible* (1985); The New *Revised Standard Version* (1990, 1995); *The New Revised Standard Version* (1990); *The Revised English Bible* (1989), a revision of the New English Bible (1962, 70); *The New American Standard Bible* (1995); and *Tanakh* (1999). In addition, the *New Living Translation* appeared in 1996, along with revised editions of the individual books in works like the *Anchor Bible*. The last decade of the millennium also witnessed a series of fresh approaches to individual books and sections, most notably Everett Fox's *The Five Books of Moses* (1995), Ariel and Chana Bloch's *Song of Songs* (1995), and David Rosenberg's *The Book of J* (1990). Rosenberg had already published a number of translations, including his impressive *Job Speaks* (1977).

Ironically, this vast explosion of editions and translations has occurred as secular influences on culture have expanded with the Bible playing a decreasing role in shaping society. What for centuries had been a great dialogue centering on the King James became a series of parallel conversations whose center has shifted to the original Hebrew, Aramaic, and Greek texts. This shift makes such a clear line of demarcation at the beginning of the twentieth century that any study of the translations of the past hundred years requires an entirely different frame of reference from those which preceded it. On a purely practical level, access to twentieth-century works is widely available, unlike many of the translations discussed in this work.

In *The Cambridge History of the Bible* (1963-70), C.F. Evans and his fellow editors offer a wide ranging history of attempts to translate the entire Bible into English. Peter J. Thuesen traces the doctrinal motives and responses to the major translations, especially the King James and its revisions, in his *In Discordance with the Scriptures* (1999), while Willis Barnstone provides an impressionistic account of the King James as a paradigm of the intersection between translation theory and practice in *The Poetics of Translation* (1993). And in two impressively detailed volumes David Norton's *A History of the Bible as Literature* (1993) examines the growth of the Western, especially British and American, awareness of the Bible as a literary text susceptible to both literary appreciation and analysis. This study of *Job* is a reflection of that tradition. Norton inevitably focused on the New Testament and the Psalms in his highly readable, comprehensive discussion. My goal is far narrower. As both St. Jerome and Martin Luther pointed out, the unique stylistic, linguistic, and theological qualities of *Job* have made it a special challenge for translators, a challenge that has fascinated a surprisingly large number of men and women. This work is a study of that fascination.

Job's appeal to translators has covered a broad spectrum, from lords spiritual to lords temporal, from scholars seeking accuracy to men of leisure seeking applause. They range from a member of parliament to a beggar, from a Kentish wool merchant to the Earl of Winchilsea, from the first woman to translate a book of the Bible to the Metropolitan of Canada, from a chronologer of the City of London to the secretary for the American Continental Congress, and from the Roman Catholic Archbishop of Philadelphia to a British officer of the Raj. And these men and women have used their translations for everything from royalist apologetics to dissenting polemics, from orthodox endorsements of traditional beliefs to highly heterodox speculations, and from idiosyncratic metrical theories to curious experiments in spelling and syntax. Few, however, have taken so light a view as the dairy firm of H.A. Job which named its in-house journal *The Book of Job*.[2]

From a homily by Aelfric, the scholarly abbot of Eynsham whose work began defining the English language near the end of the first Christian millennium, to the translation of the dissenting scholar Hugh Broughton in 1610, much of the first stage of bringing the *Book of Job* into English represents a single movement in the larger pattern of translating the entire Bible, an effort which culminated in the King James and Douai-Rheims versions. Like a benevolent but forbidding parent, the King James or Authorized Version[3] would profoundly affect all future attempts at translation. At the very least, all translators would recognize that their work would be measured against it and, to a great extent, judged by that competition.

The King James would prove so dominant that it shaped even Roman Catholic and Jewish translations. Richard Challoner, the Bishop of Debra who would revise the Douai-Rheims translation in 1750, was himself a convert to Roman Catholicism. Raised on the King James as a Presbyterian, he relied heavily on its stately rhythms and accessible phrases in his revision. And when Jewish scholars in Britain prepared an English translation during the Victorian era for their rapidly assimilating communities, they largely reprinted the King James.

During the religious and political struggles to determine the future of the Stuart monarchy in the century which followed the translation inspired by the first of that dynasty, King James I, Job became a popular symbol for all sides. Dissenters appealed to broad audiences with paraphrases which envisioned him, like John Bunyan's Christian in *Pilgrim's Progress*, as a man zealously loyal to his God, struggling constantly to make sense of the relationship between them. Royalists, on the other hand, responded with versions that emphasized patience and reason while depicting Job as a graceful prince, noble in suffering and glorious in restoration.

By the eighteenth century, Job had metamorphosed into a philosopher king, capable of both elegantly neoclassical discourse and sublime flights of poetry. At the same time, his story became an essential part of the theological debate over the limits of reason and God's providential intervention in the world. While the rise of biblical scholarship introduced new texts and new ways of envisioning those texts, cultural tides like the emergence of women's voices, the migration of Jewish scholars, England's fascination with the orient, the secularization of culture, and the growth of romanticism all offered new opportunities for reinventing the text. By the end of the nineteenth century, Job had become even more polymorphic, with translators depicting him as an exotic Arabic prince, a skeptical modernist, a classical tragic hero, a sublime poet, and a divinely mad Romantic rebel, kin of Shelley and Prometheus.

The first part of this work examines the colloquy from which these versions emerged. Translating secular texts has always involved a complex interplay of knowledge and art, sources and commentary. Homer's *Odyssey* and *Iliad*, for example, "the texts most frequently translated into English" (Steiner, *Homer* xv), suggest this historical pattern. In an anthology of those translations, George Steiner has pointed out that, from George Chapman, Alexander Pope, and Alfred, Lord Tennyson to T.E. Shaw, Robert Fagles, and Derek Walcott, all translators have engaged "more or less openly" in a triangular competition with their originals and their immediate predecessors (xxvi). Like other biblical books, *Job*, of course, adds an additional dimension. Until the beginning of the twentieth century, translators had to respond not only to the original texts and their immediate predecessors, but to the King James Version as well.

Those responses clearly reflect a wide variety of motives. Some translators of *Job* were attempting merely to improve or clarify the Authorized Version; others sought to reconceive it, to orientalize it, to versify it, to modernize it, or simply to encounter it. For many, clarification and improvement meant ensuring that the English version provided the correct (i.e., their) theological, political, or literary values. After all, as William Warburton, the iconoclastic eighteenth-century bishop whose interpretation unleashed a torrent of invective, observed, "Orthodoxy is my doxy; heterodoxy is someone else's doxy."

My goal in tracing the history of these translations is to celebrate their diversity, while placing them in particular moments of British political history or within particular stylistic moments of literary history. I have discussed the chief theological issues implicit in the translations because those issues often profoundly shape what finally results. What emerges from all of these translations is not any single movement but a wide and fascinating conversation on all aspects of the *Book of Job*, and, to some extent, on the King James Version.

In Part Two I have combined over fifty of these versions into a composite translation. The first ten chapters trace the movement from the early Wycliffe Bible to the King James. From Chapter 11 through the end, including material from the Coptic addendum and the *Testament of Job*, I have included as wide a variety of voices and styles as possible. Most of these are unknown today, even though they include such extraordinary versions as those by Thomas Heath (1756), Elizabeth Smith (1810), and Rabbi Isaac Leeser (1853). While such a collective *Job* might never serve for simple devotional purposes, its very eclecticism and creativity show how complex, compelling, and paradoxical the colloquy on *Job* has been.

For those interested in comparing the same text in different hands, Part Three, which consists of a bibliography of translations into English through 1900, includes each translator's interpretation of 20:22, an unremarkable but ambiguous verse. Although the goal of the bibliography is to provide all of the major translations of at least a full chapter, including such noteworthy and idiosyncratic editions of those translations as Noah Webster's and Joseph Smith's editions of the King James, the evidence of those translators' practice demonstrates that, however broadly they reconceived *Job*'s form, most willingly accepted the guidance of the King James Version in its meaning. I have also included a few English versions and variants like William Caxton's *Golden Legend* and the *Testament of Job*, works which have proven influential in the ways people view *Job*.

For people like myself who have come to the Bible fairly late in life and are still puzzling through two millennia of biblical scholarship, interpretation, and polemics, I have added to the introduction a *Job* primer to outline some of the background which many of the translators brought to the text. My only *caveat* about that primer is to remember that every assumption about *Job* has been questioned and every assertion challenged.

Although all of the following questionable assumptions and challengeable assertions are my responsibility, I am profoundly grateful to those who have sparked my interest in *Job* and to those who have encouraged me to pursue that interest. Aubrey Williams introduced me to the providentialist debate almost two decades ago, and his extraordinary knowledge and careful scholarship have continued to offer a model few could hope to rival. Equally impressive have been my colleagues at Rollins who have always proven far better comforters than Job's. Karen Slater, the English Department's Administrative Assistant, has always found time for helping with the details that both research and manuscripts demand. Rollins College has provided financial support through its Ashforth and Critchfield funds, and creative librarians like Lynne Phillips and Dianne Walton have proven brilliant at uncovering the most deeply buried sources. And Linda M. Watson has been invaluable in helping to tame and edit material I have gathered over almost three decades. My students have consistently brought that quality of skepticism to their discussions which has made me constantly reexamine my views. My family, especially my son, Quinn, have indulged my whims with far more than Job's patience, for which I am, as always, indebted.

I read *Job* for the first time only after I had become a college professor. During that reading, I realized how much his comments echoed those of a group of insomniac inmates I had spent one college summer listening to as a jail guard working the late shift. All of them--from the most sociopathic to the most remorseful--had a deeply abiding sense of their own fundamental goodness and the essential injustice of life. As I found those same words and dilemmas reoccurring among my friends, my students, and in my own life, I came to realize how truly challenging and comforting this remarkable book can be.

When my marvelous younger son, Brendan, died less than a month after graduating as valedictorian at the University of Florida and only three months before he was scheduled to enroll in graduate school at Oxford, Job echoed even more profoundly in my life. Unlike Job, however, I found many true comforters among friends like Larry and Margaret DeVaro, Barry and Marilyn Lundin, and Marvin and Myrna Newman, along with my neighbors and colleagues, especially Rita Bornstein. While mourning Brendan, I realized that, like all who feel they and their loved ones suffer far out of proportion to any evil they may have committed, I am Job. Although I have not yet found the comfort in his book, I often turn to it for its truth.

And so I dedicate this work to my beloved Brendan Aren Micah O'Sullivan (1977-1999). May he rest in soft peace.

Maurice J. O'Sullivan
Winter Park, Florida

A JOB PRIMER

> [As] no History is more various, then *Iobs fortune*, so is no phrase, no style, more ambiguous, then that in which *Iobs history* is written; very many words so expressed, very many phrases so conceived, as that they admit a diverse, a *countrary* sense.
>
> John Donne, Sermons III, 189.
> January 7, 1621

There is little about the *Book of Job* on which scholars and critics have agreed. They have dated it everywhere from the Age of the Patriarchs (2100-1800 B.C.) when the story apparently occurs to the Hasmonean dynasty of the second century B.C.[4] They have found parallels to its form in everything from epic and Greek tragedy to lyrics and Platonic dialogues. And they have discovered analogues in Babylonian, Sumerian, and Egyptian texts. This primer, which outlines a number of issues to which various translators allude, offers a fairly simple introduction to the complex of issues surrounding this diverse, contrary book.

Language and Vocabulary

While all the books of the Hebrew Bible provide textual challenges, *Job* has proven the most challenging of all. The problems begin with the text. Of all the biblical books, *Job* has the largest number of *hapax legomena* (i.e., words used only once) and rare words. Because so many of these words appear to be a version of Hebrew strongly influenced by other Semitic languages, scholars and translators have made a linguistic act of faith in building interpretations based on cognate words or forms. Its distinctive language has even encouraged speculation from the medieval Rabbi Abraham Ibn Ezra through Thomas Carlyle to the contemporary Israeli scholar Naphthali Tur Sinai that Job may have been translated--or partly translated--into Hebrew from one of those other languages.

Usually alternative early versions of the Bible can help sort out such difficulties. In the case of *Job*, however, those versions simply provide additional challenges. The Greek Septuagint translation, for example, often provides a way of clarifying the Hebrew text. But the Septuagint, almost 400 lines shorter than the Hebrew, is less helpful than for other biblical books. Moreover, the uncertainty about the date of composition of the work's various sections profoundly affects the way even fairly common words might have been used.

A very simple example of the problems with *Job*'s language occurs in 1:5 when Job sacrifices for his children. The Hebrew explains that he does so because they might have "blessed God in their hearts." But this literal reading makes little sense. Most translators assume that the "bless" should actually be "curse," with the author--or a copyist--using either an idiomatic expression or a euphemism to avoid placing a word like "curse" next to a word for God. Moreover, in the Hebrew Bible the heart normally represents the source of ideas rather than emotions. Thus, Marvin Pope interprets this expression in the Anchor Bible as "cursed God in their minds" and a Jewish Publication Society translation offers "blasphemed God in their thoughts" (Greenberg, 3). Such linguistic cunundra led John Edwards in 1694 to conclude, with a playful turn on the nature of Hebrew, that in *Job* "the Sense sometimes as well as the Letters must be read backwards" (II, 343).

Perhaps the most dramatic textual issue revolves around one of the most important verses in literary and doctrinal terms. Because the received Hebrew text had only consonants and because Hebrew words change meaning with a change of vowels, between 500 and 1000 A.D. a group of rabbinic scholars, scribes, and editors created a system of vowel signs and accent markings to create a standard pronunciation and intonation. Known as the Masoretes (from *masora*, the word for tradition), these scholars worked not only to ensure a standard text but also to help preserve traditional pronunciations for reciting and singing the text during the diaspora. Most of the translations discussed in *The Books of Job* relied on the cumulative product of their scholarship, the Masoretic edition. That editing, however, affects a number of interpretations, most notably 13:15. The King James translation of this verse, arguably the most famous line in Job, became for Christians both an emblem of his patience and a motto for his faith: "Though he slay me, yet will I trust in him." But the Masoretes only created their text by mistaking a negative particle for a preposition. Once scholars reestablished the original text, the result, like the interpretation in the Revised Version of 1885, reflected a less patient, more rebellious figure as in the Revised Standard Version's translation: "Behold, he will slay me; I have no hope."

Organization

Obvious differences in language, form, and philosophy have long made scholars question the relationship of the prose frame of the prologue and epilogue with the verse body. Over time this discussion broadened to debate the relationship of sections within dialogues to each other. Although positions have become extremely complex, ranging from those who argue for a single author similar to Homer or the Beowulf poet creating a unified work of art out of multiple sources to those with various interpretations about how a composite text might have been compiled by different hands, almost all scholars recognize significant differences among various sections.

1. The Prologue (1-2) and Epilogue (42:7-17): Generally regarded as the oldest part of *Job*, these prose sections provide a fairly simple story of an

idealized man heroically and patiently enduring a profound test of his faith, reveal a belief in terrestrial justice, emphasize the importance of sacrifice, and use the names Yahweh and Elohim for God. Believed by many interpreters to have their roots in an ancient folk tale, these sections appear to represent the Job known to Ezekiel (14:14, 20) and celebrated by James (5:11). If the prose version existed before the Babylonian exile, Satan (the Adversary) may well be a later addition, a product of some interaction with Zoroastrian beliefs during the post-exilic Persian period sometime after 538 B.C.E.
2. The Dialogue (3-31): The consistency of tone and language in Job's monologue (3) and the three cycles of speeches in which his friends challenge Job's innocence while he defends himself suggests a single author for this section. Even here, however, some structural problems exist. In the first two cycles (4-14 and 15-21), the book has each friend present an argument followed by a response from Job. In the third cycle (22-31), on the other hand, Bildad's third speech is abbreviated and Zophar's is missing. Moreover, during this cycle Job presents his friends' arguments in a way which suggests some confusion in editing the material.
3. The Hymn to Wisdom (28): Although similar in style and language to the dialogue, this poem, admitting that man cannot fathom divine wisdom, scarcely seems consistent with Job's arguments through the dialogues. Some critics suggest it comes from a different section of the book; others argue that it may be a separate poem by the same author which became folded into *Job*.
4. The Elihu Speeches (32-37): Elihu's abrupt appearance, his apparent knowledge of the older friends' arguments, the failure to mention him in either the prologue or epilogue, Job's lack of a response, and God's lack of either a commendation or a condemnation for his argument all suggest that this section may be a later addition.
5. The Theophany (38-42:6): Critics have seen God's appearance and two speeches both as the artistic and thematic climax of the book and as an inferior afterthought or addition. Although most readers admire the first speech (38-39), some judge the second, with its emphasis on Behemoth and Leviathan followed by Job's abject submission, as unnecessarily cruel and redundant. And some passages seem to need editing. In Job's final submission (42:1-6), for example, the first part of verse three and all of verse four are taken from God's speech. Either they were accidentally included here or they indicate that Job has paid close attention and now demonstrates his obedience by quoting from God's speech

Genre

Finding that *Job* did not fit neatly into any single genre and not content with regarding it as *sui generis*, critics have struggled to work it into most traditional forms while rationalizing its idiosyncracies. As with so much of the writing about *Job*, most of these attempts reflect assumptions about the age, culture, and author based on possibilities within the text. Among English commentators and translators, four main traditions exist. The oldest, part of the tradition in which early Church Fathers saw much of the Hebrew Bible as a typological foreshadowing of Christ and the Christian Church, views it as an allegory. Reading *Job* allegorically, a practice which parallels the third-century C.E. Palestinian amora Rabbi Simeon ben-Lakish's argument that the work should be read as a parable, would later evolve into Bishop William Warburton's detailed providentialist allegory and such other emblematic, allegorical readings as that of Thomas Dowglass in 1853 who saw the entire book as an allegorical history of the Christian Church with Job's boils representing the condition of the faithful when the Church is torn by heresy and schism and his three friends the Roman, Greek, and Protestant churches.

John Milton's assumption that *Job* offered "a brief model of the epic" (*Reason of Church Government*, 813) carried significant weight for the following two centuries in works ranging from Sir Richard Blackmore's heroic version in 1700 to the Earl of Winchilsea's romantic interpretation in 1860. As an equally classical alternative to the epic, numerous critics and translators from many of the seventeeth-century Stuart supporters to H.M. Kallen's *The Book of Job as a Greek Tragedy Restored* (1918) have followed the fourth century Theodore of Mopsuestia in regarding *Job* as a drama, most often as a tragedy. Other forms of drama have been suggested from John Dennis who suggested that the work resembles "Poesy in which Persons are introduc'd who are talking in Dialogue" ("Preface," n.p.) and John Garnett who concluded that "it is a drama of a single act" (300) to Robert Frost who presented it as a masque.

By linking dramatic elements with an emphasis on *Job*'s poetic quality, Dennis points the way to the fourth tradition, while suggesting that these traditions need not be mutually exclusive. Regarding *Job* as first and foremost a poem, translators often adapted it to their preferred forms, as Milton had with the epic. St. Jerome and Thomas Aquinas, clearly influenced by Greek and Roman models, concluded that the original was in hexameters, just as many of those influenced by Milton and the neoclassicists opted for blank verse or heroic couplets. But a number of translators, believing the poem essentially a lyric or a series of related lyrics, experimented with other forms, as in the elegiacs of Thomas Wemyss (1839) or the odes of Arthur Brett (1661) and Henry John Marten (1869).

Many have tried to merge categories, as when John F. Genung suggested similarities to everything from Robert Browning's monologues to epic, classical tragedy, legend, saga, debate, and lyric. The twentieth century has provided even better analogues, especially, for me, in the highly Joban plays of Samuel Beckett.

Meaning

Much of *Job*'s appeal lies in its essential ambiguity. It has provided a text both for those who would argue for a divinely providential vision of life as well as for those who would challenge Albert Einstein's oft quoted comment that God does not play dice with the universe. At the heart of the difficulty is the essential question of *Job*: during the eighteenth century Bishop Francis Hare defined it as "cur malis bene, et bonis male" (Spence I, 389). If the universe is essentially moral, why do bad things happen to good people? And why do the evil seem to prosper? (In our less classical age, Rabbi Harold Kushner captured this most frustrating of human problems in the rather more pragmatic and temporal title of his bestselling meditation *When Bad Things Happen to Good People* [1981].)

From the very opening of the *Book of Job*, there is little doubt that its hero is a good man. Even God singles him out for admiration. But why would a benevolent, omnipotent deity allow such an emblematic moral human being to suffer so much physical, emotional, and psychological pain? And why does God seem to provoke Satan into initiating the suffering? The various characters in *Job* appear to offer at least five very different responses to this dilemma:

1. Satan, literally translated as the Adversary, views the suffering as both a test of Job's loyalty and a challenge to the God who boasts so broadly about his servant's admirable qualities.
2. Job's three older friends--Eliphaz, Bildad, and Zophar--argue for a terrestrial eschatology, a kind of poetic justice in which happiness and suffering come to us in direct proportion to our goodness and sinfulness ("Remember. I pray thee, who *ever* perished, being innocent? or where were the righteous cut off?" [4:7]). Because they also believe the corollary (i.e., a person's goodness or sinfulness can be inferred from his or her physical and material condition), they conclude that Job must be sinful ("If thou *wert* pure and upright; surely now he would awake for thee, and make the habitation of thy righteousness prosperous" [8:6]). And so they beg him to repent ("If thou return to the Almighty, thou shalt be built up, thou shalt put away iniquity far from thy tabernacles" [22:23]) and receive his reward from a just God.

Although all three of his older friends present the same argument, some readers see differences among their approaches. Eliphaz, perhaps the eldest because he speaks first, seems the most sympathetic and often draws on experience to make his case. Bildad, the second speaker and perhaps next oldest, believes in traditional authority. In contrast, Zophar appears the least sympathetic and most absolute in his theology. As their dialogue continues, all become markedly less sympathetic. Eliphaz even cites Job's sins (22:5-9), including dishonesty, cruelty, and lack of charity (e.g., "Thou hast sent widows away empty, and the arms of the fatherless have been broken" [22:9]). One highly regarded critic, Sir Arthur Quiller-Couch, summarized his impressions of this curious trinity in an essay in *On the Art of Reading*: "I find Eliphaz more of a personage than the other two; grander in the volume of the mind, securer in wisdom; as I find Zophar rather a mean-minded greybeard, and Bildad a man of the stand-no-nonsense kind" (204).

3. Rejecting his friends' arguments and charges ("God forbid that I should justify you: till I die I will not remove my integrity from me" [27:5]), Job assumes that God has abandoned him ("Behold, I go forward, but he *is* not *there*; and backward but I cannot perceive him" [23:8]). He can only conclude that God does play dice with mankind and, therefore, cannot be just: "Behold, I cry out of wrong, but I am not heard: I cry aloud, but *there* is no judgment" (19:7). He supports his position by pointing out that, contrary to his friends' argument, the wicked are not always punished and, indeed, occasionally prosper ("Wherefore do the wicked live, become old, yea are mighty in power?" [21:7])

4. Elihu, while repeating many of the other friends' arguments, also makes a case that suffering may be both disciplinary and cautionary. It is not necessarily a response to our actions but a lesson to help us towards greater self-awareness ("To bring back his soul from the pit, to be enlightened with the light of the living" [33:30]).

5. The theophany presents Job with a series of unanswerable questions which imply that human suffering, like so many of the mysteries of the universe, is an enigma which man cannot comprehend. God offers a final irony in this ambiguous conclusion by condemning the three older friends for their argument of terrestrial justice ("Ye have not spoken of me *the thing that is* right" [42:7]) before offering rich earthly rewards to Job, apparently for his goodness. What seems to be God's insistence on faith in the presence of the unknowable inspired the remarkably powerful conclusion to Alexander Pope's first *Essay on Man* (1733), a poem which, in turn, inspired William Warburton's extraordinarily controversial and highly idiosyncratic reading of *Job*:

> Cease then, nor ORDER *Imperfection* name:
> Our proper bliss depends on what we blame.
> Know thy own *point*: This kind, this due degree
> Of blindness, weakness, Heav'n bestows on thee.
> Submit--in this, or any other sphere,
> Secure to be as blest as thou canst bear:
> Safe in the hand of one disposing Pow'r,

Or in the natal, or the mortal hour.
All nature is but art, unknown to thee;
All chance, direction which thou canst not see;
All discord, harmony not understood;
All partial evil, universal good:
And spight of pride, in erring reason's spight,
One truth is clear; "Whatever *Is*, is RIGHT."

(I, 273-86)

PART ONE: TRANSLATION AS COLLOQUY

CHAPTER ONE

Oh That My Words Were Now Written! Oh That They Were Printed In A Book! (19:23)

Thei wil saye [the Bible] can not be translated into our tonge, it is so rude. It is not so rude as thei are false lyers.
William Tyndale, The *Obedience* of a *Christian* Man (1528)

Tyndale's thunderous denunciation of all who opposed an English translation of the Bible epitomizes both the spirit and the substance of that epic process. Although the evolution of an English Bible often appears an arc from John Wycliffe to King James, it more clearly reflects a dialectic with the established English Church slowly but methodically appropriating work from those either on its fringes or in formal doctrinal opposition. Eventually, translations by Lollards and Calvinists, moderate dissenters and clerics burnt for heresy would shape the rhetoric and vision of what was to become known as the Authorized Version. The very nature of this dialectical process encouraged polemical commentaries rather than systematic discussions of literary technique. Caught in a web of ideological, doctrinal, and personal battles, translators invariably focused less on defining their methodology than on disparaging their foes.

Any discussion of the process of Englishing the *Book of Job* must reflect this larger dialectic in which authorized translations mediated among competing interpretations. But the very ambiguities in *Job* which had encouraged a tradition of typological and symbolic interpretation among theologians offered an additional set of perspectives not only on the way the Bible became translated but also on the ways those translations reflected political, religious, and cultural assumptions, assumptions which influenced and were, in turn, influenced by each new translation of this richly complex book. The first stages of this process began with the earliest attempts to provide English versions of the Bible and concluded at the end of the seventeenth century as the religious wars subsided with the defeat of the Catholic James II at the Battle of the Boyne and the broad acceptance of an

Act of Settlement ensuring a Protestant succession to the throne.[1]

During this first stage, as the King James Version not only emerged but achieved hegemony among its many rivals, translators, whatever their actual practice, publicly adhered to a set of common principles. But the *Book of Job*, widely recognized as the most ambiguous and the most difficult to translate of all the biblical texts, offered a significant challenge to theory as well as practice. Even as the King James became the Established or Authorized Version during the seventeenth century, its supporters and opponents found it necessary to qualify its version of *Job*. Debates over the language and meaning of this knotty, complex book allowed it to assume a distinctive role in the political and religious struggles of the century, a role that built upon much earlier traditions.

I

> This blessid man Iob thankyd God of His excellence
> That yt pleasid His incomprehensible deite
> So to indwe hym with the spyrite of recistence
> In pacience to withstonde the devell his iniquyte.
> And of his restoracion proude was never he,
> But ever thankyd God in well and in sorowe,
> For to-day a man may be and none in morowe.
>
> *Life of Job* (c.1473)

Despite occasional distinctions between secular and religious works, translators of both shared a common heritage in a loosely accepted set of assumptions about the nature and practice of translation, assumptions which gained authority from the two leading Roman arbiters of literary style and St. Jerome (c347-419), author of the Vulgate, the canonically mandated Latin version of the Bible.[2] Both Cicero's *De optimo genere oratorum* ("non verbum pro verbo")[3] and Horace's *Ars Poetica* ("nec verbo verbum")[4] warned against literal translations, counseling instead a creative role for the translator in capturing the spirit or sense of a work rather than providing a simple word-for-word version.[5] For those who sought guidance from religious rather than secular authority, the writings of Jerome, a man well versed in both Cicero and Horace, offered an extensive, scholarly commentary on the philosophy and practice of translation.

Jerome's most famous discussion of translation occurs in a letter to Pammachius, a Roman senator who had renounced the world to become a monk. "Epistola LVII," a curious blend of scholarship and paranoia--Jerome in a remarkably bitter outburst attacks a colleague who had copied one of his translations as a false monk and second Judas--cites Cicero and Horace as models and "freely confesses that in translating from the Greek (except in cases of the holy scriptures where even the order of words is a mystery) I express sense for sense and not word for word" (*Lettres*, III, 59).[6] Despite this exclusion of scripture, Jerome eventually turns to the practice of New Testament writers to justify the classical tradition of preserving the sense rather than the words:

> There is clear evidence that the apostles and evangelists, in translating the old testament scriptures, have sought to preserve the sense not the words, and that they have not taken great care to preserve the original forms or constructions, so long as the point was clear to the understanding.
>
> *Lettres*, III, 69.[7]

In the preface to his Vulgate *Job*, Jerome acknowledged the distinctive literary qualities and linguistic challenges that encouraged a similar approach in mazing through the difficulties of this particular text:

> The present translation follows no ancient translator, but will be found to reproduce now the exact words, now the meaning, now both together of the original Hebrew, Arabic, and occasionally the Syriac. For an indirectness and a slipperiness attaches to the whole book, even in the Hebrew; and, as orators say in Greek, it is tricked out with figures of speech, and while it says one thing, it does another; just as if you close your hand to hold an eel or a little muraenam [i.e., a small fish] the more you squeeze it, the sooner it escapes.
>
> (491)

Following the tradition of the third-century Alexandrian biblical scholar Origen, St. Jerome identified those passages missing or mangled in the earlier Latin translations with asterisks, a practice similar to the italics which would mark those words added to the King James Version to complete the sense of a thought or phrase. Earlier, in his "Preface" to the *Chronicle of Eusebius* (c382), after praising the poetry of *Job*, he pointed out how awkward and incoherent these early Latin translations seem:

> When we read [Deuteronomy, Isaiah, Ecclesiastes, or Job] in Greek, they have some meaning; when in Latin they are utterly incoherent. But if any one thinks that the grace of language does not suffer through translation, let him render Homer word for word into Latin. I will go farther and say that, if he will translate this author into the prose of his own language, the order of the words will seem ridiculous, and the most eloquent of poets almost dumb.
>
> (484)

Even though, from most modern perspectives, Jerome advised more latitude than he took--and he may have, in his usual defensive mode, simply been preparing himself for attacks--his validation of the classical latitudinarian philosophy established a basis for connecting the practice of biblical translation with the traditions of secular translation. Following in this spirit, Martin Luther, whose German translations proved both an inspiration and a model for the British reformers, defined his own goal in terms of audience and language: "I have constantly tried, in translating, to produce a pure and clear German, and it has often happened that for two or three or four weeks we have searched and inquired for a single word and sometimes not found it even then. In translating Job . . . I labored so, that sometimes we scarcely handled three lines in four days" ("On Translating," 188).[8] Later, in an addition to his "Preface to the Book of Job," Luther makes his case for *sententia* even more explicit, although he apparently cannot help himself from slipping into the anti-Semitism that so often pervades his polemics:

> The language of [*The Book of Job*] is more vigorous and splendid than that of any other book in all the Scriptures. Yet if it were translated everywhere word for word--as the Jews and foolish translators would have it done--and not for the most part according to the sense, no one would understand it.
> (252)

In England, the secular rejection of word-for-word translation, even among those engaged in providing English versions of prose works, suggests a broad agreement in viewing translation as an art rather than a craft and relying on inspiration more than rules.

Although a sophisticated, detailed discussion of secular translation would not appear in England until John Dryden's prefaces at the end of the seventeenth century,[9] the rare and unsystematic discussions of translation--as opposed to the frequent debates over the need for and propriety of translation--reflect a rough consensus. Within this fairly informal dialogue, the two most influential commentators, George Chapman (?1559-?1634) and Sir John Denham (1615-1669), described a set of values that helped shape British attitudes toward translations in general and literary, poetic translation in particular. The essential harmony between their views testifies to the continuity at the core of British translation through the end of the eighteenth century. Both poets fall into the tradition of privileging the sense over the word. In discussing his popular and highly influential translation of Homer--the complete *Iliad* appeared in the same year as the King James Version--Chapman's fairly abstract and highly metaphorical comments emphasize not technique but empathy. In his *Euthymiae; or the Teares of Peace* (1609), for example, Homer's ghost speaks of a mystical communion between his soul and his translator's

> . . . a sweet gale
> Brought me upon thee; and thou didst inherit
> My true sense (for the time then) in my spirit;
> And I, invisiblie, went prompting thee
> To those fayre Greenes where thou didst english me.
>
> ll. 82-86

This emphasis on both sense and spirit, as well as Chapman's note that literalism "hath made even th' ablest Agents erre" ("To the Reader," l.94), prepared the way for the profoundly individual and literary tradition of classical translation that would flourish in England after the Restoration of 1660.

Well known for imitating portions of Virgil's *Aeneid*, Sir John Denham's greatest influence on English translation occurred in commendatory verses for Sir Richard Fanshawe's version of Baptista Guarini's *Il Pastor Fido* (1648). In emphasizing both the novelty and achievement of his friend's work, Denham's poem, one of the most cited documents in discussions of English translation, echoes and extends the language of Horace and Cicero:

> That servile path thou nobly dost decline
> Of tracing word by word, and line by line.
> Those are the labour'd births of slavish brains,
> Not the effects of Poetry, but pains;
> Cheap vulgar arts, whose narrowness affords
> No flight for thoughts, but poorly sticks at words.
> A new and nobler way thou dost pursue
> To make Translations and Translators too.
> They but preserve the Ashes, thou the Flame,
> True to his sense, but truer to his fame.
>
> (143-44)

In much the same metaphoric tradition as Chapman, Denham's emphasis on this "new and nobler way" actually continues the literary argument for avoiding simple literal translations. Denham appears, however, to go beyond even Chapman by preferring an author's fame to his sense, suggesting that the translator's primary responsibility lies in discovering a way to recreate within the language of the translator analogues to the original work's distinctive style rather than in preserving its ideas. This point reappears in a passage which Dryden would cite from the "Preface" to Denham's *The Destruction of Troy* (1656), a passage whose language explicitly acknowledges the authority of both Horace and Chapman:

> It [is] a vulgar error in translating Poets, to affect being a *Fides Interpres*; let that care be with them who deal in matters of Fact, or matters of Faith: but whosoever

> aims at it in Poetry, as he attempts what is not required, so he shall never perform what he attempts; for it is not his busines alone to translate Language into Language, but Poesie into Poesie; & Poesie is of so subtile a spirit, that in pouring out of one Language into another, it will all evaporate; and if a new spirit be not added in the transfusion, there will remain nothing but a *Caput Mortuum*.
>
> (159)

Just as Jerome had not always followed his own principles, Stuart translators of *Job* would not always abide by Denham's distinction between works of poetry and works of faith. Like the faithful royalist Fanshawe, secretary of war to Prince Charles, and Denham himself, famous for his fiercely satiric verses against Presbyterians and parliamentarians, they often emphasized the poetic qualities of the book and the regal attributes of its hero. Puritans, on the other hand, tended to envision both a text and hero of simple, sincere, abiding faith, expanding it through paraphrase only to make it accessible as broad an audience as possible.

II

> The Scripture is the Paradise, the garden of God upon earth: and these Poeticall Books are (as I may say) as so many goodly knots in the midst of that garden.
>
> Arthur Jackson, "Dedication,"
> *Annotations upon the Five Books Immediately Following the Historicall Part of the Old Testament* (1658), n.p.

While British translators inherited a set of common assumptions about the nature and practice of translation that stretched from the classical world through the end of English neoclassicism, the Christian vision of *Job* had not been so simple, coherent, or consistent. Judaism had had a long and rich tradition of analysis, debate, and dialogue, but Christianity, for the most part, had largely ignored Jewish scholarship as its view evolved from allegorical exposition to doctrinal debates.[10] Working from the allusion in the Epistle of James, the Christian Job became an exemplary saint and type of Christ. Because the prologue and epilogue were far easier to reconcile with this view than the dialogues, the prose sections helped to establish the popular image of a patiently suffering and richly rewarded *exemplum*. Until the Bible became widely available in England, even the clergy tended to view *Job* through a set of prisms created by the prose sections, by apocryphal traditions like the pseudipigraphal Greek *Testament of Job*,[11] by liturgical uses, and by the commentaries of his most influential interpreters like St. Jerome, Pope Gregory the Great, Thomas Aquinas, Martin Luther, and John Calvin.[12]

Even though the commentators agreed on such personal qualities as Job's sanctity and patience, they often struggled with the text to reconcile these virtues with his actual words. Jerome and Gregory resolved this dilemma by focusing their discussions less on the text than its allegorical and typological possibilities.[13] In his *Moralia*, Gregory (c540-604) had described his approach in a prefatory "Epistle to Bishop Leander": "But be it known that there are some parts which we go through in a historical exposition, some we trace out in allegory upon an investigation of the typical meaning, some we open in the lessons of moral teaching alone, allegorically conveyed, while there are some few which, with more particular care, we search out in all these ways together, exploring them in a threefold method" (I, 7). Although Jerome tended to be a bit more literal and historical in his discussion, his interest in typological reflection profoundly affected his conclusions.

Attempting to establish an orthodox Christian *Job*, medieval theologians often found themselves compelled to focus their attention on extratextual readings, concluding, as one anonymous twelfth century letter advised, that the *Book of Job* has "no useful literal meaning and should be interpreted, forthwith, of Christ and the Church" (Smalley, 89). Such expositions, reinforced by the work's inherent complexities in language and meaning, both encouraged the role of authority in interpretation and legitimized subsuming the text into broader arguments, preparing for the emblematic interpretations through the end of the seventeenth century that focused as much on politics and power as on theology and philology. Just as the Calvinists' paraphrases attempted to demystify *Job*, scholarly complexity clearly offered a justification for authority in interpretation. In *A Discourse concerning the Authority, Stile, & Perfection of the Books of the Old and New Testament* (1694), for example, John Edwards argued that the more typological and mystical the sense of scripture, the more need of an authority like the Church of England to unravel them.

As the Church of England became more Protestant and less Catholic, many of its clergy found such concerns of the Church fathers increasingly dated and misguided. By the middle of the nineteenth century, Jerome and Gregory's typology could only garner a bemused scorn from such pillars of the established church as the Rev. George Croly, Rector of the united parishes of St. Stephen's, Walbrook, and St. Benet's:

> Jerome in his *Interpretation*, regards the Book as typical of Christianity; Job as the type of Christ; the Land of Uz as the Virgin Mary; the seven sons of Job as the seven forms of the Holy Spirit; the three daughters as the Law, the Prophets, and the Gospel; the Camels as the Gentiles; and the oxen as the Jews!
>
> Pope Gregory the Great (about AD 604) in his *Morals on the Book of Job*, also regards Job as a type of Christ, but apportions the other characters with

> a different exercise of imagination. His wife is the carnality of the world; his friends are the heretics inveighing against our Lord under pretence of giving him counsel; the name of Job, which he interprets "Grief," exhibiting the Passion of the Redeemer, or the Sufferings of the Church; and the reward and reconciliation of Job the general conversion of mankind.
>
> (4-5)

Croly's ironic summary suggests how far traditional typology had fallen into disrespect among many of the Victorian clergy. What had occured by then, however, represent more a metamorphosis than a fundamental shift in approach as Victorians substituted the idea of Job as a symbol for Job as a type or allegory. Thus, Croly presents Job as the romantic quester, like Byron, Shelley and Browning's Childe Roland, offering his admiration in language that our age, in its own turn, might find uncomfortable: "The true reason for his trial appears to have been the necessity of making him acquainted with his own heart. He was *self-righteous*" (43). As with all preceding ages, the Victorians found in Job a model of their own ideal.[14]

Unlike Jerome and Gregory, Thomas Aquinas (1225-1274) focused entirely on the text itself to demonstrate that "human events are ruled by divine providence" (ii). Although Aquinas occasionally offers a comment on the characters' behavior as when he observes that "Yahweh chided Job for his incautious speech" (533),[15] he excuses himself from having to deal with matters other than divine providence by observing that Pope Gregory "has so subtly and clearly exposed the mysteries of this (book) there seems to be nothing beyond, that must be added" (iv). Indeed, in his absolute focus on the role of God, Aquinas is almost singular in never mentioning Job's patience. Martin Luther agreed with Aquinas about Job's sin--"Finally, however, God decides that Job, by speaking against God in his suffering, has spoken wrongly" ("Preface to Job," 252)--but shifted his emphasis to Job's essential humanity as the occasion for that sin while providing an implicit argument for his doctrine of justification by faith:

> But this is written for our comfort, that God allows even his great saints to falter, especially in adversity. For before Job comes into fear of death, he praises God at the theft of his goods and the death of his children. But when death is in prospect and God withdraws himself, Job's words show what kind of thoughts a man--however holy he may be--holds toward God: he thinks that God is not God, but only a judge and wrathful tyrant, who storms ahead and cares nothing about the goodness of a person's life. This is the finest part of this book. It is understood only by those who also experience and feel what it is to suffer the wrath and judgment of God and to have his grace hidden.
>
> ("Preface to Job," 252)

As the Church of England's biblical translators followed Luther's example, their challenge would be to integrate his scholarship with the traditions of the classical Church fathers by finding a vocabulary and rhetoric that would preserve the essence of scripture in a language that would appeal deeply and broadly to a British audience.

III

> Men speke of Job, and moost for his humblesse,
> As clerkes, whan hem list, konne wel endite,
> Namely of men, but as in soothfastnesse,
> Though clerkes preise wommen but a lite,
> Ther can no man in humblesse hym acquite
> As womman kan, ne kan been half so trewe
> As wommen been, but it be falle of newe.
>
> Geoffrey Chaucer
> The Clerk's Tale. IV, 932-38

Aside from a brief paraphrase of the prologue and epilogue in a sermon by Aelfric, the Benedictine abbot of Eynsham who died around 1020, and nine passages used as lessons in the Office of the Dead,[16] popularly known as the *Pety Job*, the first English translations of *Job* appeared as part of efforts to translate the whole of the Bible. While that epic process which began with John Wycliffe and culminated in the King James and Douai-Rheims Bibles has been extensively documented, a brief review of it suggests the context which would affect all future biblical translators.[17] From Wycliffe to the King James Version, that process reflects a dialectical pattern in which the established church continually found ways to absorb the initiatives of dissenters. *Job* represents a microcosm of this dialogue to define an effective and theologically accurate language for the word of God.

Underlying the attempts to find an English voice for scripture lay a dedication to explication as well as translation. This concern with explaining the text led translators both to annotate extensively[18] and to adopt consciously and unconsciously the principles and language of Cicero, Horace, and Jerome. John Purvey himself argued that "the best translation out of latin into English is to translate after the sentence and not only after the words, so that the sentence be as open, or opener, in English as in Latin" (194). His emphasis on the importance of *sententia* or meaning as well as *verbum* was echoed even in the preface to the Geneva Bible, which noted, "[W]e have by all meanes indevored to set forthe the puritie of the worde and right sense of the holy Gost, for the edifying of the brethren in faith and charitie" (iv). In elaborating on their heirarchy of values, the

Geneva translators clearly, though respectfully, rank sense before word: "Now as we have chiefely observed the sense, and laboured alwaies to restore it to all integritie: so have we moste reverently kept the proprietie of the wordes. . ." (iv). In practice, this meant a text whose diction and syntax would appeal to common English readers and listeners.[19] As participants in a literary as well as theological and political endeavor, translators drew from all three realms in vigorously defending their approaches. In his preface to *The Obedience of a Christian Man*, Tyndale, with his characteristic hyperbole, had claimed, "They will saye it can not be translated in to oure tonge, it is so rude. It is not so rude as they are false lyers for the greke tonge agreeth moare with the english then with the latyne and the properties of the hebrue agreth a thousand tymes moare with the english then with the latyne" (n.p.). And attempting to put everything into perspective, the preface to the King James Version justified its latitudinarian approach with an eloquent rhetorical question: "For is the kingdome of God become words or syllables?"

Making the Bible English began as an act of protest as well as affirmation. The Oxford theologian John Wycliffe (c.1320-1384), while attacking authority and excess in the Church, charges for which he was impeached by Pope Gregory VI, completed a fairly literal, almost word-for-word manuscript translation from the Vulgate of the New Testament by 1380 and parts of what was then known as the Old Testament by his death in 1384. The entire Old Testament, completed with the help of others, most notably Nicholas of Hereford, a canon of the Abbey of St. Mary of the Meadows, appeared by 1388. In preserving the Latin syntax of the Vulgate, Wycliffe followed the tradition of Aelfric and the *Pety Job*.[20] By 1395 a revision, known as the Later Wycliffe and generally attributed to John Purvey (c.1354-1428), Wycliffe's secretary, appeared which turned the original's awkwardly Latinate syntax into more idiomatic English. While manuscript copies of these translations inspired Wycliffe's followers, who were disparagingly labelled Lollards,[21] English ecclesiastical authorities found both the translation and its adherents threatening and established the Constitutions of Oxford prohibiting translations in 1408. To emphasize the Church's objections to Wycliffe's legacy, in 1415 the Council of Constance ordered his body removed from holy ground. Richard Fleming, Bishop of Lincoln, disinterred Wycliffe's body, burned it, and threw the ashes into the Swift River, a tributary of the Avon.[22]

Such an inauspicious beginning clearly discouraged attempts at Englishing the Bible for well over a century. Aside from the copies of the Wycliffe Bibles circulating in manuscript, access to the story of Job in English during the fifteenth century appears to have been limited to versions of the *Pety Job*, two metrical portraits of Job, and William Caxton's translation of *The Golden Legend*, a miscellany of saints' lives, sermons, and other ecclesiastical materials. Around 1410 an anonymous author wrote a middle English metrical paraphrase of the Old

Testament but the poem appears, like the miracle plays, part of the popularizing of the traditional legends rather than any attempt at textual translation. While that brief account of Job centers on the temptation and justification of the prologue and epilogue, suggesting Job as a model of a Christian saint, a 182 line *Life of Job* (c.1473) in rhyme royal combines the same hagiographical material with traditions that appear to emerge from such folklore works as the pseudepigraphal Greek *Testament of Job*, originally written sometime between the first century B.C.E. and the fifth century A.D. In addition to his biblical virtues of patience and faith, the Job of folklore epitomizes hospitality and generosity and displays a marked interest in music. Caxton's translation of Jacobus de Voragine's *Legenda Aurea* offers what has become the conventional patient Job of the prologue and epilogue.

The expatriate William Tyndale (c.1492-1536) decided to challenge the bans by publishing his translation of the New Testament in Cologne and Worms in 1525. Copies soon appeared in England, smuggled into the country, according to legend, in bales of cloth. The recent past had provided Tyndale, a fine scholar, with a wealth of original materials. Using such sources as the Masoretic text of the Hebrew Bible printed in Soncino (1488), the *Complutensian Polyglot* (1514)[23], and the great Dutch humanist Desiderius Erasmus's Greek version of the New Testament (1516), Tyndale began work on an English translation of the Hebrew Bible. By 1536 when he was convicted of heresy, strangled and burned at the stake in Vilvorde near Brussels, he had completed the Pentateuch, the book of Jonah, and a section of the historical books through 2 Chronicles. Before his death Tyndale, considered far too Lutheran for the established British clerical authority, entered into a lively debate with Sir Thomas More, who objected to the exile's use of such Protestant terms as "congregation" for "church, "repent" for "do penance," "senior" for "priest," and "love" for "charity." Tyndale's greatest contribution to biblical translation, however, stems from both his commitment to original sources and his recognition that an effective translation should mediate between the original and English by preserving such elements of Hebrew style as redundancies and verbless clauses at the end of poetic statements while recognizing the need for phrases that resonated in English.

In 1535 a sometime Augustinian friar, Myles Coverdale (1488-1569), believing that Henry VIII's break with Rome would negate the 1408 Constitutions of Oxford's sanctions against translating and reading vernacular versions of the Bible, published the first complete printed English Bible, a text largely based on Tyndale's translation. Because Coverdale's Greek and Hebrew were no match for Tyndale, to translate those passages his mentor had not completed, such as the *Book of Job*, he relied on various Latin sources as well as Luther's German translation. In 1537 John Rogers (c.1500-1555), often described as Tyndale's secretary, who, in fact, shared his master's fate as the first person burnt alive when Queen Mary ascended the throne, revised Coverdale's work, possibly using texts he had from Tyndale, and added a series of controversial notes. For reasons never fully uncovered, Rogers, who retained Coverdale's version of *Job*, ascribed his work to Thomas Matthew, which has led to its being known as the Matthew's Bible. In 1539 the lay Greek scholar Richard Taverner (1505-1575) published a revision of the Matthew's Bible with slight textual changes, but it gained little recognition due to the excitement caused that same year by the appearance of Coverdale's own revision of the Matthew's Bible known as the Great Bible due to its size. Thomas Cromwell, Henry VIII's chief adviser on religious affairs, and Thomas Cranmer, the Archbishop of Canterbury, had encouraged this version to eliminate the fractious notes in the Matthew's Bible; and they arranged to have the Great Bible formally appointed for use in churches.

Although Bishop Edmund Becke edited a Bible combining Taverner's Old Testament and Tyndale's new Testament in 1551, a far more important work was to arrive at the beginning of the following decade. In 1560 the Geneva Bible appeared, a version based on work by the English colony of Calvinists at Geneva, led by William Whittington, Anthony Gilby, and Thomas Sampson. In addition to a revision of Whittington's translation of the New Testament, these dissenting scholars attempted a completely new version of the Hebrew Bible, especially those passages not translated by Tyndale. As a guide for readers, the Geneva Bible became the first to divide verses into separate paragraphs and italicize those English words added to the text to complete a thought. Like the Matthew's Bible, it also included a series of doctrinal notes from a decidedly Calvinist perspective. Even though this version was not published in England until 1576, its idiomatic, vigorous prose, its use of a more readable roman type rather than the Black Letter associated with other translations, and its appearance in quarto rather the larger folio volumes attracted a broad audience; and it went through 120 editions before 1611. To counter the popularity of this dissenting Bible, Archbishop Matthew Parker led a group of bishops and lay scholars in a complete revision of of the Great Bible, a work published in 1568 and popularly known as the Bishops' Bible. Although this edition eliminated many of the Vulgate interpolations from the earlier translations, especially Coverdale's, its occasionally awkward language and wordiness never earned it broad support.

Recognizing the growing appeal of the various English translations, Roman Catholic priests at the English College at Douai in northern France chose to counter with a translation of the Vulgate, the text established by the Council of Trent in 1546 as the source of Catholic biblical teaching. In 1582 Gregory Martin, William Allen, and Richard Bristow published a New Testament at Rheims, where the English College had moved. Finally in 1609-10, after the college had returned to Douai, the Douai Old Testament appeared to complement the Rheims New Testament. Despite its extensive annotations, notes which, in addition to their refutations of Lutheranism and Calvinism, provided one of the first truly accessible explanations of Catholic theology in English, the text's highly Latinate vocabulary and occasionally Latinate syntax never found a broad audience, even after extensive revisions in 1750 by Bishop Richard Challoner, the Apostolic Vicar in London,[24] and between 1849 and 1860 by Francis Patrick Kenrick, Archbishop of Philadelphia

When Queen Elizabeth died in 1603, her crown passed from the Tudor line to the Stuarts with James VI, King of Scotland. The following year, the newly titled James I, searching for ways to assert his Englishness and uncomfortable with the popularity of the Geneva Bible, especially its divisive notes, began appointing scholars to work on an acceptable translation. Although the popular number of those participating in this work has always been set at 54, only 47 have been identified.[25] As David Norton has pointed out, their task was fundamentally different from their predecessors: "they were not pioneers but revisers" (I.144).

When the product of this collaborative labor appeared in 1611, it became the standard translation which would not only dominate British and American perceptions of the Bible but profoundly affect the language of both cultures. This hegemony was to have two primary effects on approaches to *Job*. On the one hand, even as the King James translation drew on its predecessors, it established the norm against which all other translations would invariably and inevitably be judged. (In practice, as Part Three reveals, many of what would be presented as new translations are little more than slight modifications of the King James text.) On the other hand, the absence of substantive notes left it to individual readers to puzzle through the literary and theological complications of what was universally perceived as a dauntingly dark work. To avoid the kind of doctrinal squabbles which erupted with the Matthews and Geneva Bibles, the King James Bible included in its text only marginalia which referenced other biblical passages and discussed variant readings.[26]

Endnotes

[1] Clearly the Act of Settlement in 1701 and the Act of Union in 1707 only symbolized a temporary pause in England's religious wars. Political conflicts in Ireland and Scotland and cultural clashes throughout the United Kingdom during the past three centuries suggest that the forces underlying England's Civil War remain in play today. It does seem evident, however, that with these acts, the coronation of Anne in 1702, and the Hanoverian succession in 1714, the rhetoric of politics changed to a more explicit emphasis on

nationalism, economics, and imperialism.

[2] Of the four periods into which George Steiner divides literature on the theory of translation in *After Babel*, this work examines only the first two. The first period, which Steiner defines as lasting from Cicero to Alexander Fraser Tytler's *Essay on the Principles of Translation* (1792) and Friedrich Schleirmacher's *Ueber die verschiedenen Methoden des Uebersetzens* (1813) centered on the "immediate empirical focus" stemming "directly from the enterprise of the translator" (236). The second period, lasting until 1946 "is one of theory and hermeneutic inquiry. The question of the nature of translation is posed within the more general framework of theories of language and mind. The topic acquires a vocabulary, a methodological status of its own, away from the demands and singulariites of a given text" (237). The last two periods, which Steiner finds existing simultaneously, involve, first, the movement inspired by machine translation to examine the relations between formal logic, models of linguistic transfer, structural linguistics, and information theory, and, secondly, "a reversion to hermeneutic, almost metaphysical inquiries, into translation and interpretation" (238). Recent scholars have begun reconsidering the history of translation in works like Willis Barnstone's *The Poetics of Translation* (1993) *Lawrence Venuti's The Translator's Invisibility* (1995).

[3] In recounting his translations from Demosthenes and Aeschines, Cicero wrote: "nec converti ut interpres, sed ut orator, sententiis isdem et earum formis tamquam figuris, verbis ad nostram consuetudinem aptis. In quibus non verbum pro verbo necesse habui reddere, sed genus omne verborum vimque servavi. Non enim ea me adnumerare lectori putavi oportere, sed tamquam appendere." "I translated them not as a simple translator (or broker) but as an orator, with the same ideas and forms--or so called figures of speech--and with words fitting our customs and culture. I did not try to translate them word for word, but to preserve the essence and the vigor of the words. For I did not think to count them to the reader {like coins} but to weigh them out {like bars} instead" (IV.14).

[4] "Nec verbo verbum curabis reddere fidus/interpres" [A faithful interpreter will not try to translate word for word] (ll.132-33).

[5] From the beginning, debates about translation have always worked across a spectrum from literal to interpretive. Those who support literal translation, today generally called formal correspondence, see the process as a science that attempts to preserve the formal characteristics (e.g., syntax, imagery) as precisely as possible in order to allow the reader to experience the world from which the work emerges as accurately as possible. At the other end of the spectrum are those who view translation as an art in which the translator needs the freedom to interpret the original for contemporary audiences so that the audiences can respond in ways similar to those which the original readers might have. This approach, today called dynamic equivalence, focuses on the spirit, effect, or meaning rather than the letter. As the discussion throughout Part One shows, most attempts at theory tend to provide apologias for practice.

[6] "Ego enim non solum fateor, sed libera uoce profiteor me in interpretatione Graecorum absque scripturis sanctis, ubi et uerborum ordo mysterium est, non uerbum e uerbo sed sensum exprimere de sensu."

[7] "Ex quibus uniuersis perspicuum est apostolos et euangelistas in interpretatione ueterum scripturarum sensum quaesisse, non uerba, nec magnopere de ordinatione sermonibusque curasse cum intellectui res paterent."

[8] A little later in the letter, Luther describes the specific kinds of adjustments he has had to make with individual words and phrases, pointing out that at times, "I must let the literal words go and try to learn how the German says that which the Hebrew expresses. . ." (193).

[9] While the first English book length study of the theory of translation, Tytler's *Essay on the Principles of Translation*, did not appear until 1791, it merely summarized the principles of a rich tradition that had been defined by earlier practitioners. For a more detailed discussions of the development of an English theory of translation, see Sir Walter Scott's "The Life of John Dryden in *The Works of John Dryden*, ed. Sir Walter Scott and George Saintsbury, I (1882); George Saintsbury's *Dryden* (1881); William Frost's *Dryden and the Art of Translation* (1955); Thomas R. Steiner's "English and French Theories of Translation in the Seventeenth Centuries" (1970) and his *English Translation Theory 1650-1800* (1975); and my "Running Division on the Groundwork: Dryden's Theory of Translation," *Neophilologus* (1980).

[10] Robert Gordis offers a valuable survey of the rabbinical tradition in *The Book of God and Man: A Study of Job* (1965). The two clear exceptions to Christian scholarly ignorance of this tradition appear to be Jerome, who studied Hebrew with Jewish scholars, and Thomas Aquinas. Susan E. Schreiner's carefully detailed analysis of Joban exegesis from Gregory the Great through Calvin, *Where Shall Wisdom Be Found* (1995), is especially valuable in explaining the influence of Maimonides on Aquinas.

[11] Although not translated into English until 1897, the incidents described in the *Testament* had become such an integral part of western folklore that many of them (e.g., a fairly negative view of women, including an extended portrait of his wife's involvement with Satan's temptations, and strong associations of Job with music and magic) reinforce imagery in the Septuagint translation and survive to this day.

[12] Lawrence Besserman offers a valuable exploration of the ways biblical, apocryphal, patristic, and exegetical traditions of *Job* affected popular imagery during the Middle Ages in *The Legend of Job in the Middle Ages* (1979). See also Schreiner's *Where Shall Wisdom Be Found* (1995).

[13] In her examination of medieval influences on Calvin, Schreiner examines Gregory's argument of the relationship between spiritual suffering and self-knowledge in moral development (*Where Shall Wisdom Be Found*, 22-54).

[14] Allegorical interpretations have never fallen completely out of favor with some readers, as William Warburton's *Divine Legation of Moses (1741)* and David Wolfers' *Deep Things out of Darkness* (1995) attest. Chapter Three has a discussion of Bishop Warburton's heterodox reading, while Wolfer's essay and translation, a product of a lifetime of study, have as their goals both correcting the view of a book "misunderstood and mistranslated with unerring consistency for as far back as our knowledge stretches" (25) and establishing Job as "primarily an allegorical figure representing the people of Judah and their King Hezekiah in the time of the Assyrian conquests" (14-15).

[15] Aquinas points out that while God "refuted Job himself on his excessive manner of speaking" in Chapter 38 (461), his final judgments draw on the traditional Roman Catholic distinction on the gravity of sins: "Elihu erred through inexperience, and Job through inconstancy. Neither had sinned mortally" (535).

[16] The nine lessons from *Job* in this liturgy--7:16-21; 10:1-7; 10:8-12; 13:23-28; 14:1-6; 14:13-16; 17:1-3, 11-15; 19:20-27; and 10:18-22--appear in three English translations, a suggestion of their liturgical popularity. All of these translations, popularly known in France and England as "le petit Job" or *Pety Job,* have an English syntax and diction that clearly reflect the Latin original.

[17] The rich and complex story of the development of an English Bible has been told often and well. My brief treatment of it relies heavily on such scholars as Willis Barnstone, *The Poetics of Translation* (1993); F.F. Bruce, *The English Bible: A History of Translations* (1961); *The Cambridge History of the Bible*, vol 3: *The West from the Reformation to the Present Day*, ed. S. L. Greenslade (1970); T. H. Darlow and H. F. Moule, *Historical Catalogue of Printed Editions of the English Bible. 1525-1961*, revised and expanded by A.S. Herbert (1968); Jack P. Lewis, *The English Bible from KJV to NIV: A History and Evaluation* (1981); Geddes MacGregor, *A Literary History of the Bible* (1968); William F. Moulton, *The History of the English Bible*, new revised edition (1911); A. C. Partridge, *English Biblical Translation* (1963); and Alfred W. Pollard, *Records of the English Bible* (1911). Of special value to those interested primarily in literature and culture is David Norton's excellent *A History of the Bible as Literature* (2 vols, 1993).

[18] Textual and theological commentary become an integral part of Tyndale, the Matthews Bible, the Geneva Bible, and the Doway-Rheims Bible.

[19] One fairly extreme example was Sir John Cheke (1514-1557) who served as both Regius Professor of Greek at Cambridge and Secretary of State. Cheke attempted to rely on words with roots in Anglo-Saxon rather than Latin (e.g., "uprising" and "moond" rather than "resurrection" and "lunatic") and tried to make spelling reflect pronunciation. His gallant effort in 1550 covered only Matthew's Gospel and the opening of Mark's Gospel and was not published until 1843.

[20] The English Hexapla identifies his practice with the tradition of medieval scholars like

Richard of Hampole. In translating from the Vulgate, Wycliffe has most faithfully adhered to that version; he seems to have adopted Hampole's principle: "In this work y seke no straunge englishe, bot esieste and communeste, and siche that is moost luche to the latyne, so that thei that knoweth not the latyne by the englishe may come to many latyne words." (8)

[21] An Irish monk, Henry Crump, first labelled Wycliiffe's followers "Lollards" during a sermon attacking them. The term appears to come from a Flemish verb, "lollen" (i.e., "to mutter"), applied ironically in much the same disparaging spirit as members of the Society of Friends were mocked as Quakers.

[22] Ironically, Bishop Fleming is also remembered for founding Lincoln College, Oxford, where John Wesley studied.

[23] This polyglot edition, named after Complutum, the Latin name for Alcala in Spain, printed the Hebrew, Septuagint, and Vulgate texts of the Hebrew Bible in parallel columns, along with the Greek and Vulgate texts of the New Testament. Because of the limited number of older biblical manuscripts, both the Septuagint (also known as LXX from the tradition that Ptolemy Philadelphus invited seventy-two Jewish scholars to translate their Bible into Greek for the library at Alexandria during the third century B.C.) and the the Vulgate (St. Jerome's Latin translation of the Hebrew Bible from Hebrew and Aramaic and the New Testament from Greek completed about 405 A.D.) have been regarded as essential sources in establishing an accurate text of the Bible.

[24] The New Testament had only four editions (1582, 1600, 1621, 1633) and the Old Testament two (1610, 1635) before Bishop Challoner's revision in 1750. Challoner would actually continue to work on his revisions through 1772.

[25] One result of this limited information is the freedom it has given writers to speculate about the role in that process of the British Renaissance's most famous literary classicist, Ben Jonson, and his great rival, William Shakespeare. Rudyard Kipling's "Proofs of Holy Writ" (1932) and Anthony Burgess"s "Will and Testament" (1976) provide very different but equally clever interpretations of Jonson's and Shakespeare's possible contributions.

[26] In their "Preface" the translators had noted, "Doth not a margine do well to admonish the Reader to seeke further, and not to conclude or dogmatize upon this or that peremptorily?" The continuing popularity of the Geneva Bible, especially among British Calvinists, appears to stem as much from its occasionally polemical commentary as its Calvinist diction

[26] In their "Preface" the translators had noted, "Doth not a margine do well to admonish the Reader to seeke further, and not to conclude or dogmatize upon this or that peremptorily?" The continuing popularity of the Geneva Bible, especially among British Calvinists, appears to stem as much from its occasionally polemical commentary as its

CHAPTER TWO

Knowest Thou The Ordinaces of Heaven? Canst Thou Set The Dominion Thereof on Earth? (38:33)

> The late Bible, Right Worshipful, was sent me to censure: which bred in me a sadness that will greeve me while I breath. It is so ill done. Tell his Maiest that I had rather be rent in pieces with wild horses, then any such translation by my consent should bee urged upon poore Churches.
>
> Hugh Broughton, *A Censure of the Late Translation for Our Church: Sent unto a Right Worshipfull Knight, Attendant upon the King* London (1612), n.p.

The king's printer Robert Barker continued issuing Geneva Bibles until 1616 and some fifteen editions of it appeared between 1611 and 1644, despite a ban on producing it after 1618. However, those editions were overwhelmed by the 182 printings of the King James Version during the same period. But the King James inevitably failed to satisfy everyone. In addition to such individual voices as Dr. John Lightfoot who in 1645, the year after the last printing of the Geneva Bible, called for a stylistic and doctrinal review of the King James in a sermon before the House of Commons and Robert Gell who recommended radically amending it in 1659, the Parliamentarians made at least two formal attempts to provide an alternative. *The Souldiers Pocket Bible*, issued in 1643 for the use of Oliver Cromwell's army, consisted of a selection of extracts from the Geneva Bible; and the Long Parliament established a committee in 1653 to consider a new English translation. Some opposition continued even after the Restoration, as when England's Presbyterian ministers presented eighteen "Exceptions against the Book of Common Prayer" to the bishops, including a request for a new translation.[1]

Such lingering challenges to the King James help explain the popularity of reinterpreting some of the books, including *Job*, especially among Calvinists and Parliamentarians. These dissenting alternatives, in turn, generated new orthodox responses. The various versions quickly became codes, with Job serving as an emblem for all camps in the political struggle played out through the Civil War, the beheading of Charles I, the Cromwell Protectorate, the Restoration of Charles II, the accession of his brother, the Catholic Duke of York James II, and, finally, the Revolution of 1688 which brought William and Mary to the throne and ensured the Protestant succession. Throughout the political turmoil of the century, Job came to symbolize for royalists a conservative force opposed to rebellion, murmuring, and impatience; for disssenters, he offered a radical model of hope, promising a material, terrestrial reward and public exoneration for endurance and integrity.

In translations, the dissenters' goal, strongly influenced by Calvin's emphasis on Job's personal qualities and rejection of unnecessary elaboration, focused on clarifying a knotty work and personalizing it by making the text easy for the average reader to understand and embrace. In practice, this meant a rise in the popularity of paraphrases which not only relied regularly on such terms as "zeal," "saints," and "plain," but also envisioned the book's protagonist as a sincere and simple man with a profoundly personal experience of God. Royalists countered with translations that depicted Job's public status as an ideal prince, suggested the inherent complexity and sophistication of the text, and emphasized the virtues of reason, patience, and order. Such Stuart loyalists felt free to create paraphrases in either prose or poetry as vehicles to attack "conscience quacks" who would challenge the divinely ordained order of God's universe, as canvases to portray a wise and patient prince either in exile or in triumph, and as opportunities to embellish the text with extensive allusions to the classics and theater so that Job's world might more closely resemble the cultured, sophisticated world of the cavalier court.

In spite of the virulence of their polemics, when their fortunes shifted parties easily altered their emphases. Once the Protectorate had been firmly established, the puritan M.P. Thomas Manley could boast of *The Affliction and Deliverance of the Saints* in 1652, while the reissue of a Royalist Catholic translation had to invoke *The Pattern of Patience: in the Example of Holy Job* (1657). When Charles II returned from exile in France, however, his ardent supporter Arthur Brett could glory in *Patientia Victrix*, with both his Latin title and elegant pindarics a slap at the Puritans' emphasis on simple, direct English. This contest of emblems would culminate in Simon Patrick's attempts to find a middle ground, a fairly direct paraphrase which elaborated not on style but motive and meaning.

I.

From top to toe
I feele with woe
  that sorrow is my meat,
Put to exile

With Botch and bile
          and dunghill is my seat.

My kins folke talke
And by me walke
          wondring at my fall,
They count my fate
Unfortunate
          and so forsake me all.
A Godly Ballad of the Just Man Job (c.1645)

During the popular religious debates of the Stuart Age, *The Book of Job* became emblematic of both the suffering and reward of the true man of God. Raging in sermons, popular pamphlets, and ballads, this debate centered on which party might control images of Godliness, righteous suffering, and redemption to justify either preserving the status quo or shifting not only the nation's theological orientation but its political and economic values as well. While Puritans and Royalists differed rather violently in defining that iconic true man of God, they easily exchanged arguments depending on whether they were in or out of power. For Royalists, for example, Charles I could represent either the blameless man beloved by God or the victim of unjustified persecution, just as his son, the future Charles II, could represent a Job exiled to the dunghill of Europe or the triumphantly justified victor of the epilogue. Even Charles I himself appeared to encourage the association with Job in *Eikon Basilike*, the autobiographical apologia and spiritual meditations published on the day of his burial, February 9, 1649.[2] As the book's subtitle, "The Pourtraicture of His Sacred Majestie in His Solitude and Sufferings," suggests, the entire work provides a detailed image of Joban fortitude captured in the emblem accompanying the frontispiece portrait:

So triumph I. *And* shine more bright
In sad Affliction's Darksom night.

Despite also comparing himself to David, Joseph, Noah, Jacob, and Jesus, Charles regularly returns to Job, as in his final meditation on Death when he conflates the two most popular Christian passages in *Job*: "Though I die, yet I know that Thou my Redeemer livest for ever: Though Thou slayest me, yet Thou has encouraged me to trust in Thee for eternal life" (219).

Puritans, however, could draw as easily on the same text to explain their strategies for coping with unenlightened governments. In the case of clergymen comfortable with both sides, like Nathaniel Hardy, Minister of St. Dionys Back-Church, a cleric who could be invited to preach to Charles II in the Hague although his congregation consisted largely of Presbyterians, they could offer hope in recalling the redemptive value of Christian suffering. Hardy selected Eliphaz's questions from 4:7 "Remember, I pray thee, who ever perished, being innocent? or where were the righteous cut off?") for his sermon on the Restoration, *A Sad Prognostick of Approaching Judgment* (1660), while Charles Harriss reminded his readers that "Job stood firm in his Religion" (11) before justifying passive disobedience to royal authority in *A Scriptural Chroncle of Satans Incendiaries* (1670). One of the few dissenting clergy to be arrested, imprisoned and banished after the Restoration, John Brown showed remarkable faith in his posthumously published *The Swan-Song or the Second Part of the Life of Faith in times of Trial & Affliction* (1680). Dedicated to "the poor suffering Remnant of the Church of Scotland," Brown reminds his flock of their similarity to scriptural figures: "How oft do we finde the Saints of God, in Scripture, cry out of the hiding of God's face, when outward trouble was lying heavy upon them? As in *Job* and *David*. . . " (51).[3] Brown offers his contemporary saints a pragmatic approach to occasional bursts of frustration: "for albeit there was much Impatience to be observed in *Job*'s carriage; yet his patience is taken notice of by the Spirit of God, and we are bidden look to that, as if we had never heard of one of his impatient expressions" (174).

The New World was not immune to the struggles in the old. On July 23, 1640 ("a day of publike humiliation, appointed by the churches, in behalf of our native countrey in time of feared dangers"), William Hooke, an independent Puritan minister who served congregations in Taunton and New Haven, chose *Job* 2:13 for his sermon *New Englands Teares for Old Englands Feares* (1641). After implying an equation between civil strife and parricide by recalling David, "under a great affliction by the rebellious insurrection of the sonne of his owne loynes against him" (2), Hooke attacks those who rejoice at the afflictions of others. Although he admits that "there are no warres that Englands sinnes have not deserved" (15), he calls for civil obligation to Charles and attacks war as an unnatural evil in vivid, detailed descriptions :

> Here ride some dead men swagging in their deep saddles; there fall others alive upon their dead horses; death sends a message to those from the mouth of the Muskets, these it talkes to face to face and stabbs them in the fifth rib: In yonder file there is a man hath his arme struck off from his shoulder, another by him hath lost his leg; here stands a Souldier with halfe a face, there fights another upon his stumps, and at once both kils and is killed.
>
> (11)

In 1676 Samuel Scattergood, preaching on Job 28:28 before the King at New Market, makes Charles sound very much like Job, "who but a while before had been a mighty Prince, was all of a sudden reduced to most extream poverty" (5). Such reduction will prove only temporary, for "Our wounds must be cleansed with a Corrosive before we pour in Oyl" (10). The great villain is, of course, the archetypal rebel and anarchist Satan who not only "overthrew our first Parents" (2) but in other guises sounds much like the rebellious Calvinist and Presbyterian divines as he sows "abuse in the maintaining of wrangling Disputations, and unnecessary (and sometimes dangerous) Controversies. By which means he rents the seamless Coat of Christ, divides the Church into Schisms and Factions, and shakes all into disorder and Confusion" (4).

As Charles II's reign drew towards its end, fears of Roman Catholicism intensified with the prospect of his brother, the Catholic Duke of York succeeding to the throne as James II. On February 15, 1684, almost exactly a year before Charles's death, the Dean of St. Paul's, Edward Stillingfleet, could find in *Job* 23:15 spiritual rewards for supporting the status quo: "they who serve their Prince and their Country, and follow their lawful Imployments, with an honest and conscientious diligence, and neglect no necessary Duties of Religion, do carry on the great ends of Religion. . . " (35). With a similar sense of loyalty to the Stuart cause, Thomas Long, who had endured sequestration during the Commonwealth, preached *A Sermon against Murmuring* on 29 May 1680, equating murmuring with anti-Royalist sentiments. Even the strongly anti-Papist curate at Brislington and Queen Charlton advised restraint, when John Moore's preached *Of Patience and Submission to Authority* before the Lord Mayor, cautioning Londoners that "Patience is that blest temper of mind which enables us with all cheerfulness to doe and suffer the will of God" (5).

Murmuring apparently related to attacks on the status quo, because Simon Patrick, the Bishop of Ely and one of the first to take an oath of loyalty to the new queen and her consort, offered *A Sermon against Murmuring* on the fifth sunday of lent (17 March 1689), immediately after William and Mary had succeeded James. Although Patrick, the great commentator on *Job*, never mentions that work, his definition evokes the language of his *magnum opus*: "[Murmuring] signifies something more than meerly an inward repining and dissatisfaction of the Mind; denoting withal, the outward Expressions of that discontented Humour in undutiful words. . . " (4).

II

This is true glory and renown, when God
Looking on th'Earth, with approbation marks
The just man, and divulges him through Heaven
To all his Angels, who with true applause
Recount his praises; thus he did to *Job*,
When to extend his fame through Heav'n and Earth,

As thou to thy reproach mayst well remember,
He askd thee, hast thou seen my servant *Job*?
. . . .
They err who count it glorious to subdue
By Conquest farr and wide, to over-run
Large Countries, and in field great Battels win,
Great Cities by assault: what do these Worthies,
But rob and spoil, burn, slaughter, and enslave
Peaceable Nations, neighbouring, or remote,
Made Captive, yet deserving freedom more
Then those thir Conquerours . . . .
But if there be in glory aught of good,
It may by means far different be attaind
Without ambition, warr, or violence;
By deeds of peace, by wisdom eminent,
By patience, temperance; I mention still
Him whom thy wrongs with Saintly patience born,
Made famous in a Land and times obscure;
Who names not now with honour patient *Job*?

John Milton
Paradise Regain'd (1671),
III, 60-95

Within this highly charged political environment, the translations themselves inevitably became part of the theological and political skirmishes. The earliest versions, inspired by Calvin's teachings, confronted a major obstacle in the traditional view of Job as a perfect man, a condition inconsistent with the essential Calvinist view of man's fallen nature. Calvin himself had addressed this issue in setting the twin themes that would dominate his followers' interpretations: Job's moral character and the book's literary character. The first, in the language of Arthur Golding's 1574 translation of his 159 sermons on the book, described Job as an ideal Calvinist:

> It is said, that *He was a sound man*. This word *Sound* in the scripture is taken for a *playnnesse*, when there is no poynte of fayning, counterfayting, or hypocrisie in a man, but that he showeth himself the same outwardly that he is inwardly. . . . The sayde worde hath also bene translated *perfect*, as well by the Greekes as by the Latins. But for as muche as the woorde *perfect* hath afterwarde bene misconstrued: it is much better for us to use the worde *Sound.*
>
> *(3)*

Calvin's second theme reflects his admiration for plainness, in consistently mocking artistic elaboration as essentially diabolical.[4]

The earliest of these Calvinist versions was the *Job Expounded by Theodore*

Beza Partly in the Manner of a Commentary, Partly in the Manner of a Paraphrase (?1589). As the successor of Calvin in Geneva, the French classics scholar and theologian Theodore de Beze (1519-1605), popularly known as Theodore Beza, developed close ties with British Calvinists, especially those at Cambridge where he donated the New Testament manuscript known as Codex Bezae or Codex D in 1581. A widely respected poet for his *Poemata juvenilia* (1548), he is often identified with his *Du droit des magistrats sur leurs sujets* (1574), which expanded the Calvinist argument supporting the right of the people to rebel against tyrants. Evidently one of his British disciples, perhaps Thomas Cartwright (1535-1603), who made a pilgrimage to Geneva after being removed from his chair as Lady Margaret Professor of Divinity at Cambridge in 1571, "faithfully translated" Beza's Latin into English in this volume which was published at Cambridge. Part of the broad Protestant effort to make the Bible accessible to all people, Beza's translation helped establish *Job* as a commentary on contemporary political conditions. In his "Epistle Dedicatorie," which he offered to Queen Elizabeth, an "example of unfeigned zeale," Beza makes the connection explicit:

> Seeing the troubles of these times and the daungers wherein this common wealth now standeth . . . I am therefore minded to expound the historie of *Job*, in which, as in other bookes of holie Scripture, there are many darke and hard places, insomuch that I must here of necessitie sometime sayle, as it were, among the rocks: and yet I hope I shal not make any shipwracke. . . .
>
> (n.p.)

Beza recognizes the problem of genre, but he has a clear sense of the work's underlying structure: ". . . if it were not that it is shut up with a ioyfull and wished ende, it might rightly both for the matter, (then which nothing can be thought or imagined more graue and weightie) and also for the exceeding worthinesse of the persons, that here talke and reason together, be called a Tragedie. . . ." Once he has established that point, he assumes its dramatic nature, as when he begins discussing the *dramatis personae*: "The Actors or speakers herein, are God him selfe. . . ."

One of Beza's most fervent critics published an alternative *Job* the year before the appearance of the King James Bible. Hugh Broughton (1549-1612), a fellow of St. John's and Christ's at Cambridge, followed the tradition of Jerome and Luther as an odd mixture of precise scholar and vitriolic polemicist. A highly respected rabbinical scholar and minister who lobbied James's court for a new translation of the Bible, he was not included among the 54 translators chosen for the task. Once that version did appear, however, he became its most stringent critic: "The late Bible . . . was sent me to censure: which bred in me a sadness that will grieve me while I breathe, it is so ill done. Tell His Majesty that I had rather be rent in pieces with wild horses, than any such translation by my consent should be urged upon poor churches. . . . The new edition crosseth me. I require it to be burnt" (*Censure*, n.p.). Unfortunately, he died before completing his own alternative, a translation based on the Geneva Bible. A puritan preacher who believed in the apostolic nature of the episcopacy, he was, according to legend, so respected among the Roman Catholic heirarchy for his scholarship that he was offered a cardinal's hat.

In 1610 Boughton's translation and paraphrase of *Iob* dedicated to the king as a "Colon-Agrippina studie of one moneth for the metricall translation: but of many yeres for the Ebrew difficulties"[5] justified expanding what he saw as a knotty text: "God would have this book as a Iewel hid in the ground, not seen playn without paines" (Dedication, 3). Broughton's most eloquent passages, which capture the cadenced parallels of the original in vivid, earthy language, come in descriptions of Job's suffering:

> 25. Did I not weep for the hard of day: did not my soule burne for the poore?
> 26. But I looked for good, & evil came: and I wayted for light, and myrkenes came.
> 27. My bowels seethed & rested not: dayes of affliction came upon me.
> 28. I walked black out of the sun: I stood up in the Church: I cryed.
> 29. I am a brother to the Dragons; and a felow to Estrich kind:
> 30. My skin upon me is black, and my bones are brent without hoat-drought.
> 31. And my harp is made a mourning: and pleasant soundes be weepers voice.
>
> XXX:25-31 (6)

To help even the least sophisticated reader understand the text, Broughton creates a menu of alternatives for his reader, offering his translation in simple, direct English, followed by a summary of each chapter, followed in turn by a paraphrase in dialogue form. For example, his fourth chapter opens with clarity and power:

> Then answered Eliphaz the Themanite, and sayd:
> 2. If we make a speach to thee, wilt thou hold it wearysome: and who can refrain from speaking?
> 3. Behold thou hast instructed many: and strengthened the weary hands.
> 4. Thy words have lift up the falling, & thou hast confirmed bowing knees.

5. But now, it comes to thee, thou faintest:: it touches thee and thou art troubled.

(11)

In his paraphrase, these lines become even more direct, eliminating much of the need of working through the imagery: "Eliphaz. May I speak my mind? Thou hast comforted many others in sorow: Thy religion knoweth the right way of hope in Gods mercy: and thou knowest how to make thy ways right, by seeking unto God" (106).

The four royalist versions which followed Beza and Boughton took a decidedly different tack. All are dedicated to Charles, the earliest two while he was still a prince. Interlacing meditation and narration, the first two, Joshua Sylvester and Francis Quarles, reject Calvin's aesthetics of plainness, relying heavily on literary embellishment and allusion. While less elaborate, the anonymous *Iob's Pietie* and George Sandys *Job* reinforce Sylvester's and Quarles' emphases on the value of order and the dangers of rebellion.

In 1614 the Kentish wool merchant and translator Joshua Sylvester (1563-1618), who had established his reputation by translating Guillaume Salluste Du Bartas' *Divine Weeks and Works* (1592-99), dedicated his *A Divine & True Tragi-Comedy; Iob Triumphant in his Triall: or the Historie of His Heroicall Patience, in a Measured Paraphrase* not to the king but his son, Charles. In the tradition of Du Bartas, Sylvester added occasional reflections into his narrative. One of the first to conceive of the work as both drama and epic, Sylvester not only rejects Calvin's hostility to stellar embellishment by calling on Urania for inspiration and portraying Job blessing his sons by "Aurora's rosie beames," he also invokes an heirarchical world of privilege and obligation in describing Lucifer as an "ambitious Prince" and concluding with God's release of Job from his "Thral-full State." Sylvester's classical heritage becomes most apparent when he appears to reject it, as in this passage from the Proem which emphasizes what he sees as the major theme, the value of patience for the public good, an association that Thomas Hobbes would later reiterate when he drew the title and controlling imagery of his *Leviathan* from *Job*:

If any Spirit, inspir'd with Holy-mood,
Carefully-curious of the Publike Good,
Would lively limne th'immortall Excellence
Of such a Pattern of such Patience;
As neither Elements displaced quight,
Nor envious Starres, nor angry Foes despight,
Nor all the Fiends insatiate Furie fell
(By fraud or force) could ever quail or quell:

Twere labour lost, to fable (Homer-like)
The strange long Voyage of a wily Greek;
The Paines, the Perills, and extream Disease
That he endured, both by Land and Seas;
Sith sacred Truthe's Heav'n prompted Books present
In Constant Iob a worthier Argument.

(2)

With these heroic couplets in that mildly Euphuistic style which Dryden rejected as "abominable fustian" (*Spanish Fryar*, 101), Sylvester divides the original into four books, setting the entire work into poetry. He can overemphasize, as when Job begins his lament in the beginning of Chapter 3:

Iob therefore straining his obstructed voice,
Began thus, sadly with a shivering noise:
O! Wo be to the Day when I was born:
O! be it ever of the light forlorn:
O! may it ever under Darknes lie,
And never Sun vouchsafe its cheerfull eye;
Nor God regard it: let a deadly Shade
O're-clowde it aye, as ever Dismall made.

(10)

Despite his call for constancy, Sylvester never loses sight of genuine problems, even though in doing so he suggests a less than omniscient deity:

But, can it be (How can it other be?)
But that the Times of the Divine Decree,
(Concerning Judgements more or less severe;
When, Why, and Who, and How, & What, & Where)
Hidden from God, and hidden from his Owne;
Should to the World and wicked be unknown.
They shift the Land-marks from their ancient seat:
They take by force Mens Flocks, to feed, or eat:
They drive away the silly Orphans Asse:
They take for Pledge the Widowes Oxe (alas!)

(62)

As his title suggests, however, Sylvester sees Job as ultimately triumphant in his trial and his capacity for enduring as heroic.

A more orthodox writer and even more partisan royalist, Francis Quarles (1592-1644) followed Sylvester in alternating meditation with narration. Quarles, a member of Princess Elizabeth's court when she married the Elector of Palatine, became secretary to James Ussher, the Archbishop of Armagh who atttempted to establish the historical dates for every event from the creation of the world to the dispersion of the Jews under Vespasian,[6] and was appointed Chronologer to the City of London in 1539. A fierce partisan who called parliamentarians a "viperous generation" (Stephens and Lee, XVI, 537), Quarles eventually saw his property sequestered and his manuscripts destroyed by Cromwell's army. He began his writing career with a series of biblical paraphrases before publishing his popular *Emblems* in 1635. As the titles of his paraphrases often suggest, from *A Feast of Wormes set forth in a Poeme of the History of Jonah* (1620) to *Sions Elegies wept by Jeremie the Prophet* (1625), his emphasis on terrestrial suffering often shaped both his choice and treatment of subjects.

In 1624 Quarles published *Iob Militant: with Meditations Divine and Morall*, "in part, Periphrased; in part, Abridged." Using heroic couplets, his vision of the work combines epic similes with imagery that recalls classical drama,[7] all with the purpose of applying Job's message to the current political environment, as his Proposition suggests:

> Would'st thou discover in a curious Map,
> That Iland, which fond worldlings cal, Mishap,
> Surrounded with a Sea of brinie Teares,
> The rocky Dangers, and the boggie Feares,
> The stormes of Trouble, the afflicted Nation,
> The heavy soyle, the lowly situation?
> On wretched Iob, then spend thy weeping eye,
> And see the colours painted curiously.
>
> (71)

As social and political problems become subsumed into the tragedy of daily life, Christian fortitude, confidence in an ultimately benevolent Providence, and obedience become man's only hope for survival and salvation. Underlying this tragic vision is his essentially theatrical sense of *Job*:

> Would'st thou behold a Tragick Sceane of sorrow,
> Whose wofull Plot, the Author did not borrow
> From sad Invention? The sable Stage,
> The lively Actors, with their Equipage?
> The Musick made of Sighes, the Songs of Cryes,
> The sad Spectators, with their watry Eyes?
> Behold all this, comprized here in One,
> Expect the Plaudit, when the Play is done.
>
> (71)

The opening lines of the text, with their strong sense of allusion and their soft rhymes, manage to imply the ironies of both ambition and the lack of self control:

Not far from Casius, in whose bountious wombe,
Great *Pompeys* dust lies crowned with his Tombe,
Westward, betwixt Arabia and Iudaea,
Is situate a Country, called Idumaea;
There dwelt a man (brought from his Linniage,
That for his belly, swopt his Heritage,)
His name was Iob, a man of upright Will,
Iust, fearing heaven, eschewing what was Ill;
On whom his God had heap't in highest measure,
The bountious Riches, of his boundlesse Treasure.
(73)

Throughout his version he weaves meditations which call on both his theatrical imagery (the illusion of this world) and an Elihu-like argument for the instructive power of suffering, as in this "Digestion of the whole Historie":

Art thou advanc'd to thy supreme Desier?
Be still the same; Feare Lower; aime no Higher:
Mans Play hath many Sceanes, but in the last,
Heaven knits up all, to sweeten All that's past:
  Affliction is a Rod, to scourge us Home,
  A painfull Earnest of a Heaven to come.
(98)

Although Quarles' popular *Emblems* were to go through over fifty editions, leading to Horace Walpole's ironic quip that "Milton was forced to wait till the world was done admiring Quarles" (*Correspondence*, 215), only rarely does he develop the potential of the couplet for nuanced reflection through balance and parallelism. When he does, as in perhaps his most powerful lines, his interpretation of 13:15, he achieves the kind of complex relationships which foreshadow Dryden and Pope:

My soule is on the Rack, my teares have drown'd me,
Yet will I trust my God, though God confound me.
(84)

In *Iob's Pietie, or the Patience of a Perfect Man* (1624), the author, identified only as R. H. (R. Humphrey?), offers a series of dialogues broadly based on the original. Dedicating the work to "All Princes and Potentates," R. H. focuses less on the suffering than on the ubiquitous role of Satan, who appears even in Job's dialogues with his comforters ("I have stirred up his Friends" [52]) and on the ideal of a "compleate and perfit good man, such, as amongst the Greekes Homer faymed his Achilles to be, and Plato strove to lay the foundation of an happie Commonwealth; such, as amongst the Romans, Virgil made his Aeneas; and Tully (labouring for an honest Man) framed his offices" ("Dedication," n.p.). Setting Job's classical sophistication against the common grumbling of his friends, R. H. provides an ideal model of the loyal Stuart subject.

It was the last of this wave of Royalists, George Sandys (1578-1644), who won admiration from subsequent poets for his mastery of couplets, including Dryden's praise as "the best versifier of the former age" (*Fables*, 20) As treasurer of the Virginia Company, Sandys completed an expurgated translation of Ovid's *Metamorphoses* (1626), generally accepted as the first literary work by an English settler. His *Job*, dedicated "To the Best of men, and Most Excellent of Princes, Charles," offers a more direct and forceful version than Sylvester, Quarles, or R.H. by not attempting to reach after effect or tie the text into classical antecedents. Compare, for example, his opening lines with those of Quarles:

> In Hus, a Land which neare the Suns uprise,
> And Northern confines of Sabaea lies,
> A great Example of perfection reign's:
> His Name was Iob; his Soul with guilt unstaind.
> (1)

He does, however, in the finest royalist tradition, find more subtle ways to comment on his patron's political difficulties with the rebellious Puritans and their financial imperatives:

> Why are the punishments by God decreed
> To wicked men, and their rebellious Seed,
> Since times to come are present in his sight,
> Conceal'd from those who in his Lawes delight?
> Some slily markes remove from bordering Lands;
> Feed on the Flocks they purchase, with strange hands:
> The Orphants only Asse they drive away;
> And make the Widowes morgag'd Oxe their prey:
> Who force the frighted poore to turne aside;
> Whom milder Rocks in their darke Cavernes hide.
> (31)

Throughout his work, Sandys emphasizes two lessons in *Job*: the value of order (Job symbolizes the "Master of a mighty Family,/Well ord'red and directed by his Eye" [1]) and the forgiveness of those who repent. In a similar spirit, Sandys' conclusion suggests the harmony of a well-ordered kingdom. After chastizing Eliphas of Theman not only for his argument but, in much the same spirit as Royalists denounced the fervor of puritan preaching and absolutism, for his motives--"Since you, unlike my servant Iob, have err'd;/And Victory before the Truth preferr'd" (54)--he leaves Job reigning in the best of Stuart patriarchal imagery:

> The Master of a mighty Family;
> Well ord'red, and directed by his Eye.
> None was more opulent in all the East;
> Of greater power; yet such as still increast.
>
> (55)

In a far more partisan spirit, George Abbott (1603-49),[8] who was to fight with the Parliamentary forces against Prince Rupert, published in 1640 *The Whole Booke of Iob Paraphrased, or Made Easie for Any to Understand*, a title which clearly reflects his primary goal. Abbott, who was to serve as an M.P for Tamworth from 1645 until his death, took a strict Calvinist approach to his work, as he points out in his prefatory note:

> A Paraphrase (and not a commentarie) is the thing that I endeavour, which is a bare rendering of the sense plaine and easy, the better to enable the Reader to be a Commentator to himselfe.
>
> ("To the Reader," n.p.)

In order to achieve this goal, however, Abbott recognized the need to provide his audience with some assistance, the extent of which he describes in an elegant metaphor:

> The Booke of Job in respect of the dialect of those times, being of quaint expressions, must needs be explained by other and more familiar language: and being also difficult in the coherence, (which is very materiall, many texts or verses besides their proper senses must in their explications carrie their dependent, and coherent meanings in them, else they cannot bee fully rendred, nor the discourse by its right joints and ligaments continued, and knit together; but must needs be imperfect, blind, and lame, which I have laboured the cure of, by perspicuity of phrase and dependencie.
>
> ("To the Reader")

His achievement, significantly simpler and more direct than the earlier paraphrases, places a great deal of emphasis on emotions and human relationships. Unlike a Royalist like Sandys who defines an elegantly heroic world in the order and harmony of his imagery, Abbott presents his protagonist as "a faithfull and upright-hearted man" (5) attacked by a diabolic foe in vivid, dramatic prose: "Satan, seeing all these temptations would not make *Job* blaspheme, puts him at last directly upon the very point it selfe, by the desperat counsell and provoking suggestion of his bosome-friend, his wife. . ." (13).

The Royalist response during these times of Parliamentary triumph was a translation of a translation by a French father of the Oratory. Jean Francois Senault's paraphrase on *Job* appeared in 1648 with a telling prefatory note, "Sure, it cannot be unsuitable to the condition of these Times to publish a Discourse of Patience" ("The Translator to the Reader," n.p.). Senault's "Preface," which identifies Job with other biblical victims, emphasizes qualities that echo the Royalist vision, including Jesus' "Princely qualities and suffering, as well as betrayals by brothers (Jacob & Esau, Joseph & brothers)" (n.p.). For Senault, Joseph became an especially important model whose life appears to offer a telling parallel: "Joseph was sold by his Brethren, and mounted not upon the Throne of Egypt, but by the Staires of Servitude and Prison" (n.p.).

Twice removed from its original, this translation lacks the vitality of Broughton and Abbott, partly because its elaborate syntax, which relies too frequently on conditional clauses, carries an appeal that is far more rational than affective. Consider, for example, the following two comments by Eliphaz:

> (4.2) "I know not if in the griefe which afflicts you, you are capable of hearing us; and whether our reasons will not exasperate your evils, instead of sweetening them. But who can hinder a discourse from coming forth, which is already conceived? who would conceale from his friend those sentiments which are profitable to his soule, and which coming from a good intention, ought in reason to produce a good effect?
>
> (30-31)

> (15.2) "If you were as wise as you think you are, you would not speak with so much vanity, but you would command anger which transports you, and you would not cast so many unprofitable words into the aire for to exaggerate your griefes."
>
> (134-5)

In contrast to Broughton's simple, clear interpretation of the first passage, the English version of Senault, with its awkward syntax, complex periods and latinate diction, was unlikely to develop a broad popular audience.

This first English edition of Senault's *Paraphrase* acknowledged a very odd couple in its introductory material. Stamped with the imprimatur of James Cranford, a scholarly Presbyterian divine who served as a licensor of the press from 1643 to 1648, the work is dedicated on its title page to Cardinal Richelieu (i.e., Armand Jean du Plessis, duc de Richelieu), who as France's Secretary of State from 1624 through 1642 had broken the power of the Huguenots. When the work was reissued near the end of Cromwell's reign in 1657 under the title *The Pattern of Patience*, all mention of Senault, Richelieu, and Cranford had disappeared. However, the opening of the preface became even more appropriate to the decade of royalist exclusion:

> Though all be Princely in the Person of Jesus Christ; though his Actions, as well as his sufferings deserve to be adored, and his greatnesse exacts from me as much respect, as his Humility; yet it seems that his father hath taken delight to make his pains more glorious than his Miracles.
>
> ("Preface," n.p.)

In direct contrast to such Catholic Royalist sentiments was Thomas Manley's celebration of the Parliamentary victory, *The Affliction and Deliverance of the Saints* (1652). Emphasizing the success of the righteous who suffer, Manley, a lawyer who would publish a poem on Cromwell the following year,[9] makes the applicability of *Job* explicit in his "Epistle Dedicatory" to Thomas Challoner (i.e., Chaloner), one of Charles I's judges, a man who both signed the king's death warrant and, in a remarkable shift in loyalties, published a speech in 1659 containing a plea to reestablish the monarchy:

> The troubles of the Times are so great, and all men by them such sufferers; that England had need to be a Nation of *Iobs*, that with patience they may run through the extremities which daily begin to coast us. And truly, if we would make *Iobs* example our Precept, it is to be beleeved we should endure our sufferings with more Christian-like alacrity, and have a more Saint-like deliverance out of our troubles.
>
> (n.p.)

Manley selects metaphrase rather than paraphrase for his task in order to achieve clarity and remove the excresences previous paraphrases have gathered:

> The reason of my Metaphrasticall Translation was, that I would not, as neere as I could, deviate from the very Letter of the Text, which I have as little as possible; yet where the sense was darke, comparing severall Translations together, and all with the originall, I made them easie to the most illiterate understanding: conceiving it better than a Paraphrase, they often losing, or at least darkening halfe the sense in their circumlocutions, whereas this wholly keepes the sense, and avoids its prolixity. ("To the Reader," n.p.)

Prolixity, however, marks some sections, especially when he promulgates his puritan ideology. That ideology appears first in the opening lines, when he privileges the term "zeale," one of those linguistic differentiaters among the religious wars.

There was a man in Uz, for zeale whose fame
Merits beyond an equall, *Job* by name:
Perfect and upright, such the world ne'r knew,
Who feared God, and evill did eschew.
(1)

In contrast with Sandys' opening for Chapter 24, which focused on the dangers of rebelliousness, Manley shifts his emphasis to the personal experience of God:

Can the All-knowing God, to whom obey
Dayes, times, and houres, be ignorant how they
Do passe or circle? whence proceeds, if then
That those who know him not, most wicked men,
Can see his daies, and think to force his will,
To bear their crimes, and luxuries fulfill?
The Land-markes some remove, and take aweay
The flocks, and feed upon them as their prey.
The Orphans Asse they drive away unbought,
And take the widdowes ox to pledge for nought.
(56)

His vocabulary becomes broader in a concluding meditation on the necessity and inevitability of suffering--"Bastards go free, he chastens whom he loves" (98)--as he warns of the possibility of reverses and the need for constant vigilance. Manley concludes with a final vision of the kind of paradise often envisioned by Puritans, not so much a democracy as one in which the true believers would gain the trappings of royalty:

The Prophets take,
And your example the Apostles make:
Who held this rule, that many crosses bring
To heaven, where every Saint[10] shall be a King.
(99)

The Saints' victory, however, proved short lived. The Rev. Mr. Arthur Brett (d.1677), who had received his B.A. and M.A. from Oxford, celebrated the return of the Stuart monarchy in 1660 with *The Restauration. Or, A Poem on the Return of the Most Mighty and Ever Glorious Prince, Charles II, to His Kingdom*. The following year, the Catholic *Pattern of Patience* turned into Brett's *Patientia Victrix*, a version of *Job* that excoriated Puritans and celebrated the deliverance of a patient prince. Never successful in his hopes of preferment, Brett eventually gave up his living as vicar at Market Lavington to move to London, where he survived by begging on the streets, especially from Oxford men.

To signal the new age with its revival of classical learning and continental elegance, Brett rejected the heroic couplets which had dominated since Broughton in favor of "the happily reviving Pindarick strain." In his "Preface," Brett shifts the terms of the work's theme of "Ruine and Restauration" to the Royalist camp, explicitly connecting Job with Charles while taking swipes at his enemies, including a demonization of Martin Luther:

> Whether Job was an Absolute prince or no . . . we are sure that part hath in this Age been acted by a Mighty *Monarch*; against whom there have risen up such as by their actions surely meant to prove the Sabaean plunderers unskilful in their own art, and the Chaldean robbers conscionable men; whose stately Pallaces have been thrown down by the violence of a blasting Vote from out of a thin, desolate, and *Desert house*; whose goods, and every thing in which he might justly delight or glory, have been destroyed by the help of that Artificial fire, which, through the Grand enemy of mankind were not in every piece of of iron that vented it, yet some are resolved to believe he first found out in the shape of a German *Monk*; who, in short, has been a most notable example to demonstrate (as it were) that to heaven's Favourites Loss is Gain, and that Patience is a Crowning vertue; for, his Friends are double the number they were at the first, seeing those who not many years ago were his (because his Father's) Enemies, have kinly faced about, and been successful practitioners in Loyalty; how much his Treasures are increased, let his Exchequer speak; and how his Territories shall be more and more inlarged, I leave to future Victories, and the year 1666 to declare.
>
> (n.p.)

Brett's pindarics underline the resurgence of a cavalier temperament in England. Like Sandys, he focuses more on the social effects of rebellious behaviour ("Some men their ant'ent bounds w'ont keep,/But throw the common stakes away" [81]) rather than Manley's emphasis on the cause in the failure to experience God His language occasionally takes digs at the dissenters, the recent establishment, as when Job's wife comments sarcastically in 2: "What ails this everlasting Puritan?" or when Job himself calls his comforters "*Conscience-quacks*" in 13.4. And an image in Chapter 4 offers him an opportunity to adapt the original for some ironic commentary on recent history. :

> The fiercest Lions roaring voice,
> It proveth but an empty noise
> The lusty Lion in his vig'rous youth
> Has much ado
> His meat to chew
> With scarcely half a tooth;

While the decrepit one
Oft pines away
For want of prey
His kind provider being gone;
And the stout old ones whelps are thrown.[11]

(16)

In his additions to the text, however, Brett's typological reading can make significant differences, as in Job's remarkably precocious confession of faith in 19:25

For on my Sav'our I rely
A *Second Person* in the *Trinity*
I have his Pass'on in my eye,
I ken the top of *Calvary*
Hither (me thinks) I hear him cry,
Eli, Eli, Lamaschabactany!

(66)

This tradition of paraphrase culminates with the work of Simon Patrick, Bishop of Ely. As one of a series of paraphrases of Scriptures, Patrick's work became part of his attempt to defend the Church of England by establishing a middle ground between the extremes of Roman Catholicism and Calvinists. Like many of his predecessors, he finds appealing the contemporary applicability of *Job* "Which I could never have presented to . . . the world more seasonably than now; when the state of our affairs is so dangerously perplexed that we cannot stand upright, nor preserve our souls from sinking into the saddest fears or discontents, or some such troublesome passion without a strong confidence in the most wise, just, and merciful providence of the Almighty; which orders things, in unsearchable ways, to the good of those that steadfastly adhere unto him in faithful obedience" (737).

Patrick's Job, a rational man of late seventeenth-century sensibility, finds his plight more puzzling than unfair. Printing his paraphrase below the King James text, Patrick consistently expands the legal imagery--terms like "judge," "sentence," and "bar" become far more frequent--to emphasize the inevitablility of God's achieving a just and rational conclusion. In fact, Patrick introduces the theophany in Chapter 38, when God himself appears as a judge "(according to Job's repeated desires) to decide this great controversy." Although his comments show a taste for the melodramatic, especially his frequent use of "Alas!," he shows his own impatience for witnesses like the comforters (e.g. XX:1 "Here Zophar, though he had no new thing to produce, hastily interrupted Job"). In portraying a dynamic

Job slowly reaching a fuller understanding of his relationship to God, Patrick constantly includes parenthetical references to other passages to clarify the ideas and in both his prefatory "Argument" before each chapter and in the paraphrase itself: XIX:25: "For my hope, which was as dead as myself (XVII:13, 15. XIX:1) begins to revive, because, though I seem for the present to be forsaken of God, yet I know that he can hereafter deliver me out of this miserable condition, since he lives for ever; and will, I doubt not, at last appear victorious over all the enemise which now oppress me." Both Job and his young friend Elihu demonstrate a sense of social proprieties within their debate (e.g., XXXIV:35 "Job seems to be very much mistaken;" Argument to XXXV: "Job still keeps silence . . . because he was sensible he [i.e., Elihu] meant him well").

Such referential ambiguity occasionally becomes confusing, as in the pronominal thicket in the "Argument" to Chapter 25: "The foregoing discourse of Job, in the twenty-fourth chapter, was so undeniable, that Bildad begins to break off the dispute. For he says not a word to it, but only advises him to speak more reverently of the majesty of God, than he imagined he had done in his appeal to him." Despite such lapses, Patrick shows a high degree of sensitivity for the needs of his audience, as when he expresses concern with the length of some commentaries in which the parts distract readers from the whole: "I have therefore taken quite another course, and only given the sense of it in a compendious but perspicuous Paraphrase (or Metaphrase rather, as the ancients would have called it), which is not much longer than the text. . ." (737).

As support for James II waned, James Warner, who identifies himself only as "a Protestant," preached *The Surest Way to the Safest Peace, in Troublous Times* before the Lord Mayor on September 3, 1688. Despite focusing on Elihu's argument in Job 34:29 that troubles could be a warning, Warner argues that times of disquiet reflect not so much a test as a judgment: "Provocations . . . which when found among any people, do provoke the Holy God to hide his Face from a people; which being too visible among us, must be reformed, or we shall be destroyed" (19). The greatest provocation ("When a People leave God and turn to Idolatry" [20]) seems like a clear criticism at the emerging Catholic culture at court. Warner's conclusion that the city and nation need "to Repent and Reform" actively appears in his 'Epistle Dedicatory": "The more we strive to avoid Trouble, the more we are encompassed with it, until we repent: This has been a practice fatal to all ages" (n.p.).

England's act of repentance occurred when James II was forced into exile by his Protestant daughter Mary and her consort, William of Orange. After the Battle of the Boyne and the final defeat of James, with the Protestant succession and parliamentary primacy secured, *Job* could begin serving other purposes. In one last reflection on the politics of his century, Henry Rider, the Bishop of Killaloo in

Ireland could use Job 8:13 in 1695 to commemorate the anniversary of the defeat of the Irish Rebellion in 1641. Although he begins with a bloody account of that revolt and its defeat, he moves quickly on to the most recent rebellion. Invoking the growing hostility to the corrupting influence of the stage on British morals, Bishop Rider contrasts the deposed king, whom he titles "the Hypocrite" with patient, virtuous Job. James,the "foolish Actor, who was to personate a King" (9), as well as his brother and his father, all become the superficial creations of illusion: "take him but to the tiring Room, strip him, and lay aside his Robes, pull off his Mask and Vizard, that Paint and Fucus which he lays on with so much Art and Cunning, he will then be seen as he is, a deform'd shrivel'd Piece; a miserable Spectacle indeed. . ." (7-8). In contrast with such artificiality, the bishop presents William of Orange as both product and producer of nature: "we have yet a Gracious King, a Nursing Father to the same Church they made such Havock of, and Persecuted with so much Rage and Violence. That Vine which Gods own Right hand hath Planted, Flourishes in the Land, and after that excellent way which they still call heresy, we even now Worship the God of our Fathers" (15).

Endnotes

1 Among the many doctrinal objections dissenters had to the King James Version was language which privileged the established church, its heirarchy, and its practices. For example, in the KJV its translators had preferred the term "church" to "congregation," had emphasized the role of bishops with only a single use of "presbyter," and had reinforced the material sense of religion by adding such phrases as "robbers of churches" in Acts 19:37.

2 While most scholars now accept the view that John Gauden, Bishop of Worcester, was actually responsible for much of the *Eikon Basilike*, patching together and expanding material the king had sketched out during his final imprisonment, the book, with its portrait of a king heroic in suffering, captured the popular imagination and was frequently republished as the king's own book, even during Cromwell's rule. Charged with refuting its imagery and argument, John Milton portrayed it as a "civil kinde of Idolatry" (III. 343) in his awkwardly scholastic *Eikonoklastes* (1649).

3 Schreiner points out Calvin's extensive allusions to David in his sermons on Job: "Between the tragic figures of Job and David, Calvin sees an existential connection, which he transforms into a hermeneutical device" (96). She also suggests a source for Calvin's

connection of the two figures in Ambrose's four fourth century sermons "On the Prayer of Job and David" (97-99).

4 His comments on Arcturus and Orion (9.9) are fairly typical: "There are twoo Starres that are named here: And the Poets have feyned many fables and fond things of them. Whereof commeth such unreasonablenesse? Of the vaynnesse and naughtiness of men. They have said that such a Starre was the crounet or Garlond of a woman, or else the woman hirself. Lo here a cow [lo there an ox,] Lo here this, and lo there that: to be short, Lo a sort of dotages. Neverthelesse we have to mark that these dotages are sprung out of Satans suttlest wylinesse. For his desire was (so far as was possible to him) to deface this fayre lookingglasse wherein Gods will was to be seene and knowen" (157). Note here Calvin's eco-logic for not portraying the world as it is. The most valuable contemporary discussion of Calvin's sermons on Job appears in Susan E. Schreiner's *Where Shall Wisdom Be Found*, 91-155.

5 Broughton's title acknowledges his admiration for Heinrich Cornelius Agrippa von Nettesheim of Cologne (1486-1535), whose interest in esoteric literature, Cabalistic, Hermetic, Neoplatonic, and magical, inspired his *De occulta philosophia* (1510), an argument that magic offers the best path to God. In 1526 von Nettesheim's second major work, *De incertitudine et vanitate scientiarum et artium*, reintroduced skepticism to Europe by rejecting all human learning and placing total faith in the Bible.

6 In his *Annales Veteris et Novi Testamenti* (1635), which finds creation to have begun in 4004 B.C., Archbishop Ussher placed Job immediately after Joseph's date on the same day in 2369: "Hoc tractu temporum Job fuit, legem naturae & agnitionem Dei & omnem justitiam complexus: praedives opibus; atque eo illustrior, quod his neque integris corruptus, neque amissis depravatus est. Nam cum per Diabolum exutus bonis, filiis etiam esset orbatus, ad extremum diris ulceribus affectus; non potuit vinci, ut prae doloris impatientia aliqua in parte peccaret. Mercedem denique divini testimonii consecutus, sanitati redditus, omnia quae, amiserat in duplum recepit" (9-10).

7 Perhaps in keeping with his catholic view of genre, Quarles selected his headnote for *Iob Militant* from Horace's Ode XVII: "Diis, pietas mea;/Et Musa, cordi est."

8 This George Abbott was not the George Abbot, Archbishop of Canterbury, to whom Sylvester dedicated one of the prefatory poems in his *Iob Triumphant*. Clearly a believer in the art of acknowledgment, Sylvester also offered dedicatory poems to the Lord High Chancelor, the Lord Chamberlain, the Chief Justice, and all Parliamentarians ("the Right Honourable Lords Spirituall & Temporall; [and] the Knights and Burgesses of the Lower House"). In his letter to Parliament, he demonstrated his interest in the public good by listing fifty-five bills which *Job* justified, ranging from "An Act against Atheisme & Irreligion" to "An Act against Wandring & Wanton Eyes."

9 The title of his Cromwell poem reflects both his essentially heroic vision and the influence of the Renaissance on him: *Veni; Vidi; Vici: The Triumphs of . . . Oliver Cromwell.*

10 Job as a model of the new Parliamentary saints on earth also appears in the work of George Hutcheson of the Church of Scotland who preached 316 sermons on the text, through which he holds the man of Uz as a model, occasionally with some curious theology: "Yea, his very Infirmities and the discovery of his dross in the furnace, are recorded for the advantage of weak Believers, when they observe that perfection of most eminent Saints, within time, consists not of sinlessness but in sincerity . . ." (1).Frustration with the last years of the Commonwealth became tied into commentaries on Job as in the indirect observation of John Trapp, Pastor of Weston upon Avon in Gloucestershire, in his *A Commentary or Exposition upon the books of Ezra, Nehemiah, Esther, Job, and Psalms* (London, 1657): "Job never had any suites in Chancery; no; but he had far sharper trials; and if he had been judge in that Court (as he was in his own Country, Chap. 29.12,17.) he would have made as good dispatch there, as ever Sir Thomas Moror did, who calling once for the next cause, was answered, That there was none" (2). Trapp's lively, witty commentary captures the tensions in the text with a wonderful colloquial style as when he points out that Job was "in a pitifull pickle" after his wife's advice (24) or that "It is a blessed thing to have a stomack for God" (279).

CHAPTER THREE

And Now Am I Their Song (30:9)

> Mr. Pope is now employed in a large design for a moral poem. There will be several behaviours of men flung into fables: one in particular on the misery of affluence (planned just like that of Job, only with the contrary point of view), which Mr. Pope says he foresees already will take up at least a thousand lines.
>
> Joseph Spence, *Anecdotes*
> (1730) I, 129

With the final resolution of the civil wars of the seventeenth century in the Acts of Settlement of 1701 and of Union in 1708, doctrinal disputes could shift into new arenas. Simon Patrick had established a model for a middle ground with a popular paraphrase which could help, in his words, "those who have little leisure, or less money" (737) through the complexities of *Job*; and in 1701 Bishop William Lloyd inserted Archbishop Ussher's biblical chronology and an index into an edition of the King James Version, preparing the way for a series of enormously popular editions with explanatory notes which began to appear during the century, such as John Brown's *Self Interpreting Bible*.[1] As theological disputes moved to the margins of the text, despite King James' instructions that it be printed without notes, the Authorized Version could became every denomination's English Bible.

When the collected sermons of John Tillotson (1630-1694), the latitudinarian Archbishop of Canterbury admired for both his common sense and graceful literary style, appeared, they began with a sermon on Job 28:28 about the wisdom of being religious against atheists, an increasingly popular term for deists. By the turn of the century deism had replaced dissent as the primary perceived threat to orthodox hegemony, and Anglican churchmen focused their arguments on the providence of God and the limits of human reason. In a sermon on 38:4, Richard Marsh in *The Vanity and Danger of Modern Theories* (1699) pointed to the connection between the earlier challenges to the state and current ones to the church in warning, "Men are turning Levellers in Religion, as they were of old in Government; and nothing now must pass for an Article of their Faith, but what is of the same Height with their Reason" (8). He concluded,"Tho a good use may be made of Philosophy in Religion, yet 'tis not Safe, nor Prudent to venture it much upon that Bottom" (23).[2]

While restating the classic British position on translation, John Dryden defined it broadly enough to provide adequate justification for a wide range of experiments. *Job* translations became more self-consciously literary with traditionalists developing a heroic strand based on Milton and Dryden and experimentalists exploring the possibilities of pathos in lyric forms. Shaped by such choices, Job evolved from a classical epic hero modeled on the ideal prince to a man of acute sensibility, a perfect model for Samuel Richardson's *Clarissa* and Oliver Goldsmith's *Vicar of Wakefield*. And as interest shifted from politics to theology, genre, and style, a pair of Anglican bishops published two of the most important British works on *Job*: William Warburton's reinterpretation of the story's religious allegory and Robert Lowth's structural analysis of Hebrew poetry.

I

As moody Job, in shirtless case,
With collyflowers all o'er his face,
  Did on the dunghill languish,
His spouse thus whispers in his ear,
Swear, husband, as you love me swear:
  'T will ease you of your anguish.

An Anonymous Satire on William Sherlock's Decision to Switch Allegiance from James II to William III from Thomas Babington Macaulay's *History of England* (1849-61), IV, 163n.

Ever since Thomas Aquinas, *Job* had been a traditional citation for theologians demonstrating God's general and particular providence. William Sherlock (1641-1707) merged that providentialist tradition with an acceptance of England's new political order. Sherlock, the Dean of St. Paul's, had become an emblematic figure among his contemporaries for his Anglican orthodoxy, a theological commitment that made his willingness to swear allegiance to William and Mary extraordinarily difficult. After his suspension as a non-juror following James II's overthrow, his acceptance of the new Protestant succession allowed other members of the Church of England, especially those suspicious of the Calvinist and Lutheran leanings of many of the anti-Jacobites, to accept the new order. In his *History of England*, Macaulay presents Sherlock as an essential figure in the established church's psychological shift toward acceptance of the new regime.[3] In Sherlock's most famous work, *A Discourse concerning the Divine Providence* (1694), often read as his apologia for submitting to the reality of the new political order, he regularly draws on examples from *Job*:

> [L]et us consider how that man must suffer, who suffers with Submission to God; and that is the Submission which we owe to Providence. Now a man who suffers with Submission, must not reproach and censure the Divine Providence, but think and speak honourably of God, how hardly soever he deals with him; he may complain of what he suffers both to God and men, but he must not complain of God: this was *Job*'s Behaviour; *Naked came I out of my mother's womb, and naked shall I return thither: the Lord gave, and the Lord hath taken away, and blessed be the name of the Lord: in all this Job sinned not, nor charged God foolishly*, I Job 21,22.
>
> (350)

As heterodox thinkers like Thomas Hobbes and Bernard Mandeville found leviathan an effective metaphor for their nominalist, pragmatic visions of society and the deists discovered in Job's dialogues a justification for reasoning even with God, providentialists became even more forceful and explicit.

With confidence in reason and an almost ingenuous fascination with the new science, the deists proved an especially troubling threat to orthodox thinkers during the eighteenth century. In his *Christianity as Old as Creation or The Gospel, A Republication of the Religion of Nature* (1731), Matthew Tindal found in *Job* an argument for the primacy of reason over revelation: "And cou'd God & Man reason together, except there were some notions in common to both; some foundation for such reasoning? Otherwise how cou'd *Job* say, *I desire to reason with God*? And certainly, the next thing to reasoning with God, is reasoning with one another about God & Religion; that being the chief end, for which our reason was giv'n us" (174). Providentialists like William Derham turned to the dialogues for additional proof of their case. For Derham, even God's description of the ostrich (39:14-17) offers "Demonstrations of the Wisdom, Care, and especial Providence of the Infinite Creator and Conservator of the World" (*Physico-Theology*, 354).[4]

In the tradition of Aquinas, Sherlock consistently turns to Job as an example of the unsearchable wisdom of God's works and ways: "For God many times serves the wise ends of his Providence by the wickedness of Men, to punish the wicked, and to chastise the good; to exercise the Graces and Vertues of good men, or to give terrible Examples of his Vengeance on the wicked; and all this, how severe soever it may be, proves the Goodness of Providence, because it is for the general good of the World, that bad men should be punished, suppressed, destroyed, and that good men should be made better, and become great and eminent Examples of Faith and Patience" (261).[5]

As part of the orthodox establishment's attempt to refute deism, William Warburton (1698-1779), who served as both Alexander Pope's literary executor and the Bishop of Gloucester, created the century's most curious and controversial work about *Job*.[6] Warburton's *The Divine Legation of Moses* (1737-1741 but revised regularly until his death) ostensibly focused on the differences between Mosaic Law and Christian Revelation to demonstrate the inadequacies of the deist position.[7] But the book's most popular and controversial section involved his allegorical reading of *Job* as a drama written "to remove all Errors concerning the supreme Cause, from amongst a People now about to come under the *ordinary Providence* of God, who had long been accustomed to the *extraordinary*" (II. ii.533). For Warburton, the importance of *Job* stems primarily from its historical period. In a drama set just after the Babylonian captivity, Job's friends err by not realizing the end of their former relationship with God, a relationship characterized by a covenentally established extraordinary providential care, and the beginning of a new association as a people governed by ordinary providence. In the bishop's intricately detailed argument, every component of the original plays a part in his interpretation; Satan's assault on Job, for example, represents "the very Assault that the Prophet Zechariah tells us he made, at this Time, on the People" (528). By challenging the orthodox interpretations, Warburton opened the way for a wide range of writers to re-consider *Job*.

Warburton bases much of his analysis on the demands and conventions of *Job*'s genre. The friends' persistent attacks, for example, seem at first reading hardly credible: "But suppose now the Work to be *Dramatical*, and we immediately see the Reason for their Behaviour. For had they not been indulged in their strange captious Humour, the Author could never have produced a Piece of that Integrity of Action, which a scenic Representation demanded" (487). Dramatic conventions allow Warburton to resolve every problem from potential inconsistencies between the date of composition and the piece's apparent setting (i.e., playwrights often set their work in earlier historic periods to discuss contemporary issues) to the theophany (i.e., that "common Expedient of Dramatic Writers," a true *deus ex machina* [487]). Once he reaches these conclusion, the critic can reject the historical and literary accuracy of the words; after all, even this divine "Interposition was only a Piece of Poetical Machinery. And in that Case we see the Reason why the Knot remains untied: For the sacred Writer was no wiser when he spoke *poetically* in the person of God, than when in that of Job or his Friends" (489). Freed from any need to deal with the book's literal meaning, Warburton can address the divinely inspired symbolic meaning of *Job*.

This idiosyncratic re-consideration would begin a merging of literary and theological scholarship. *Job* still offered opportunities for fairly conventional sermons against the deists, but theologians might just as easily draw upon the century's fascination with literary form and even upon the pose of common sense adopted by the deists themselves to argue with them, as the Rev. Mr. Henry Grove did in a 1773 sermon on 21:5 titled "The Reasonableness of Religion." Grove, seeking to regain control of disputed terms by redefining them, reminded his audience that "religion is grounded on good reason" (135). In his far more elaborate *Dissertation on the Book of Job* (1749), John Garnett, Lady Margaret's Preacher and a fellow of Sidney College at Cambridge, could acknowledge the practical problem with the prologue to *Job*: "Such an interview as this between God and Satan was too inviting an one to escape the profane wit and raillery of a Tindal and a Chubb. . ." (59). His conclusion is that in fashioning the material into a play, the author took some liberty. After asking, "How far the poet may venture in the alteration of a true story, in order to fit it for the stage?", he responds "the variations should rather be in the circumstances than in the principal facts; but without some variation, from the letter even of these, without image and incidents, dialogue and episodes, occasionally scattered, and properly disposed throughout the work, it could be *no drama* at all, but an unanimated cold piece of history" (291).

II

> There are a Set of Religious, or rather Moral Writers, who teach that Virtue is the certain Road to Happiness, and Vice to Misery in this World. A very wholsome and comfortable Doctrine, and to which we have but one
> Objection, namely, That it is not true.
>
> Henry Fielding, *Tom Jones*
> (1749), Book XV, Chapter 1

By the turn of the century, John Dryden (1630-1700) had established a sophisticated dialogue about the theory and practice of translating. Unlike France, which had an extensive history of discussing the subject, beginning with Estienne Dolet's *La Maniere de bien traduire* in 1540, the first book length study in English would not appear until 1791 with Alexander Fraser Tytler's *Essay on the Principles of Translation*.

Dryden's earliest extended discussion of the art which came to occupy more and more of his time until his death two decades later appeared in his "Preface" to *Ovid's Epistles* (1680) and established not only definitions but models for his major terms:

> All Translation I suppose may be reduced to these three heads. First that of Metaphrase, or turning an Authour word by word, and Line by Line, from one Language into another. Thus, or near this manner, was *Horace* his Art of Poetry translated by *Ben. Johnson.* The second way is that of Paraphrase, or Translation with Latitude, where the Authour is kept in view by the Translator, so as never to be lost, but his words are not so strictly follow'd as his sense, and that too is admitted to be amplyfied, but not alter'd. Such is Mr. *Wallers* Translation of *Virgil*'s Fourth *Aeneid.* The Third way is that of Imitation, where the Translator (if now he has not lost that Name) assumes the liberty not only to vary from the words and sence, but to forsake them both as he sees occasion: and taking only some general hints from the Original, to run division on the ground-work, as he pleases. Such in Mr. *Cowleys* practice in turning two odes of *Pindar*, and one of *Horace* into *English.*
>
> (I, 114-15)

After discussing both the practices and practitioners of these techniques, he reaches the inevitable conclusion his moderating political rhetoric had taught him: "Imitation and verbal Version are in my Opinion the two Extreams, which ought to be avoided: and therefore . . . I have propos'd the mean betwixt them . . ." (118). He easily dismisses metaphrase, borrowing John Denham's lines praising Fanshawe's *Il Pastor Fido* and asserting that "verbally" and "well" are mutually exclusive terms (117-18). In rejecting imitation, he struggles with both his respect for Cowley's achievement in matching Pindar's "wild and ungovernable" odes (117) and his admiration for Denham's metaphor on the need for transfusing "a new spirit" when translating poetry from one language to another. While concluding that imitation is generally a distortion of the original, he excuses Cowley as a unique case and Denham who "advis'd more Liberty than he took himself" (117).

Dryden's subsequent writings, as he attempted to define his own practice and synthesize some of the elements he had opposed in his preface to Ovid, emphasize greater and greater interest in recreating the style of the original. His continual redefinition stems not only from his practical experience as a translator but from his essential rhetorical technique. By framing his ideal as a search for a *via media* and by constantly redefining his terms--in his "Dedication of the Aeneis, for example, metaphrase comes to mean a fidelity to style rather than to ideas--Dryden justified a broad range of practices and bequeathed the dynamic ideal that any English theory of translation would need to develop from practice and constantly rebalance its components to recognize their essential interdependence.

This emphasis on balance reappears consistently through the eighteenth century. The period's great intellectual synthesist, Alexander Pope, reiterates it in the "Preface" to his extraordinarily popular translation of the *Iliad* (1715-16):

> It is certain no literal Translation can be just to an excellent Original in a superior Language: but it is a great Mistake to imagine (as many have done) that a rash Paraphrase can make amends for this general Defect; which is no less in danger to lose the Spirit of an Ancient. . . . I know no Liberties one ought to take, but those which are necessary for transfusing the Spirit of the Original, and supporting the Poetical Style of the Translation. . . .
>
> (17)

By 1780 Samuel Johnson invoked the same spirit to defend Alexander Pope's additions to Homer (e.g., "Pope wrote for his own age and his own nation" [ii, 240]). Johnson's own practice, however, from his first published work, a Latin translation of Pope's *Messiah* in 1731, through his great Juvenalian imitations *London* (1738) and *The Vanity of Human Wishes* (1749), shows a marked taste for extending the boundaries of translation. By the end of the century, Tytler's *Essay on Translation* did little more than restate the traditional British view that had stretched from Chapman through Denham and Dryden to Pope and Johnson.

Late in his career Edward Young (1683-1765), who had offered a version of *Job* almost half a century earlier, expanded on the spirit of freedom in using other writers' materials in his famous letter to Samuel Richardson, *Conjectures on Original Composition* (1759). In this essay, which takes the tone of the neoclassic familiar dialogue, Young points out the superiority of original work to imitation:

> Must we then, you say, not imitate antient authors? Imitate them, by all means; but imitate aright. He that imitates the divine *Iliad*, does not imitate Homer; but he who takes the same method, which Homer took, for arriving at a capacity of accomplishing a work so great. Tread in his steps to the sole fountain of immortality; drink where he drank, at the true helicon, that is at the breast of nature. Imitate; but imitate not the *Composition*, but the *Man*.
>
> (226)

A little later Young offers the same point, but with the addition of the term "emulation": "Imitation is inferiority confessed; emulation is superiority contested, or denied; imitation is servile, emulation generous; that fetters, this fires; that may give a name; this, a name immortal" (238). Even though he wrote this long after his *Job*, he retained a strong sense of the importance of that work. In 1739, in a curt letter to the publisher Edmund Curll, he clearly regarded his *Job* as the most telling example of his genius: "You seem in the collection You propose to have omitted what I think has claim to the first place in it, I mean a Translation from Part of Job. . ." (74-75). The persistence of the traditional language of Joban translation may well account for Young's continuing to use the term paraphrase to describe his efforts.

Although Dryden, like Denham, had followed Jerome in distinguishing between works of faith and poetry, that distinction became somewhat blurred by the next generation of *Job* translators who, regarding it as a work of both faith and poetry, sought not only to distill the poetic spirit of the original but to demonstrate their own poetic powers as well. Until the end of the eighteenth century, most believed they had the sanction of authority and the example of history to continue reinterpreting the spirit of *Job* for their own age.

III

> When *Job* says in short, *He wash'd his Feet in Butter*, (a Circumstance some Poets would have soften'd, or past over) hear how it is spread out by the Great Genius.
>
> With Teats distended with their milky Store,
> Such num'rous lowing Herds, before my Door,
> Their painful Burden to unload did meet,
> That we with Butter might have wash'd our Feet.
>
> How cautious! and particular!
>
> Alexander Pope's critique of Sir
> Richard Blackmore's *Job*.
> *Peri Bathous* (1727), 34

In 1700 two versions of *Job* appeared which offered strikingly new approaches. The better known translator, Sir Richard Blackmore (d.1729), who would become physician to Queen Anne, prefaced his version with an essay that reveals both his confidence in the stability of the political order and his reservations about the theater.[8] Blackmore begins, with his characteristic rhetoric of balance, praising William and calling for a shift in the nation's attention from the political to the spiritual arenas: "notwithstanding we have by His Majesty's unrivall'd Courage, and most prudent Conduct, surmounted our fears of Foreign Enemies, the Nation is still in greater Danger from our Vices and Immoralities, our more formidable ones at Home. His Majesty, therefore, to put a stop to the progress of this dreadful Evil, and after he has sav'd us from our Enemies to deliver us from our Selves, (his last and hardest Task) has been pleas'd to recommend from the Throne the Suppressing of Vice and Irreligion. . ." ("Preface," n.p.).

Enlisted in this task, Blackmore's *Job* offers an exemplum for the nation. In order to fulfill this responsibility and in keeping with the heroic values of a poet who had already presented *Prince Arthur, an Heroick Poem* to his fellow citizens in 1695, Blackmore dismisses the tradition that Job emerges from tragic drama. Building on attacks on the theater by the Society for the Reformation of Manners and in such works as Jeremy Collier's *A Short View of the Immorality and Profaneness of the English Stage* (1698), Blackmore points out that contemporary poets have "corrupted the Stage" and then moves quickly on to quote scholars who "affirm that this Poem of Job is of the Epick kind." He then elaborates on this view with a curious redefinition of the epic:

> But whether this be an Epick, or barely an Historical Poem, which I leave undecided, the Character of Job may in my Opinion be every way proper for the first. The Hero is indeed a passive one. . . . But if we . . . reflect on the End and Design of an Epick Poem, which is to instruct the World in some important Moral Truth, by the Narration of some great and illustrious Subject-Matter, there is no question but that the relation of the Sufferings, as well as the Actions of great Persons are very conducive to that end; and indeed what else is the Subject of the Odysses? . . . Job then is a hero proper for an Epick Poem . . . a most noble Example of passive Fortitude, a Character in no way inferiour to that of the active Hero.
>
> ("Preface," n.p.)

Once he has established his perspective on the character of Job, Blackmore acknowledges the need for latitude in translation ("we can't translate verbatim a good Poem from one Modern Language into another . . . without a mighty diminution of its Excellence" ["Preface"]). Although he selects the work for its moral quality, he here clearly conceives of it in literary rather than theological terms. And aside from his evident intelligence, his tenure as a schoolmaster,[9] and his work ethic, Blackmore made no pretense to specialized knowledge in either theology or the biblical languages. Lack of experience, however, rarely hindered him, for as Dr. Johnson, an occasionally biased interpreter, reports, "[Blackmore] had read, he says, 'but little poetry throughout his whole life; and for fifteen years before had not written an hundred verses. . .'" (*Lives of the Poets*, II, 237). Later in his career he continued with his English epics, *Eliza, an Epick Poem* (1705) and *Alfred, an Epick Poem* (1723), and added a few philosophical poems, *The Nature of Man* (1711) and *Creation* (1712).

Despite his call for a new type of hero, much of Blackmore's work actually presents Job in more traditional epic terms. His opening lines, for example, echo Dryden's *Absalom and Achitophel* in establishing Job's heroic credentials:[10]

> In ancient Times, e'er Moses Wonders wrought,

And murmuring Israel back from Egypt brought,
A Prince of great Renown, and wide Command,
Whose name was Job, dwelt in Arabia's Land.
He in the Heav'nly Paths of Virtue trod,
And fear'd to Sin, because he fear'd his God.
Sev'n goodly Sons that Admiration bred,
And Three Fair Daughters crown'd his Nuptual Bed
With gracious Heav'n's peculiar Favour blest,
The prosp'rous Man unmeasur'd Wealth possest.
His Fleecy Flocks o'er all the Hills were spred,
And in his Stalls a Thousand Oxen fed.
When he decamp'd to find a new Abode,
Three thousand Camels bore along the Road
His precious Goods, and groan'd beneath the Load.
No Lord was found thro' all the Spicy East,
Whose Herds and Stored so vastly were increast.[11]
(1)

Blackmore's preoccupation with proving the work epic leads him to a diction more appropriate to Achilles or Odysseus than Job: "When the various Efforts to make this mighty Man's invincible Constancy prov'd ineffectual, he is at the latter end of the Poem acquitted by God himself, and rewarded highly for his Patience and perseverance. . ." ("Preface," n.p.). Even Job's death appears in as positive a light as Blackmore could shine on it ("ripe with Hoary Age, and fully pleas'd,/He dyed, or rather, he from Living ceas'd" [187]).

This effort to ennoble both Job and God appears perhaps most clearly in Blackmore's elaboration of 13:15, couplets which sound far more like chivalric fealty than either self submission or self-justification:

Tho'God yet hotter Anger should express,
And with redoubled strokes my Pains increase;
Tho' he advances with his glitt'ring Dart,
And o'er me stands to strike me to the heart;
I on his Truth and Justice would rely,
And with strong Faith would to his Mercy fly.
(55)

As these lines show, the poet's tendency to amplify, relying on two words where one would suffice, led to a significant expansion of the poem. At the same time, however, Blackmore deletes much of what would diminish his hero's stature. In Job's last speech, expanded from the original five verses (42:2-6) to forty-four lines, the good knight omits the repentence in dust and ashes, scarcely appropriate action in epic, and substitutes for it a heroic summary:

My arrogant Discourses I repent,
And charges brought against thy Government,
Which, delug'd in my Tears I now lament.
I grieve, that grown impatient of thy Rod,
I justified my self and censur'd God.
(185)

With its four uses of "I" and three of "my," Job seems scarcely humbled in this example of passive fortitude. While the translation can be easily dismissed as a product of that flawed sensibility Pope so wittily dissects,[12] Blackmore's commitment to epic portraiture established a model for both the heroic and literary approaches to *Job* that would dominate the following half century.

That same year another remarkable translation appeared, *The Book of Job in Meeter* by R. P., identified only as a "Minister of the Gospel." Although the preface notes, "I do not pretend to poetry, neither do I much Paraphrase upon the Words, but for the most Part keep close to them as they are translated," R.P.'s practice is to rearrange the text radically. He begins, for example, with 5:9-17 and then moves to 9:4-16. By relying on the King James for most of the language, R.P. can focus on arranging the text into either tetrameter lines or ballad measure. His awkward attempts at rhyme unfortunately lead him into a confused and confusing syntax that too often creates a confusing rather than pathetic effect. In 38:2, for example, he reveals some unconscious humor:

Who is this that my Counsel dares,
To darken, and misrepresent?
And that by Reasonings so weak,
And without Knowledge, Words doth vent.
Come then, if thou wilt Cope with me
Gird up thy Loyns, and let me see:
Thy Man-hood, for I will of Thee,
Demand, and do thou answer me

His ballad meter has a similar sense of forcing the syntax

Rest in the Grave
Job 3:17,18,19
In th'Grave from troubling wicked cease,
At Rest the weary are:
There Prisoners Rest together, an
Oppressors Voice don't hear.

The small and great are there, for Death
Seizes on all Degrees:
And there who was a Servant here,
Is from his Master free.

R.P.'s work, however, does reveal a movement away from regarding the text as sacrosanct. To achieve his end, R.P. felt comfortable with reconceiving the structure to create both literary and emotional effects. Like Blackmore, the goal is no longer to preserve the word but to achieve a comparable effect, even if this requires a radical revision of the original.

Traces of the older tradition of paraphrase persisted, but they generally took a slightly different direction from the works of the previous century by focusing on literary rather than political issues. In 1716, for example, a person identified only as "a Presbyter of the Church of England" published *A Short Paraphrase on the Book of Job* which placed additions in brackets, while Edward Wells's *An Help for the More Easy and Clear Understanding of the Scriptures* (1727) includes a paraphrase of *Job*, but adds an aid for his readers by italicizing his additions, as in 42:1: "Then Job answer'd the Lord, and said, 2. I know thou canst do every thing, and that no Thought *or Design* can be withholden from thee, i.e. *can be hinder'd from being done by thee, if thou pleasest.* 3. *I am sensible also of the Justice of the Reproof, which thou gavest to me in those words, Chap. 38:*2 Who is he that hideth Counsel without Knowledge." And in 1748 Daniel Bellamy's *Paraphrase of Job* echoes Blackmore's belief in the protagonist's passive fortitude and emphasizes the pervasive goodness of both God and man.

But paraphrase had clearly taken a back seat to poetry. In 1706 Daniel Baker, the Rector of Fincham in Norfolk, offered *The History of Job: A Sacred Poem in Five Books*. Baker noted that he had not seen Blackmore's work until he had finished his own, but agreed with Blackmore on the need for a change in the concept of the hero: "In the old Heathen World those gentle passive Virtues, which the Christian Religion recommends to our Esteem and Practice, were hardly known, or, if known, despised and slighted, so that their Poets lay under a necessity of choosing some bold, active, fighting Man for their hero. . ." ("Preface," n.p.). Replacing such heroes with figures who epitomize those gospel values embodied in the beatitudes has become his goal. Baker also admits that he has some personal motivation for selecting this text: "It having pleas'd Almighty God to afflict me (as He did his Servant Job) with great Losses, and other Occasions of Sorrow, I resolv'd to make that Holy Man my Pattern. . ." ("Preface," n.p.).

Thus Baker opens his poem with a charge to his reader that moves Job from Blackmore's more traditionally heroic image to a figure capable of claiming identification for his pathos:

You that at ev'ry trifling Cross repine,
And tax the Ways of Providence Divine
You that to ev'ry soft Temptation yield,
And leave your Captain in the doubtful Field;
Weak Souls, unable to resist the Charms
Of the fond World, or stand her rude Alarms;
Whom Wealth and Want do equally destroy,
By ev'ry Grief undone, and ev'ry Joy:
Come, and behold a valiant Hero, whom
Nor Fortune's Smiles, nor Frowns could overcome.
'Gainst whom the Infernal Pow'rs in vain conspir'd,
Who all their Wit, and all their malice tir'd.
(1-2)

While his nicely balanced couplets prevent his work from moving too much in the direction of sensibility which would soon come to dominate the poetic efforts to English Job, that balance occasionally collapses, as when he reintroduces a strong dose of the medieval misogynist tradition by adding a long temptation of Job's wife. In the following catalogue about her by Belial, his lines adopt an enjambed Miltonic organization:

Her Sex's Dow'r she wants not, Envy, Pride,
Revenge, and Forty glorious Names beside.
Lustful and Covetous, she hates her Lord
Now Poor and Sick, nor able to afford
What would content her, and she longs to be
From such an inconvenient Marr'age free.
(33-34)

In fact, Baker adopts a good deal from Milton, including debates in hell and extensive allusions, while sharply cutting Job's dialogue with his comforters.

Such freedoms marked an even more talented poet in 1719, when Edward Young presented his *Paraphrase on Part of the Book of Job* to the British public.[13] Despite his title, he acknowledges, "I use the Word Paraphrase, because I want another which might better answer to the uncommon Liberties I have taken. I have Omitted, Added, and Transpos'd." Samuel Johnson suggested a pattern in Young's selections when he pointed out that the poet "favoured himself by chusing those parts which most easily admit the ornaments of English poetry" (iii, 395). In order to reach his primary goal, God's speech, Young races through the rest of the story in a mere three pages. The opening lines suggest this contraction:

Thrice Happy Job long liv'd in Regal State,
Nor saw the Sumptuous East a Prince so Great;
Whose Worldly Stores in such Abundance flow'd,
Whose Heart with such exalted Virtue glow'd:
At length Misfortunes take their Turn to reign,
And Ills on Ills, Succeed; a Dreadful Train!

(1)

Young, who was to help shape the sensibility of sentiment and the Graveyard Poets, especially with *The Complaint; or Night Thoughts on Life, Death, and Immortality* in 1742, focuses in *Job* far more on the imagery of God's speech than either the apologetics or melancholic detail of that later poem. And in recreating that imagery, he transposes rather dramatically, reorganizing the imagery into a taxonomic crescendo from less significant creatures to the climactic behemoth. Only in describing Job's fall does he establish some of melancholic tone which would mark his subsequent pieces:

What Now but Deaths, and Poverty, and Wrong,
The Sword wide-wasting, the reproachful Tongue,
And spottted Plagues that mark'd his Limbs all o'er
So thick with Pains, they wanted Room for more?
A Change so sad, what Mortal heart could bear?
Exhausted Woe had left him nought to fear,
But gave Him All to Grief: Low Earth He prest,
Wept in the Dust, and sorely smote his Breast.

(2)

Although Young compresses the dialogue into eight lines, perhaps his most suggestive deletion occurs at the end, when Job's submission is not followed by a reward:

O'erwhelm'd with Shame, the Lord of Life I see
Abhor my self, and give my Soul to Thee:
Nor shall my Weakness tempt Thine Anger more:
Man was not made to Question, but Adore.

(26)

William Thompson, a fellow of Trinity College, Dublin, went a step further in 1726 with *A Poetical Paraphrase on Part of the Book of Job in Imitation of the Style of Milton* by omitting the opening of *Job* altogether. His version begins fairly abruptly:

Job silent stood, when from a thick'ning Cloud
Impetuous rush'd a Whirlwind Blast, the Voice
Of God, and said, Impetuous Man, prepare
To own thy Ignorance of Counsels high
My secret Purposes and deep Desires
From utmost Reach of Men or Angels Sight
Remote. . . .

(1-2)

Part of his Miltonic style involves the use of blank verse, a practice which he defends with a slight anti-papist note: "Whatsoever little and false Pleasure the Ear may receive from Rhime and a jingling repetition of Sound, yet it must be confess'd that it is an heavy Clog upon the Spirit of Poetry. And indeed . . . it is a thing in it self unnatural, of Gothic Invention, handed down to us by ignorant and lazy Monks. . . . But surely Heroic Poetry should walk at large and unmanacled, that it may be the better able to put forth all its Strengths" (Preface, n.p.). Thompson's justification, based on artistic rather than theological principles, reflects how readily he imagined *Job* essentially as literature. And like Young he emphasizes the rich imagery and envisions an ending with no hint of material rewards, emphasizing instead the psychological benefit:

God said, and Job
Humbled in low Prostration where he stood,
Rever'd the Voice Divine, and to his Mind
Firm Peace recover'd soon and wonted Calm.

(18)

By 1734 the ability to conceive of *Job* primarily in aesthetic terms becomes apparent in the anonymous *Complaint of Job*, which reads more like an imitation of Pope's enormously popular, proto-Romantic *Eloisa to Abelard* than *Job*. The work, like many of its predecessors, freely switches chapters and verses. The difference is that the *Complaint* offers only Job's words. The poem begins with 29:2:

Oh! that the Voice of Grief had Pow'r to raise
From Times dark Graves those dear remembred Days!
Those roseate Hours! those Moments of Delight!
Which once around me wing'd their happy Flight
And whose soft Pinions plum'd alone for Joy,
Ne'er knew the heavy Burden of a Sigh.

(5)

It continues in this vein, juxtaposing passages to pile up image on image with a diction that had appeared in some of Young's earlier works, Pope's *Eloisa to Abelard* and *Verses to the Memory of an Unfortunate Lady* (1717), and Elizabeth Rowe's *Friendship in Death* (1728) and would soon become popular in works like Young's *Night Thoughts*, James Hervey's *Meditations and Contemplations* (1746) and Thomas Gray's *Elegy* (1750).

> (30:28-31) Disconsolate, I haunt the dismal Shade,
> The Shade more dismal by my Sorrows made;
> With Birds obscene associate, and decline
> The rosy Blush of Morn and Noon-Tide shine:
> To some foul Den unobvious skulk away,
> And hate the Eye of Man, and Eye of Day.
> Where's now the sprightly Harp, and swelling Voice,
> Which late to entertain me would rejoice?
> . . . .
> (4:16) Help, help, my God! for thou alone can'st tell
> To dissipate this horrid Gloom of Hell;
> Break with consummate Splendor on my sight,
> And chear my Soul with thy reviving Light.
> (10-11)

And like Young and Thompson, the *Complaint* concludes with a final vision a sense of a spiritual rather than material resolution, but, in keeping with the poem's extravagant imagery, it does so against an apocalyptic background:

> The Light of God--then shall my Soul on flame
> Spring up to mix with his congenial Beam;
> Melted, dissolv'd, in his superior Rays,
> Whilst burning Worlds shall unregarded blaze.
> (18)

In addition to the poem's cavalier attitude toward its original, its highly secular ironic dedication to the reigning wits ("the Meek in Spirit") calls for an aesthetic rather than religious response.[14]

By 1750 the pseudonymous Eugenio can set his work clearly among the Graveyard School by dedicating his *Age in Distress: or, Job's Lamentation for his Children* to Edward Young "for his *Night Thoughts*." Eugenio's work owes relatively little beyond theme and an occasional image to its source. Relying on blank verse, he invokes all of the established imagery of pathos:

> No sooner has *Aurora* shed her Rays

And gilded o'er the gloomy Veil of Night;
But Sorrow like a Tide o'erwhelms my Mind,
And with her roaring Billows wakes my Grief:
My Eyes wax dim with Woe, and throbbing heart.
Disturbs my Rest, and spreads a dreary Gloom
Thro' all the Regions of my tortur'd Soul:
Fatigu'd with Life, and plung'd in endless Cares,
I seek the Grave and long to sleep in Death.
        Frustrate Desire! my Woe but slumbers yet,
Nor to Perfection does my Misery rise;
Distress but blooms, nor is the Hour arriv'd
To calm the surging Waves, and lay the Storm;
Death treats me with Disdain, nor will vouchsafe
To plunder Life and steal the crazy Load.
        Thro' the revolving Hours of each long Day,
Black Scenes of Horror discompose my Peace,
And spread Distraction o'er the Seat of Life;
Distress has plac'd her Empire in my Soul
And reigns despotic with a Tyrants Sway:
Frantic I seek Relief without Success
And curse Time's ling'ring Pace in Sobs and Groans.
        When Phoebus spreads his Lustre o'er the Globe,
And rouzes Slumber from her dark Retreat,
And spreads content o'er all the waking World;
I sink beneath my Woes, and ardent wish
To view his shining Pomp absorb'd in Night.
Oh foolish Wish! imaginary Hope!
To drown corroding Cares, and ease those Pains
That sport in Darkness, and exult in Night:
Night--is the Nurse of Woe, and only serves
To wake Despair and fan her glowing Coals,
Till the rekindling Embers burn afresh,
And blaze amain in purple Flames of Fire.

(3-5)

As translators experimented with alternative versions of individual books, the Roman Catholic response was an entire revision of its English translation. Unlike its Anglican rival, the Douai-Rheims version of the Old Testament, with a heavily Latinate style that often follows its Vulgate original closely, had never proved popular. Where the King James had inspired hundreds of editions, only two of the Douai Old Testament had appeared, in 1610 and 1635. Recognizing its inability to find a broad audience, in 1750 Richard Challoner, a Presbyterian convert to Catholicism who had been appointed Bishop of Debra, revised it, bringing the text closer to both standard English and the King James. Challoner's revision was to stand, with some minor revisions, for another century until Francis Patrick Kenrick, the Archbishop of Baltimore, attempted a new revision. With Challoner, Roman Catholics at last had a more readable text. In 9. 14-15, for example, where the Doway had phrased Job's question in an awkwardly Latinate syntax ("How great am I then, that I may answer him, and speake in my wordes with him? + Who although I have just thing, wil not answer, but wil besech my judge.") Challoner makes enough slight revisions in the language and syntax to make it closer to standard English usage, although the second verse remains fairly obscure: "What am I then, that I should answer him, and have words with him? I, who although I should have any just thing, would not answer, but would make supplication to my judge."[15]

Attacks on rhyme like William Thompson's, the use of blank verse, and assumptions of the epic nature of *Job* drew a response from Ralph Erskine, Minister at Dumfernline. Clearly influenced by the success of Isaac Watts (1674-1748), whose *Hymns* (1707) and *Psalms of David* (1719) had become widely popular among dissenting congregations, Erskine expressed his scorn for "modish blank verse" while drawing an important distinction between the form and substance of poetry: "It is much doubted, among the learned, whether this book of *Job* is written originally in metre, yea, or not; but though they are of different judgments on this head, yet it is acknowledged by them all, that the subject of it is treated in a poetical manner, and that therein is discovered a great air of what is called *epic poetry*" (13).

Like R.P. a half century earlier, Erskine chooses to interpret *Job* as song in his *Job's Hymns: Or, a Book of Songs upon the Book of Job*. And like R.P., his interest is less in rethinking the diction than the rhythm in what emerge essentially as a series of moral precepts:

Song VIII (Job 5:17-27)

(1)

Lo! happy is the man whom God,
  In kindness doth correct;
Then do not thou his chast'ning rod,
  Contemptuously neglect.

(2)

The more th'Almighty makes thee smart,
    To break thy carnal ease,
The more he seeks to win thy heart,
    And bring thee to thy knees.

(30)

Erskine's strict moral vision allows him to expand or contract the text with ease. His theology, simpler than Watts, often reflects the historical and cultural assumptions of his time, as in the devolutionary view of human history which he shared with Jonathan Swift:

Song XII
Time and Life Short (Job 8: 9)
(1)
We're but of yesterday's new mold,
Our life's of no regard,
When with our long-liv'd father's old
And ancestors compar'd.
(2)
No knowledge or experience we
Can ever justly boast:
Our days like shadows are that flee
No sooner had, than lost.
(35)

IV

Poor Job! what will these allegorical reformers make of thee at last?

Richard Grey, *An Answer to Mr. Warburton's Remarks on the Book of Job* (1744)

Whatever disagreement there may have been among the learned--in Erskine's words about "whether this Book of *Job* is written in metre, yea, or not"--disappeared in the same year that *Job's Hymns* appeared with the publication of Bishop Robert Lowth's *De sacri poesi Hebraeorum*, a series of Latin lectures Lowth (1710-87) had delivered at Oxford. Even though his work was not translated into English until the end of the century, Lowth's emphasis on the role of genius in art and his clear illustration of the nature of Hebrew versification made his work both influential and popular, as it not only transformed the way readers would view the *Book of Job* but also helped pave the way for the Romantics by emphasizing the sublimity of *Job* and identifying "the proper genius and character" of Hebrew poetry as "unconstrained, animated, bold, and fervid" (230).[16]

While acknowledging what could not be determined (e.g., "the real quantity, the rhythm, or modulation" and "the true Hebrew pronunciation" [33]), he clearly demonstrated that "the verses are very unequal in length" (32), which allowed translators and scholars to explore rhythmic patterns which would not rely on the Western tradition of the relationship between stressed and unstressed syllables, and that an essential component of Hebrew poetry is *parallelismus membrorum*, the development of a line through synonymous, antithetic, and synthetic parallelism:

> The Hebrew poets frequently express a sentiment with the utmost brevity and simplicity, illustrated by no circumstances, adorned with no epithets (which in truth they seldom use); they afterwards call in the aid of ornament; they repeat, they vary, they amplify the same sentiment; and adding one or more sentences which run parallel to each other, they express the same or a similar, and often a contrary sentiment, in nearly the same form of words. Of these three modes of ornament at least they make the most frequent use, namely, the amplification of the same ideas, the accumulation of others, and the opposition or antithesis of such as are contrary to each other; they dispose the corresponding sentences in regular distichs adapted to each other, and of an equal length, in which, for the most part, things answer to things, and words to words, as the Son of Sirach says of the works of God, *two and two, one against the other.*
>
> (100-101)

Discussing parallelism in Hebrew poetry has become such a commonplace that few even recognize Lowth's original role in identifying it.

Part of Lowth's objective was to replace Warburton's emphasis on the work's coded message with an emphasis on its sublimity, the affective quality Lowth identified as the measure of its greatness. For the most part, Lowth dismisses Warburton's argument with his usual, measured arguments. At times, however, he allows his irritation to show: "The truth of the narrative would never, I am persuaded, have been called in question, but from the immoderate affection of some allegorizing mystics for their own fictions, which run to such excess as to prevent them from acceding to any thing but what was visionary and typical" (357).[17]

Perhaps the least satisfying part of Lowth's analysis arises in his discussion of the work's genre. Much of the problem here lies in the frame of reference with which he examines differences between the nature and form of Greek and Hebrew drama. Lowth compares both to "the true dramatic model" (378), a model which he appears to have inherited from Aristotle, Aeschylus, and Sophocles. Once having established such a Platonic ideal inferred from Greek models, he inevitably finds *Job* limited in comparison with the very plays that helped establish that ideal. When he assigns it "a distinct and conspicuous station in the highest rank of the Hebrew poetry" (378), his context makes it clear that "Hebrew" is a sharply restricted and restrictive adjective in this context. Once he establishes that limitation, his arguments develop a labyrinthine pattern of reservation and rationalization. In one sentence he even manages to cite and attempt to excuse *Job*'s limitations twice: "But though the nice and fastidious criticism of the moderns demand variety [in the characters of the three friends], the simplicity of infant poetry will be excused by every person of real judgment; and I think this deficiency (if such it may be called) is amply compensated by the gravity and importance of the subject and sentiments" (386). Clearly recognizing the inadequacy of this part of his discussion, he suggest--although he never fully pursues--the idea that *Job* might be more accurately considered a monody or elegiac dialogue (376).

After Lowth, no serious translator could ignore the technical lessons of *De sacri*. But Lowth's contribution would prove to be more extensive than defining poetic technique. After Lowth, translators of *Job* would begin taking a far more scholarly view of the poem, often feeling free to challenge traditional assumptions. Their titles and practice reflect this search for a more authentic version of the poem, a quest which largely owes its impetus to Bishop Lowth's lectures.

Endnotes

[1] Brown's *Self-Interpreting Bible*, first issued in 1778, became the first edition published in New York in 1792, with George Washington as its first subscriber, and was reprinted in both the United Kingdom and the United States until well into the Twentieth Century.

[2] As the violence of the preceding century receded, *Job* could also offer less sectarian Anglican clergy topics for more material reflections. Preaching on *The Lawfulness of Feasting, with the Danger of Abusing It* on January 3, 1714, the Rev. Charles Wheatly used Job to remind his flock that "*Feasting, Mirth*, and Society are not inconsistent with the Practice of Virtue and Religion" (4). *Job*'s continuing popularity appears in Sampson Letsome's listing of 183 sermons on the book between 1660 and 1753 in *The Preacher's Assistant* (29-33, 279).

[3] While recognizing that Sherlock's fairly public anguish in making his change of loyalties generated a good deal of satire against both him and his wife, Macaulay more often portrays him as a figure who epitomized the orthodox position even if he rarely broke new ground: "He was not of the first rank among his contemporaries as a scholar, as a preacher, as a writer on theology, or as a writer on politics: but in all the four characters he had distinguished himself"

(*History*, III, 450).

[4] Derham's extraordinarily optimistic reading of the universe as the "Handywork" (428) of a benevolent, kindly deity clearly does not allow him to recognize either the cruelty or ambivalence in this portrait of a creature which, denied wisdom, abandons her young.

[5] For Sherlock, suffering has an essentially postlapsarian redemptive role for man: ". . . the present state of Mankind in this world [is] a state of Trial and Discipline; to reclaim and reform Sinners by the various methods of Grace and Providence, and this changes both the very Notion and Exercise of God's Goodness and Justice in the world; for we must expect no more of either, than what a state of Trial and Discipline will allow" (219). Job's case, however, was "very peculiar" for "God did not punish him for some unknown wickedness, but to exercise his Faith and Patience, and to make him a Glorious and Triumphant Example of a firm adherence to God under the severest Trials" (111).

[6] Warburton's work would inspire both heated responses and equally heated defenses. William Sherlock's son Thomas (1678-1761), a highly respected preacher who became master of the Temple, weighed in with a sharply *ad hominem* and decidedly aristocratic attack on the bishop's style: "Since some reason may be expected for having taken great Liberties with the name *Warburton*, I give this for Answer: His Language is strong and nervous; his Periods are judiciously turned; his Words run off tolerably harmonious; his Wit is lively and poignant, but it has an inbred Meaning which is utterly rude and beggarly, such as shews the Author of it wanted that early Introduction into good Company, which was necessary to have given him a Taste for the Language and Behaviour of sensible Men. He professes himself a true Church Militant; but mark him! he advances to the Combat with all the Ferocity of an untutored Barbarian" (104-5). Valuable discussions of Warburton's work and the controversy it engendered, including Bishop Lowth's responses, appear in Jonathan Lamb's *The Rhetoric of Suffering* (1995), 110-27 and "The Job Controversy, Sterne and the Question of Allegory, *Eighteeth Century Studies* 24 (1990), 1-19 and in Martin Battestin's *The Providence of Wit* (1974), 197-200. Lamb sees *Job* functioning as a trope for the eighteenth-century's "crisis of normative language" (*Rhetoric*, 6), the conflict between individual experience and systems of doctrines and interpretation.

[7] Warburton's primary argument, delivered in extensive and combative fashion, focused on his belief that Judaism did not have a sense of an afterlife until fairly late. In his discussion of *Job*, therefore, he interprets 19:25 as a reference to a temporal deliverance from affliction rather than a resurrection (II.ii.548). Valuable discussions of the controversy Warburton provoked appear in Jonathan Lamb's *The Rhetoric of Suffering* (1995).

[8] In his discussion of Pope's reading of Blackmore in *The Rhetoric of Suffering* (205-25), Jonathan Lamb points to Blackmore's political assumptions: "The politics of the *Paraphrase* are those of an ardent Williamite Whig who wishes to praise the steadiness of the Hanoverian succession during its first crisis" (205-6).

[9] A constant butt of the wits, Blackmore was ridiculed for both his time as a schoolmaster and as a physician. One contemporary satire, cited by Theophilus Cibber in his *Lives of the Poets*, comments: "His boys grew blockheads and his patients died" (V, 177).

[10] Dryden was no admirer of Blackmore the poet, whom he attacked in his last published work, the preface to his *Fables* in 1700. While angrily denouncing Blackmore's *Satyr against Wit* (1700), Dryden wittily dismisses his earlier work, "But I will deal more civilly with his two poems, because nothing ill is to be spoken of the dead. . ." (II, 272).

[11] Despite his clear influence on Blackmore's thought, Dryden completely dismissed his translation in a "Prologue" to *The Pilgrim* (1700), one of the former laureate's last works:

His man of *Uz*, stript of his *Hebrew* Robe,
Is just the Proverb, and *As poor as Job.*
One wou'd have thought he could no longer Jog;
But *Arthur* was a Level, *Job*'s a Bog.

(Poems, ll. 1758-59)

[12] See Lamb's *The Rhetoric of Suffering*, 205-25. Blackmore himself cavalierly dismissed such criticism: "I am unacquainted with the Definition of *Too Much*" (*Collection of Poems*, xii).

[13] Young dedicated his poem to the Lord Chancellor, Thomas, Lord Parker, the Baron of Macclesfield. Ironically, Macclesfield left office in disgrace

.

[14] "Gentlemen

I am conscious that I am guilty of a very perceptible Rudeness, in offering this publick Violence to your Modesties, without having first solicited *a-la-mode* for your Permission to offend you.

That innate Goodness, which is in so peculiar a manner your own, I know would immediately grant me a Pardon; but I hope you won't think I lie under any necessity of applying myself there, when I assure you that it was positively out of my power to act otherwise than I do; for tho, like your old Familiars, Content and Resignation, you are very much talk'd of, yet, I flatter myself, that I'm in no danger of displeasing you, if I venture to say, you are very little known. I have often made the strictest Enquiries, where I might have the Honour of paying you my Devoirs; but never yet could be so fortunate, as to find a Guide to that happiness: which makes me very apprehensive, that no Place of my Acquaintance has any just Claim to boast of your Residence. There are indeed some demure Rascals amongst us, who have Impudence enough to personate you; and as Folly is the Growth of all Countries, there are others, who are Fools enough to believe 'em. . . . Wherefore, since it was not lack of respect, but only my Ignorance where to pay it, that occasions this Breach of Good-manners, I hope the necessity of my Fault will entitle it to the Favour of being overlook'd, and that you won't refuse your Patronage to the following Representation of your illustrious Predecessor surprise that echoes of that tradition appear in his revision. The King James version of 9:15, for example--"Whom, though I were righteous, *yet* would I not answer, *but* I would make supplication to my judge"--clearly influenced his reading. Ironically, the first important post-Douai-Rheims Catholic translation also came from a hand and ear raised on the King James. Ronald Knox, who had been ordained in the Church of England in 1914 but become a Roman Catholic priest in 1917, published a new version of the New Testament in 1944 and the Old Testament five years later.

[16] Lowth's comment on Zophar's thoughts on infinity in 11.7-9 reflects the passion of his admiration for *Jo*b's poetry: "Here we find the idea of infinity perfectly expressed, though it be perhaps the most difficult of all ideas to impress upon the mind: for, when simply and abstractedly mentioned, without the assistance and illustration of of any circumstances whatever, it almost wholly evades the powers of the human understanding. The sacred writers have, therefore, recourse to description, amplification, and imagery, by which they give substance and solidity to what is in itself a subtile and unsubstantial phantom; and render an ideal shadow the object of our senses. They conduct us through all the dimensions of space, length, breadth, and height: these they do not describe in general or indefinite terms; they apply to them an actual line and measure, and that the most extensive which all nature can supply, or which the mind is indeed able to comprehend. When the intellect is carried beyond these limits, there is nothing substantial upon which it can rest; it wanders through every part, and when it has compassed the boundaries of creation, it imperceptibly glides into the void of infinity--whose vast and formless extent, when displayed to the mind of man in the forcible manner so happily attained by the Hebrew writers, impresses it with the sublimest and most awful sensations, and fills it with a mixture of admiration and terror" (173).

[17] Lowth is careful to make distinctions about this truth: "When I speak of the poem as founded in fact, I would be understood no further than concerns the general subject of the narrative; for, I apprehend, all the dialogue, and most likely some other parts, have partaken largely of the embellishments of poetry. . ." (357). In a note to this passage, he is even more explicit, "I feel very little doubt that the subject of the poem is altogether fabulous. . ." (358fn).

CHAPTER FOUR

Hast Thou Perceived the Breadth of the Earth? (38:18)

> A noble Book; all men's Book! It is our first, oldest statement of the never-ending Problem,--man's destiny and God's ways with him here in this earth. And all in such free flowing outlines; grand in its sincerity, in its simplicity; in its epic melody, and repose of reconcilement. . . . Sublime sorrow, sublime reconciliation; oldest choral melody as of the heart of mankind;--so soft and great; as the summer midnight, as the world with its seas and stars! There is nothing written, I think, in the Bible or out of it, of equal literary merit.
>
> Thomas Carlyle, *On Heroes: Hero-Worship, & The Heroic in History* (1841), 78-79

By the middle of the eighteenth century, England had developed an extensive admiration for Hebrew literature and culture, an admiration which Howard Weinbrot has termed "philosemitism" and identified in works as diverse as Christopher Smart's *Song to David* (1763) and Handel's oratorio *Israel in Egypt* (1739), which Weinbrot calls "the greatest Pindaric poem in the English language" (406). Other movements—an increasing fascination with the sublime and romanticism; an instinct for ambiguity which fed a taste for irony; the century's "undeniable mania for physical representations of decay" (Goldstein, 3); a growing curiosity about a world in which England had become an imperial power; the rise of a more secular scholarship; an increasing sophistication in the Church of England which allowed scholars to look more critically and creatively at a wide range of texts; and an expanding market for books generated by expanding literacy and affluence—created an environment in which the tools of scholarship became so readily available that even a woman of extremely modest means and resources like Elizabeth Smith (1776-1806) could compile an Arabic, Hebrew, and Persian dictionary.

After Alexander Tytler's summary of traditional practice, the theory of translation would take a decidedly new turn. Although no English or American theorist rose to the stature of continental writers like Johann Wolfgang von

Goethe, August Wilhelm von Schlegel, Friedrich von Schlegel, or Friedrich Schleiermacher, the occasional comments of British and American writers showed a broad agreement with the Germans. With their emphasis on individual genius and the organicism of texts, many nineteenth-century writers found themselves caught between beliefs in the need to preserve the unique quality of the original and in the right of translators to exercise their own genius. They almost invariably attempted to resolve this dilemma by calling for fidelity[2] to original works, a tendency that often manifested itself in archaic or unusual diction and syntax. Matthew Arnold based such a case for literal versions on an argument from authority. After defining the translator's primary responsibility as reproducing the effect of the original, he argued that to identify and recreate that effect the translator must take direction from scholars, "the only competent tribunal" ("On Translating Homer," 98-99).[3]

Thomas Carlyle, Dante Gabriel Rossetti, and William Morris all agreed with Arnold about the primacy of original texts in consistently regarding translation as an activity inferior to original composition. Even when they practice it, Victorian translators often allow a note of apology to creep in, as in Rossetti's reflection in his "Preface" to *The Early Italian Poets* that "the task of the translator . . . is one of some self denial" (176).[4] A singular exception was the Victorian translator whose work has proven most enduring. Edward Fitzgerald offered an impressionistic, Romantic restatement of the traditional English view in explaining his very liberal approach to the anonymously published *Rubaiyat of Omar Khayyam* (1859): "I suppose very few people have ever taken such Pains in Translation as I have: though certainly not to be literal. But at all cost, a Thing must *live*: with a transfusion of one's own worse Life if one can't retain the Original's better. Better a live Sparrow than a stuffed Eagle" (*Letters*, II, 335). But Fitzgerald's position stands out among his contemporaries as a singular voice defending translation as an art.

During the century and a half following Bishop Lowth's lectures, an experimental eclecticism came to characterize the world of Joban translations. Although paraphrase and poetry continued after the mid-eighteenth century, they developed new directions which separated them from the work of textual purists and theological traditionalists. Paraphrases became more fanciful, introducing much of the legendary Joban material, while poets, profoundly influenced by theories of the sublime and romanticism, took a more secular approach and continued experimenting with forms. But the most striking development arose among scholars and theologians. By modeling a more critical approach to the text, William Warburton and Robert Lowth inspired new efforts not just by traditionally trained clerics like Thomas Heath and Thomas Scott but by newly emerging women and Jewish scholars as well. Scholarship engendered curiosity about sources and style, which led not only to an increased interest in variants like the Septuagint and Arabic versions but also attempts at a more literal version. What combines all of these efforts is a search for authenticity either in a more historically accurate version or a more compelling contemporary one.

I

> Job, on his dunghill, far more great
> Than when he dwelt in royal state!
> He heard, before, Jehovah's grace,
> But now he sees him face to face;
> Meekly he bow'd before his God,
> He felt the smart, but kiss'd the rod.
> "In me, great God, complete thy will!
> Slay me, and I will trust Thee still."
>
> Hannah More,
> *Bible Rhymes* (1821), 28

The tradition of paraphrase lingered a bit through the end of the century in works like Lawrence Holden's (1710-1778) elaborately polite *A Paraphrase on the Books of Job, Psalms, Proverbs, and Ecclesiastes* (1763) and the appropriate named Rev. Job Orton's (1717-1783) *A Short and Plain Exposition of the Old Testament* (1790). Each of these follows in the tradition of prose attempts to clarify and simplify the story. By the next century, however, paraphrases began serving entirely different roles. With the appearance of Bibles containing extensive commentaries, they lost their role in explicating the texts; and as biblical scholarship became increasingly sophisticated, paraphrase lost its intellectual and theological respectability. John Selby Watson's didactic "Job, or Patience" in his *Sons of Strength Wisdom Patience* (1861) suggests the direction paraphrase had taken. Watson (1804?-1884), less interested in explicating the text than in explaining his vision of the story, begins his prose version with a conversation between Satan and Belial, figures who intervene often into the action of his reinterpretation. The activist role of Satan appears to have been influenced by the meditations in Francis Quarles' *Iob Militant* (1624), which Watson nevertheless dismisses as a "feeble attempt" at interpretation (vi). Watson's own vision of the diabolic presents highly civilized adversaries always a bit ephemeral in their excessive manners. Note the prose's cautious qualifications in the words and phrases I have italicized from Satan's response to the first cycle of speeches:

> Satan desired to know what impression had been made on the mind of Job by their discourse. He was *somewhat* disappointed to find that Job

> was *so little* provoked. He had *indeed* expressed thoughts that *could not but be* displeasing to the Divine power, yet they were mingled with others that were as compensations to them; and he *might be* considered *on the whole*, to have stopped far short of rebellion against heaven. The Divinity had *certainly* made no open display of wrath against him.
>
> (231)

Watson's interest in recasting Job into his own vision of Victorian civility reflects the freedom paraphrase came to symbolize. The term could justify, for example, even greater poetic freedom. In 1760 the advertisement for William Langhorne's *Job: A Poem in Three Books* describes it as a "free Paraphrase." That advertisement explains why the author does not call his work a translation: "The Title Page does not profess it such, because the Author has sometimes omitted Images unsuitable to our Times; and sometimes has ventured to add to that sublime Composition." Whether Langhorne (1721-1772), the Rector of Hawkenge, or his printer wrote the advertisement, the term paraphrase has clearly become a code for the freedom which Langhorne exercised in his greatly elaborated version of *Job*,[5] which conceives of the sublime in epic terms. Despite clearly modeling his work after Edward Young--"Had He versified the Whole, the Author of this Essay would never have attempted it after him"--Langhorne's essentially Augustan values appear even in Job's plea for death which has less anguish than a sense of balanced retreat to the Horatian countryside:

> O kind Retreat from Woes, impartial Grave!
> Where Liberty, long sought, relieves the Slave;
> Where, from the Burden freed, the Weary rest,
> Like Brethren sleep th'Oppressor and opprest.
>
> I, 37-40

The freedom Langhorne exercises, as well as his choice of heroic couplets, would mark many of the poetic paraphrases that followed, like the anonymous 1779 *A Paraphrase of the Thirty-Eighth Chapter of the Book of Job*. When friends of the American Richard Devens published his *A Paraphrase on Some Parts of the Book of Job* in 1795, they offered it "as a memorial of what the author *once was* and to preserve the remains of a noble genius--now in ruins" (v). Devens had taught mathematics at Princeton until "a disorganization of his intellectual powers ensued and his reason forsook him" in his twenty-fourth year (iv) and he retired into solitude. His paraphrase, clearly presented as emblematic of both Job's and Devens' lives, compresses much of the work in presenting Job as a good Christian with solid neoclassical values and a taste for melancholic and

Miltonic imagery:

Oh! in the clay cold horrors of the grave,
Now to be plung'd; Death, instant death, I crave!
Oh! soon to find me, in that land of night!
That region rayless all, where e'en their light
Gleams horribly; where darkness is their day:
Where method is misrule; confusion sway.

(23)

Devens' *Job*, like his own life, ended with submission not reward: "Hence my rebellious thoughts shall all be slain,/My work shall be to worship, not complain" (39).

This tradition of using the term paraphrase as a justification for broadly translated English versions continued in such works as William Carpenter's *A Poetical Paraphrase on the Book of Job* (1796) and Valentine Lumley Bernard's *A Sacred Poem in Four Books. Being a Paraphrase on the Book of Job* (1800). Bernard's poem has relatively little to do with the matter or meaning of *Job*. Although he never seems quite certain of the form he wants, he clearly has the epic in mind as his opening suggests:

I sing not arms--nor deeds of martial kind:
I sing those virtues, which adorn the mind.
The patience of a Job--the muse now sings,
Which far surpass the royalty of kings.

(3)

As in many of the Miltonic inspired Joban elaborations, various devils play multifold roles. In a council in hell, for example, Belial encourages Satan:

Let not your wrath, great prince, unruly grow,
Against that stupid wretch: we'll make him know
Our strong temptations cannot be withstood,
For he shall yet blaspheme and curse his God.

(25)

Before appearing in a dream to Job's wife as her recently deceased mother--Bernard's willingness to invent has no compunction--Belial continues his speech of encouragement to Satan. In this markedly antifeminist work,[6] Barnard also continues demonstrating his lack of facility with rhyme and syntax:

Have you forgot, how Adam was undone,
'Twas by his wife--and Job has such an one.

> She to great Satan gladly will return,
> For in her heart she Job's religion scorn.
>
> (26)

During the nineteenth century, the term "paraphrase" only appears in the title of one fragmentary translation, the 1838 *Job; or the Gospel Preached to the Patriarchs: Being a Paraphrase of the Last Ten Chapters of the Book of Job* by Mrs. Walter Birch. Birch practices some of the freedom apparent in the other paraphrases by inserting into her work passages from *Genesis*, *Exodus*, *Psalms*, the *Gospel According to John*, *Galatians*, *Hebrews*, and *Romans*. After Birch, poets no longer felt the need to justify their activity and a significant new force had taken over translations of Job.

II

> I would desire that all women should reade the Gospell and Paule's epistles, and I wold to God they were translated in to the tonges of all men. So that they might not only be read and knowne of the scotes and yryshmen, But also of the Turkes and saracenes. Truly is it one degre to good livinge, yee the first (I had almost sayde the cheffe) to have a little sight in the scripture, though it be but a grosse knowledge.
>
> Erasmus, *Novum Instrumentum* (1516)
> Translated by William Tyndale

The effects of the new scholarly approach appear first—and most impressively—in Thomas Heath's *An Essay towards a New English Version of the Book of Job from the Original Hebrew* in 1756. Heath explicitly acknowledges the influence of "the very learned Dr. Warburton" (ix) in a number of areas. Warburton's greatest influence, however, lay in convincing Heath that the work was not an autobiographical history but a poetic interpretation of that history. Heath also recognizes the problem with the original manuscripts "mouldering in the several public libraries in divers parts of Europe," a condition which suggests "that no particular providence hath attended the writings of the Old Testament beyond those of the New, or indeed the works of any other writer." And he concludes that "the only method of restoring those writings to their primitive purity, is to make use of the same helps, and the same critical acumen, which hath thrown light on the writings of all other ancient authors" (xiii). The critical methodology he suggests (e.g., collating texts, using dialects to establish the roots of the oriental languages) reflects how extensively scholarship from other disciplines has begun influencing the world of biblical studies. Although many of the best translators retained an interest in their audience, the text came to have a primacy among their concerns.

This new emphasis on fidelity to the text in both form and language becomes quickly apparent in the titles which begin to dominate *Job* translation. In 1764 Anthony Purver (1702-1777) published *A New and Literal Translation of All the Books of the Old and New Testament*, a title implicitly critiquing the King James. Seven years later Thomas Scott would use a title, *The Book of Job, in English Verse; Translated from the Original Hebrew*, which would echo through translations for the next century and a half. Thus in 1796 Charles Garden would somewhat modestly offer *An Improved Version Attempted of the Book of Job; a Poem*, while in 1805 the Right Rev. Joseph Stock, Bishop of Killalla, would publish his *The Book of Job: Metrically Arranged according to the Masora and Newly Translated into English*. Between 1810 and 1825 all four of the versions which appeared share this emphasis to at least some degree: Elizabeth Smith's *The Book of Job; Translated from the Hebrew* (1810), John Mason Good's *The Book of Job, Literally Translated from the Original Hebrew, and Restored to Its natural Arrangement* (1812), John Bellamy's *The Holy Bible, Newly Translated from the Original Hebrew* (1818), and George Hunt's *The Book of Job. Translated from the Hebrew* (1825). This tendency, which would remain in force throughout the nineteenth century in works as diverse as *The Book of the Patriarch Job* (1837) by Samuel Lee, Regius Professor at Cambridge, and the *Revised Version* of 1885, provided not only a justification for new translations but an advertisement for the purity and fidelity of their results. The actual products, however, occasionally present less than they promise.

Heath was the first translator to tackle the difficulty of the traditional reading of 13:15 ("Though he slay me, yet will I trust in him"). The problems with this passage, in which the Masoretes had substituted a preposition for a negative particle, had been recognized not only by more recent contintental biblical scholars but by such scholarly divines as the metaphysical poet John Donne while he was Dean of St. Paul's Cathedral in 1621.[7] Heath's alternative—"Lo! he will slay me, I expect nothing else"—found few adherents other than Thomas Scott in 1771: "Yes, he will slay me (other hope were vain)." In 1796 Charles Garden even softened the conditional suggestion of God's harshness in the King James: "Behold, he may slay me, I will trust in him." Others discovered creative ways of dealing with the negative particle. Bishop Joseph Stock managed in 1805 to work the negative in without questioning Job's faith: "Lo, he may slay me, I will not wait." By 1818, in a translation dedicated to the Prince Regent, John Bellamy had found a way to make the negative adverb part of Job's affirmation: "Though he slay me, shall I not hope?" The enduring influence of the dual Jamesian legacy, the Epistle's view of Job's fidelity and the equally traditional language of the Authorized Version, along with the influence of the Masoretic text affected even nineteenth-century translations for Jewish families. In 1853 Isaac Leeser drew on its language, adding only an initial interjection: "Lo, though he slay me, yet will he trust in me," while eight years later Abraham Benisch offered, "Though he slay me, yet will I wait for him." By 1880 Rabbi Hermann Gollancz would return to the very words of the Authorized Version.

Other than Scott, one of the few to follow Heath's lead was Elizabeth Smith (1776-1806), who produced what is easily the most remarkable and arguably the most graceful and compelling translation of *Job* between the King James and Revised Versions.[8] With only four and a half years of tutoring from a young governess and despite a life enduring the kind of polite poverty with which Jane Austen often threatens her heroines, she learned over a dozen languages, compiled the first comparative dictionary of Hebrew, Arabic, and Persian, and translated extensively from a variety of languages. All of her work appeared posthumously, including her *Fragments, in Prose and Verse* and *Memoirs of Frederick and Margaret Klopstock* in 1808, her *Book of Job* in 1810, and her *Vocabulary, Hebrew, Arabic, and Persian* in 1814. As her accurate and powerful translation of 13:15 suggests--"Behold he will slay me, I will not endure"--her scholarship and literary skill allowed her to create a far bleaker and more troubling vision of *Job* than the one reflected in the Epistle of James.

Although completed in 1803, Smith's *Job* was not published until 1810, four years after her death. Five years earlier, her publisher, Richard Crutwell of Bath, had released a translation of the same book by Joseph Stock, Bishop of Killala (1740-1813). Bishop Stock's workmanlike poetic version--even the prologue and epilogue are in verse--follow the King James even more closely than most translations:

King James 7:1-4

Is there not an appointed time to man upon the earth? *are not* his dayes also like the dayes of an hireling?

As a servant earnestly desireth the shadow, and as an hireling looketh for *the reward of* his worke:

So am I made to possesse moneths of vanitie, and wearisome nights are appointed to me.

When I lie downe, I say, When shall I arise, and the night be gone? and I am full of tossings to and fro unto the dawning of the day.

Stock

Is there not an appointed time for man upon the earth?
And as the days of an hireling are not his days?

As a servant swalloweth in hope the shadow,
And as an hireling looketh for his pay;
So did I possess myself before-hand of months of misery,
And wearisome nights are numbered unto me.
If I lie down, then do I say,
When shall I arise, and the dark have taken its round?
And I am full of tossings till the morning breeze.

While the bishop has clearly attempted to preserve the numinous quality of the King James, his taste for archaic rhythms ("And as an hireling looketh for his pay"), indirect expressions ("When shall I arise, and the dark have taken its round?"), and awkward syntax ("So did I possess myself before-hand of months of misery") creates a confusing effect on his reader.

Comparing Bishop Stock's translation with Elizabeth Smith's gives some sense of her achievement:

IS not man a soldier on earth?
And his days like the days of an hireling?
As the servant panting for the shade of night,
And as the hireling longing for the reward of his labour,
So am I made to inherit months of vanity,
And nights of trouble are numbered me.
If I lie down, I say, When shall I arise?
And the evening is lengthened out,

And I am weary with tossing till the morning breeze.

Beginning with a vivid image, Smith takes more freedom in reorganizing and reinterpreting her text. In her contemporary context of the tensions and eventual war--between England and France, her use of a soldier may well have been a more telling point of identification for an English audience than either the servant or hireling. True to her original, however, she directly links the soldier to both servant and hireling. With the fourth verse, she shortens the question, linking the next two clauses of increasing size into a more logical arrangement. And their rhythm, lengthened like the evening, mirrors the slow passage of time.

Clarity and dramatic effect lie at the heart of Smith's approach to *Job*. While retaining a few archaic forms, especially in the verbs, she more often modernizes the diction, integrates the syntax, clarifies arcane or awkward constructions, and transposes verses. In fact, she shifts ten verses, far more than any other translator of her time.[9] This ability to look clearly at her text allows her to simplify with a parenthetical word or phrase, as in the confusing imagery in the Hymn to Wisdom. Verse 28:3 ("Hee setteth an ende to darknesse, and searcheth out all perfection:

the stones of darknesse and the shadow of death") can then become both clearer and more powerful:

> (The miner) feels in the dark,
> And all around he seeks
> For the stones of darkness,
> And the shadow of death.

Her translation often works for such dramatic effects, as when she eliminates the italicized language the King James translators had added to elucidate the text. In 24:19 ("Drought and heate consume the snow waters: *so doth* the grave *those which* have sinned"), she achieves her effect with startling suddenness: "Drought and heat shall absorb the waters of the snow,/Hell, sinners."

While Smith's romanticism imparts an oriental flavor to her work with frequent allusions to Arabs and the substitution of "tent" for "tabernacle," her interest in science leads her to prefer "atoms" to "pieces" (16:12), to describe God causing light to "irradiate" rather than "shine" (37:15), and to eliminate the Authorized Version's classical and astrological allusions to the pleiades, Orion, Mazzaroth, and Arcturus (38:31-32). Her theology appears fairly orthodox, even when she changes Zophar's charge against Job from "lies" to "self-sufficiency" (11:3). Smith's graceful imagery, however, can offer striking insights into Job's dilemma. Where the King James has him complain to his would-be comforters, "Why do yee persecute me as God, and are not satisfied with my flesh?" (19:22), she recognizes his frailty, "Why do ye pursue me like a deer?/And are not satisfied with my flesh?"

Elizabeth Smith established a model which would be followed by five other women who attempted translations of *Job* during the nineteenth century. Although three focused only on *Job* while two included it in larger designs, none was as successful as Smith either as a scholar or poet. Mrs Walter Birch's anonymously published *Job; or the Gospel Preached to the Patriarchs: Being a Paraphrase of the Last Ten Chapters of the Book of Job*, presented as the product of the widow of a clergyman, appropriately emphasizes Job's care for "the fatherless" and "the widow's heart" (14). Birch acknowledges Bishop Lowth and emphasizes the Christian element in *Job*, especially his belief in a Redeemer. Her lines often achieve a simple majesty, as in the following couplets from the beginning of the thirty-seventh chapter, with their steady alliteration and regularly decreasing periods:

> Appall'd, man hears the elemental strife,
> And his heart trembles to the seat of life;
> The voice of God himself he seems to hear,

When the loud pealing thunder echoes near,
Reverberating through the vault of Heaven,
And to the earth's remotest region driven.
Wondrous these mighty works, and when we bend
Our thoughts to scan them, who can comprehend?
Who can the unfathom'd depths of wisdom know?
And say, whence comes the rain, or whence the snow?
(21-22)

In 1852 Sarah Hustler Fox (1800-1882) published *A Metrical Version of the Book of Job* using a dizzying variety of forms. "Designed Chiefly for the Use of Schools," as the title page explains, Fox's version seems more a primer on poetic form. Her goal, as defined in her self-deprecating introduction, appears fairly simple: "This little work has been undertaken, not with any presumptuous notion of elucidating or adorning Scripture, but simply with a hope to commend to the young mind and memory, through the medium of rhythm, the deep truths and the Divine instruction contained in the Book of Job, which appears to be a portion of the Sacred Writings, peculiarly adapted to varied metrical composition" (iii). Relying primarily on the language of the King James, although not as literally as she suggests in her introduction, Fox opens with a set of unremarkable heroic couplets that establish an essentially epic vision of the work:

Few were the ages since the world began,
When in the land of Uz there liv'd a man
Who served with upright heart and fear'd his God,
And in life's path with perfect footsteps trod.
(1)

But she quickly moves on to tetrameter and hexameter couplets, quatrains of various meters, and longer stanzas that suggest her view of *Job* as a series of lyrics. While each of Job's friends has his own form, Job himself shifts among a dizzying variety, even within the same speech. Chapter 3, for example, begins with a series of quatrains:

Oh! Why is light to misery given,
And life to souls in bitterness--
They who for death have long'd and striven
In vain distress.

Yea, more than theirs who delve the earth
For hidden wealth, hath been my care;
A grave to me were better worth

Than jewels rare.

How joyful should I close my eyes,
And make the valley clods my bed!
For why should light on him arise
Whose way is hid?
She soon switches to longer, weightier stanzas:
Oh that my grief were rightly weigh'd,
And that my sore calamity,
Were with it in the balance laid,--
Than would it heavier seem to be
Than sands the ocean tides that bound,
And all too weak my words be found.
(15)

At best, her work has a clarity of statement that others who attempt similar metrical translations never achieve. For example, her version of 10:16b-17 describes God's pursuit effectively, beginning with a series of passive constructions, ambiguous prepositional phrases, and spiraling syntactic complexity, to portray the speaker as an increasingly confused prey until the regular cadence of a rhymed iambic pentameter couplet and fairly direct syntax reestablish the certainty, inevitability, and persistence of the divine order:

For as a man pursued
By a fierce lion, am I hunted down;
By witness, renew'd
Against me, Thine increased wrath is shown
Whilst still Thy marvels ever meet mine eyes,
And war and change against me ceaseless rise.
(29)

Contrast the relentlessly compelling closure of Fox's image with the ponderous effect created by the archaic diction and awkward syntax of James Davie's interpretation of these lines almost half a century later in 1891:

Like lion fierce Thou huntest me,
Then Thou dost whelm me in dispeace!
Anon new witnesses Thou bring'st
Against me, and Thou dost increase
Thine indignation on me, so
That war and change 'gainst me never cease.[10]

The most extensive biblical translation undertaken by a woman in the nineteenth century appeared in the United States as the work of a suffragette who belonged to a small Christian sect. Although Julia Evelina Smith (1793-1886) completed *The Holy Bible . . . Translated Literally from the Original Tongues* in 1843, it was not published until 1876. After reading William Miller's apocalyptic scriptural predictions about the end of the world, she began a scrupulous study of the original texts with her four sisters, seeking evidence to support or refute Miller's interpretations. Attempting a literal translation, Smith expressed pleasure with her product: "It may be thought by the public in general, that I have great confidence in myself, in not conferring with the learned in so great a work, but as there is but one book in the Hebrew tongue, and I have defined it word for word, I do not see how anybody can know more about it than I do" (n.p.).

Much of her success occurs in books other than *Job*. In *Genesis*, for example she uses *Life* rather than *Eve* and, like Tyndale before her, translates *love* for *charity*. Elizabeth Cady Stanton was so taken by the translation that she used it as the text for *The Women's Bible* (1895-98). In the *Book of Job*, however, Smith's literalness makes her prose stiff and labored, as in her opening verse: "A man was in the land of Uz, Job his name; and that man was blameless and upright, and fearing God, and departing from evil" (720). Attempting to remain faithful to the Hebrew original, Smith's version can become confusing. The second verse of chapter 32, for example, becomes labyrinthine in its syntax, tenses, and pronouns: "And the anger of Elihu will kindle, son of Barachel the Buzite, from the family of Ram: against Job was his anger kindled, for his justifying his soul above God."

Helen Spurrell restricted herself to the Hebrew Bible in her 1885 *A Translation of the Old Testament Scriptures from the Original Hebrew*. While retaining much of the language of the King James, she occasionally shifts emphases, as in Chapter 14 when she changes a series of statements and questions into more dramatic assertions:

> Man, born of woman!
> His days cut short, and filled with disquietude.
> 2 Like as a flower he springeth up, and is cut down;
> Even like a shadow he passeth over and abideth not.
> 3 But *yet* upon such an one does thou fix Thine eyes!
> Even me dost Thou bring into judgment with Thee!

Her changes affect the work in only minimal ways, although she does have Job characterize his wife as an "ungodly women" rather than a "foolish women" (442) and she adds a distinctive sensibility to her note to 1:21 ("Naked came I forth from my mother's womb, and naked shall I return thither"): "I think Job speaks of the earth as his mother" (441n). And even though she occasionally relies on the archaic verb forms associated with the King James, when she uses contemporary forms her lines achieve an immediacy and simplicity without sacrificing the grandeur, as in 26.6:

> Hades is disclosed before Him;
> And for destruction, *there is* no concealment.
> He spread out the north sky over the void space;
> And hung up the earth upon nothing.
>
> (459)

In contrast, Samuel Sharpe's version of these lines in his *The Hebrew Scripture: A Revision of the Authorized English Old Testament* (1865) has a slightly more rhetorical and traditional tone.

> Hell is naked before him,
> And the Pit of Destruction hath no covering.
> He strecheth out the north over empty space,
> And hangeth the earth upon nothing.

Like Spurrell, Sharpe, a Unitarian minister, relies heavily on the King James translation and develops lines of varying length. He is, however, not so sensitive to women's issues and tends to be a bit more concrete in his imagery. Two years after Sharpe's translation, Joseph Smith's (1805-1844) corrected version of the King James appeared. Although Smith had begun his revision in 1830, the same year he founded the Church of Jesus Christ of the Latter-Day Saints, and been killed in 1844, his edition did not appear until 1867. While most of his corrections of the King James tend to have been made for the sake of clarity and Mormon doctrine, his only changes in *Job* involved substituting "children of God" for "sons of God" in 1:6 and 2:1.

The least effective of the versions by women during the century was Henrietta Emily Benson's "Thoughts on the Book of Job" (1882). Not so much a translation as a meditation on the King James, Benson's awkwardly didactic blank verse resembles more a homily or Christian exhortation than a reflection on her original ("There lived a man in far receding days,/Whose life, so briefly and so simply penned/On sacred page, much deep instruction yields" [156]). And she ensures that her reader will see that instruction

:

> What teaching does this narrative convey?
> . . . .
> That sin and a self-righteous spirit both
> Enfold, as with a garment's closest web,
> The darkened soul of sinful, helpless man,

Yet none but God can rend it.

(162)

As Job looks forward to "the Resurrection and the Life" (157), he encounters a redemptive "Sun of Righteousness" which heals his suffering (168).

Such blatantly Christian interpretations encouraged Jewish scholars to begin producing alternative editions and translations in the middle of the nineteenth century. The first attempt, undertaken in much the same spirit as Joseph Smith's version, was a translation of Dr. M. Budinger's abridged German edition of the Bible. Using the Authorized Version as his base, David Asher presents *The Way of Faith* (1848) primarily as a work for Jewish mothers for "the moral disposition and sentiments of her children" (iv). Sanctioned by Rev. Dr. Adler, Chief Rabbi of the British Empire, Asher offers an almost unqualified defense of the King James Version: "The authorised version is, in this country, the standard translation of the Bible; its phraseology is as familiar to the Englishman as the voice of a dear friend; the least departure from it is offensive, and startles from its novelty . . ." (xii). His only qualifications occur in the Prophets and in *Job*, books which he believes need special attention for their poetic qualities. Despite this position, he actually includes relatively little of the *Book of Job*.

In 1853 Isaac Leeser (1806-1868), who had been born in Westphalia and immigrated to Richmond, Virginia, before accepting a position as a rabbi at Congregation Mikveh Israel in Philadelphia, published the first complete English translation from a Jewish perspective. Concerned that the only versions of the Bible available to American Jews who knew little Hebrew were translations by Christians which not only followed the Christian canon but generally included notes and chapter summaries emphasizing Christian interpretation and typology, Leeser feared these editions would "assail Israel's hope and faith" (iii). In addition to eliminating the editorial material which constantly pointed readers towards the fulfillment of scripture in the New Testament (e.g., the King James's chapter heading for 19:25: "He believeth in the resurrection"), he also divided the Hebrew text, as his title points out, into *The Twenty-Four Books of the Holy Scripture* and tried to develop a distinctive language for his version. Despite its heavily Germanic and Hebraic phrasing, Leeser's work served American Jews until it was replaced in 1917 by a translation sponsored by the Jewish Publication Society.

Once Leeser had begun the process, British rabbis soon followed. Their approach differed significantly, however. Rather than trying to develop an entirely new English tradition as Leeser had, they sought to modify the familiar cadences of the King James to the needs of their congregations. In 1861 Abraham Benisch (1811-1878) published his *Job* in the second volume of the *Jewish School and Family Bible* which appeared in four volumes between 1851 and 1861. By 1872 A. Elzas consciously defined the middle ground he sought in offering the first version of *Job* for both "Jewish and Christian" audiences. While most Christian versions capitalized "Redeemer" in 19:25 to emphasize its Christological significance, Elzas substitutes "avenger," where Leeser had merely eliminated the initial capital and Benisch had offered "vindicator." When *The Holy Bible for Jewish Families* appeared in 1880, Rabbi Hermann Gollancz's introduction echoes David Asher's respect for the enduring influence of the King James Version: "it has been deemed advisable to adhere as closely as possible . . . to the excellent Anglican version of the 17th century" to the point that even "expressions and grammatical forms now obsolete have been retained so as not to affect the venerable hue of the old translation" (5).

III

> I profess to be literal, so far, indeed, as in some instances to have preferred retaining Hebraisms rather than deviating too considerably from the original, though I am not aware of having carried out this principle inconsistently with any grammatical or other strict requirement of the English language or idiom; whilst in other instances I have chosen to sacrifice mere elegance rather than not give what has appeared to me the exact rendering of a particular word or passage; and I would beg the merely English reader to bear this in mind, should he in some cases suppose that I might have selected some more high-sounding or more dignified or more apparently choice word or phrase than that which I have presented. In the case of seemingly ambiguous expressions, I have thought it best . . . to leave them as far as possible in their ambiguity, without presuming summarily to attach any definite meaning of my own to them....
>
> Carteret Priaulx Carey, *The Book of Job* (1858), Preface, x.

In the Rev. Mr. Carey's prefatory *apologia* for his translation, the assumption that local concerns, envisioned as the product of limited experience ("mere elegance" and "merely English readers"), cannot compete with the principle of scholarly fidelity reveals one of the two very different paths that translations of *Job* were to take for the remainder of the nineteenth century. Despite fundamental differences in approach and goals, both paths focused on issues of authenticity and voice. On the one hand, a growing interest in scholarly literalism spurred efforts, like Carey's, to recreate as faithfully as possible the original voice of Job. On the other, a desire to expand the effect of the Bible merged with the Romantic and Victorian fascination with poetry that speaks in "the real language of men" (Wordsworth, 384) to discover a more authentic contemporary literary voice.

To recreate a more historically accurate text, scholars first sought help from sources other than Hebrew. In 1808 the first English translation of the Greek Septuagint appeared, oddly enough, in Philadelphia. Its author, Charles Thomson (1729-1824), had been elected secretary of the Continental Congress in 1774 and served for fifteen years until he retired to devote the remainder of his life to the study Greek and Hebrew. Thomson's fairly straightforward prose version offered, for the first time in any modern European language, a glimpse of those sections that differ from the Hebrew texts. In 1844 a baronet, Sir Lancelot Charles Lee Brenton, published another version of the Septuagint together with the Vatican Text, while half a century later in 1897 John Tattersall turned the Septuagint into 309 quatrains of generally regular iambic pentameter, as in he version of 24:3-4:

CCXXII

The orphan's ass they drive forth from its fold,
And for a pledge the widow's ox they hold;
They turn the weak and needy from the way;
The poor men of the earth are bought and sold.

While these three versions of the Septuagint offered an entirely new possibility for English readers, the Roman Catholic archbishop of Baltimore made one final attempt to make the long suffering Doway translation of the Vulgate speak to his growing American flock. In 1859 Francis Patrick Kenrick (1796-1863) revised *Job* as part of his revision of the entire Doway-Rheims version between 1849 and 1860. In keeping with the scholarly recognition of the primacy of Hebrew sources, Archbishop Kenrick not only discusses "apparent discrepancies" with the Hebrew text in footnotes but moves towards "rendering [the Latin translator] in close conformity with the Hebrew" ("General Introduction," v). In doing so, he reveals that he shares the bias of his fellow Protestant biblical scholars in preferring "the soft Hebrew to the hissing Greek" ("General Introduction," vi).

In addition to these Septuagint and Vulgate *Jobs*, English and American scholars provided audiences fascinated by England's imperial adventures in the East with even more exotic sources and variants. Henry Tattam (1788-1868), the Archdeacon of Bedford, for example, published *The Ancient Coptic Version of the Book of Job the Just* in 1846. And in 1881, during the Anglo-American effort to modernize the King James, the Rev. Cornelius Van Dyck (818-1895) of Beirut sent the American Old Testament Revision Committee a very literal set of translations of passages of an Arabic version of the Book of Job which differed from the King James. The Committee published them as *Renderings of the Recent Arabic Version of the Book of Job Which Vary from the English Version* with a prefatory note from Van Dyck that the passages may well be "out of good taste in English, though perfectly classical in Arabic" (1). The resulting list of phrases and clauses, with interpretations and comments interspersed, offers an interesting gloss on other translations, as in 7.4: "my skin has become corrugated (wrinkled up in folds) and runs (like an open sore) (The Arab word is used of melted wax or pitch or earth softened like mud)" (5). One of the most interesting Joban variants, the pseudepigraphical Greek *Testament of Job*, the source of so many of the legends about Job and his wife, finally appeared in English with Kaufmann Kohler's translation in 1897.

The Hebrew text, however, clearly remained the primary concern of *Job* translators. By the middle of the nineteenth century, Robert Young (1822-1888) defined the dividing line between the two dominant approaches: "There are two modes of translation which may be adopted in rendering into our language the writings of an ancient author: the one is to bring him before us in such a manner as that we may *regard him as our own*; the other, to *transport ourselves*, on the contrary, *over to him, adopting his situation, modes of speaking, thinking, acting--peculiarities of age and race, air, gesture, voice, &c.*" ("Introduction," n.p.) Although Young acknowledges advantages to both, he finds the latter "incomparably the better of the two," and goes on with a slightly ironic characterization of the practice of his time to privilege the scholarly approach and marginalize the paraphrastic one: "All attempts to make Moses or Paul act, or speak, or reason, as if they were Englishmen of the nineteenth century, must inevitably tend to change the translator into a paraphrast or a commentator, characters which, however useful, stand altogether apart from that of him, who, with a work before him in one language, seeks only to transfer it into another" ("Introduction," n.p.).

While Young's practice, as suggested by his title (*Literal Translation of the Bible* [1862]), follows his argument, it creates a fairly confusing text, primarily as a result of his idiosyncratic theory that Hebrew tenses reflected attitudes rather than temporal relationships.[11] Young's quaintly muddled opening reflects that singular approach to verbs: "There hath been a man in the land of Uz, whose name is Job; and that man hath been perfect and upright--fearing also God, and turning aside from evil. And to him are born seven sons and three daughters. And his substance is seven thousand of a flock. . ." (343). This practice continues into the dialogues, which Young organizes as lines of different lengths, as in the beginning of Chapter 12

:

And Job answereth and saith:
2 Truly, ye *are* the people,
And with you wisdom dieth.
3 I also have a heart like you;
I am not falling more than you;
And with whom is there not like these?
4 A laughter to his friend I am;
"He calleth to God, and he answereth him;
A laughter *is* the perfect righteous one.
(347)

With an even greater commitment to literalism, Oliver Spencer Halsted (1792-1877), a former Chancellor of the State of New Jersey, attempted a translation in 1875 that would omit such idiosyncracies of English as articles. His result, a curiously primitive version of English, was even more confusing, as his opening suggests: "Man was in land of Uz, Job name of him, and was that man which he upright and just, and feared God, and turned aside from evil." Much the same occurs in the poetic part (e.g., 13.15: "Lo, should he kill me, to him will I hope/but ways of me to face of him I will argue"). Halsted's preface reveals that this new style is only part of his goal; proving that strange ideals tend to congregate, he also intends his work to reveal that the author of *Job* was himself a Jewish anti-Semite: "in his struggle with the central falsehood of his own people's creed, [the writer] must have divorced himself from them outardly, as well as inwardly; that he travelled away into the world, and lived long, perhaps all his matured life, in exile" ("Preface," iv).

Two less cranky and more successful attempts at achieving a greater literal translation were those by John Medley (1804-1892), Bishop of Fredericton and Metropolitan of Canada, and George H. Gilbert. Medley occasionally achieves effective rhythmic contrasts through his use of lines of differing lengths, as in the end of Elihu's speech (37:22-24):

22 From the North cometh a golden glow,
With God is awful majesty.
23 As for the Almighty, we cannot find him out;
He is exalted in strength, and judgment, and
plenteous in righteousness,
He will give no account.
24 Therefore shall men fear Him.
He regardeth not any that are wise in their own esteem.
(134)

Gilbert prefaces *The Poetry of Job* (1889) by arguing that the work is "rhythmical

. . . not metrical" (ix). His description of that rhythm, couched in musical terms, sounds much like Anglo-Saxon accentual prosody: "The Hebrew lines in *Job* generally have three tones, the only important exceptions being the two-toned and the four-toned lines. . . . The number of syllables belonging to a single tone varies constantly, producing what would be designated, according to our canons of meter, a mingling of iambic, trochaic, dactylic, and anapestic feet; but the rhythm is not often disturbed by this freedom" (x). In practice, Gilbert, who displays some inconsistency among his verbs--note the "flieth, and stays" below--often relies on alliteration and heavy consonantal clusters, as in the opening of Chapter 14:

The man of woman born
Short lived and full of unrest!
He comes forth as a flower, and is withered;
Like a shadow he flieth, and stays not.
E'en on this Thou has opened Thine eyes,
And brought me to judgment with Thee!
O came a clean one from unclean!
Not one!

(45)

IV

A Spirit pass'd before me: I beheld
The face of Immortality unveil'd--
Deep sleep came down on ev'ry eye save mine--
And there it stood,--all formless--but divine:
Along my bones the creeping flesh did quake;
And as my damp hair stiffen'd, thus it spake:

2.

"Is man more just than God? Is man more pure
Than he who deems even Seraphs insecure?
Creatures of clay--vain dwellers in the dust!
The moth survives you, and are ye more just?
Things of a day! you wither ere the night,
Heedless and blind to Wisdom's wasted light."

Lord Byron, *Hebrew Melodies*
(1814-15), 311.

Despite Robert Young's argument and the scholarly pursuit of more literal translations of *Job*, most of those who attempted poetic versions during the nineteenth century became primarily concerned with discovering an effective English voice for *Job*. All acknowledged the importance of the original text, but many seem more concerned with aesthetic issues like identifying the work's genre than theological ones like explicating its theodicy. Decisions about genre, after all, affected such important literary decisions as the choice of meter. Those who believed the work a primitive Hebraic combination of drama and epic tended to rely on blank verse, while those who found it essentially lyric explored a variety of traditional meters.

Two exceptions to this principle were W. C. Stather, a lieutenant-colonel who translated *The Book of Job; in English Verse* (1860) in "the solitude of the remote districts of India, beneath its almost perpetual sunshine" ("Preface," xiii), and Henry Wright Adams (1818-1891), whose *Book of Job in Poetry; or, A Song in the Night* appeared in 1864 in New York. In their prefaces, both authors emphasize one dominant characteristic. While Stather praises the work's "boldness of sublimity" (x), Adams makes the same point more elaborately and repetitively: "Like some latter, grander, sublimer mountain peak of inspiration, where storm, and darkness, and flames alternately battle, enshroud, and play; it stands alone in its own inimitable grandeur and sublimity" (xxxvii).

Oddly enough, however, after pointing out "how exceedingly difficult it is to warp, and bend, and cramp the wild, unfettered strains of Job into the tight-jacket, straight-laced, arbitrary confines of modern poetry" (xl), Adams follows Stather in warping, bending, and cramping *Job* into heroic couplets. Stather had justified his practice by concluding that "the majestic cadence of heroic rhyme seemed, at least to the author's taste, the only one becoming the dignity of the subject," excluding only the frame, "which being prose in the original, have herein, been thrown only into blank measure" (xiii). In fact, Adams' work, despite his comments, is more consciously epic, beginning with an invocation to the "Celestial Goddess" to help him "Sing how there lived, renowned in all the Globe,/A man, in Uz, that bore the name of Job" (55) In much the same spirit, Job's response to Bildad at the beginning of Chapter 9 has a more formal cadence.

The truth that Bildad, in his speech, expressed,
Was now, by Job, in frankness, thus confessed.
I know 'tis so, nor do I thus distrust,
But how alas! can man, with God, be just?
If he contend, as man with man, hath done,
Of thousand sins, he cannot answer one.
Within his heart, is he supremely wise,
And strength unbounded in Jehovah lies.
And who, resisting, hath withstood his will?
Or been rebellious, and succesful still?
He hurls the mountains from their native spot,
By force of earthquakes, and they know it not;
He overturns them, in his dreadful wrath,
When fires volcanic lift them from their path.

(101-102)

By capitalizing references to God and eliminating the maze of pronouns, Stather simplifies his text. In his attempt to achieve "a *translation* as close to the original Hebrew as English *rhyme* can possibly admit" (xiii), he is careful to bracket passages added to the original. In addition, his less qualified, more direct syntax creates a greater thrust through the lines and a more powerful sense of closure at the end of each couplet than Stather's highly mannered periods:

Full well I know it *is* so, Job replied,
And how can Man with God be justified?
Be it His pleasure with him to contend,
Can he one charge 'mid countless sins defend?
What heart so wise--so vast what mortal might,
Him to resist, and prosper in the fight?
Who heaves th'unconscious mountains from their base,
And hurls, indignant, from their ancient place;
Bids reeling Earth, upon her centre quake;
Commands the sun--the sun forbears to rise--
Seals up the stars, [and shrouds th'empyrial skies.]

(24)

In these three final couplets, Stather follows the Authorized Version in treating the passages as subordinate to the earlier introduction of God rather than following Adams' decision to make them fully independent clauses.

Even though iambic pentameter had became associated with viewing *Job* as both epic and drama since Blackmore, a significant exception appeared in Boston in 1866. Its anonymous author introduces his Whitmanesque work with an attack on tradition and a defense of individual freedom: "If the reader find in this version an evident effort to allow Job and his comforters to express their own views in their own way, it is confidently submitted that he will find in King James's version an equally evident effort to make Job stultify himself, and talk orthodoxy" (5). The translator takes a number of freedoms with the text, omitting sections like Elihu's speech and freely expanding imagery. Using lines of different lengths, the work often relies on punctuation and long, sweeping lines to achieve dramatic effects, as in its version of 31.35-37:

--Oh that someone would now listen to me!
Behold! here is my signature: let the Almighty answer!
Let him write out his charges against me,
And sign them with his initials!
If he would do it, I would bear them openly

on my shoulder,
And I would display them upon my forehead;
For they would be a crown and sceptre to me!
I would recount to him all my steps,
And as a prince would I stand before him.

(82-83)

In spite of Colonel Stather's dismissal of it, blank verse became a far more common vehicle, used for three translations in 1880 alone. In the "Preface" to one of those works, *The Book of Job: A Metrical Translation*, Henry James Clarke justified this practice on the grounds of both aesthetics and tradition. He argued that he had "selected . . . that kind of metre which has commended itself to the cultivated English ear as being for dramatic composition and for dialogue, the sort of channel best suited to facilitate the majestic flow of elevated thoughts" (xi). His analysis of the nature of English and Hebrew as languages seems to agree with Robert Young's conclusion that the two languages are fundamentally different: ". . . the genius of English . . . demands that the relations of connected ideas shall be indicated with some more of logical elaboration, a mode of expression more copious and discriminating, than chartacterizes tha language of any literary production of remote antiquity" (vi). As the connotations in that quote suggest, however, Clarke reaches a very different conclusion from Young about the appropriate mode of translation: "A closely literal translation must needs misrepresent the work" (ix).

Clarke's result often shows a directness and simplicity, as in the end of Job's lamentation in Chapter 3:

For still my sighs
Prevent my food; and like a rushing stream,
My groans escape me in continuous flow.
For something terrible I fear, and then
It comes upon me; and the very thing
I dread befalls me. I am not secure,
Nor have I any rest, nor any time
For breathing ; but fresh trouble ever comes.

(8)

The power of Clarke's concrete version becomes more apparent in contrast with the more formal, more abstract interpretation of these lines in Arthur Malet's *The Book of Job in Blank Verse* (1880):

I take no food for sighing; and I weep
Like running waters; for I feared a fear,

And it has come. That which I feared is here,
For I was neither over confident,
Nor was I passing time in careless rest
Or idle quietude; yet trouble came.

(ll. 161-166)

By substituting a meditative quality for Clarke's anguish, Malet's lines create an analytically reflective neoclassical mood. The stately quality that often results becomes most effective in passages like the formal, highly rhetorical charges in Chapter 24.12-14 which carry the quality of a legal summation:

Groans rise from out the city; wounded men
Send up their feeble cry: and yet the lord
Delayeth still His judgment on their sins.
Associate they with those who shun the light,
Hating its paths, avoiding open ways.
Murderers rising with the early dawn,
Greedy, yet poor, refraining not from blood,
And stately stealing in the dead of night.

(ll. 1166-1173

G. Cecil White's approach to the text in *The Discipline of Suffering. Nine Short Readings on the History of Job* (1880) involves severe compression to emphasize the orthodox Christian message of *Job*. In the spirit of Clarke, he clearly wishes to show the logical connection among the ideas but he attempts to do so by consolidating symbols. In chapters 23 and 24, for example, he reduces the powerful plea for social justice and imagery into a calmer, less specific, more reflective speech:

Job. Although I feel Him near, I see Him not,
But yet He knows my path and marks my steps;
And at the last He will approve my faith.
But now I cannot stay Him, His desire
I cannot alter:--This doth trouble me.
Why men reap not on earth the fruits of sin
I cannot tell. Some men pluck golden fruits
From evil seed: and float on calmly
To the shore of death: and as the grateful earth
Receives in quietness the melted snow,
So peacefully they glide into the grave.
The brigand goodly ransoms oft obtains,
Yet still remains at large, and roams at will.

(Part 2, 19

White's style suggests that he shares the common view of *Job* as essentially a dramatic piece. Performing *Job* as a play became fairly common, helped by works like Alfred Walls' *The Oldest Drama in the World* (1891) which rearranges the KJV into dramatic form. Otis Cary (1851-1932) took this a step further by revising the Revised Version into heroic couplets in his *The Man Who Feared God for Nought, Being a Rhythmical Version of the Book of Job* (1898). He even advises his readers to write out "casts of characters for the drama as it is played from time to time" ("Preface," xxix). Preferring "the term *Rhythmical* to *Metrical*" (vi) like George H. Gilbert and recognizing that "irregularity seemed to be in consonance with the spirit of the poem" (vii), however, Cary often substitutes shorter iambic lines as well as alexandrines. The result appears with full stage directions, as in the opening of Chapter 3:

> *The garden connected with Job's house.*
> *Enter Job, his garments rent, and his head shaven. He falls upon the ground.*
> *Job*. Naked from out my mother's womb I came;
> Naked shall I return.
> [*After a pause he rises and says submissively*
> Jehovah gave;--Jehovah took away;
> Jehovah's name be blessed.
>
> (4)

Most of the work, however, appears as soliloquys with theatrical allusions to acting, costumes, and dialogue. And even his shorter lines tend to be relentlessly iambic, as in 24.13-17

> Some men there are who 'gainst the light rebel,
> Who will not walk within its trodden ways,
> Nor in its paths abide.
> The murderer at early dawn will rise,
> He slays the needy and the destitute,
> And through the night he plays the part of thief.
> Th'adulterer's eyes await the evening gloom,
> "No eye," he says, "shall see me as I go;"
> A muffling veil he winds about his face,
> The burglar digs in darkness through the house,
> And in the day-time hides himself away.
> These men are strangers to the light;
> The morn to them as darkness has become;
> Yea, well they know the terrors of the night.
>
> (47)

Cary's choice of the Revised Edition suggests the success of this new version, whose very title acknowledges its homage to the King James. During the two and a half centuries in which the King James had held sway, scholars had made extraordinary advances in locating early texts, recognizing the nuances of Semitic languages, and defining the characteristics of Hebrew poetry. Even before James I had died, he received as a gift from the Patriarch of Alexandria a fifth-century manuscript of the Bible, a far more accurate text than any his translators had access to. Now known as the Alexandrine Codex, this text was only the first of many which would become available to English biblical scholars. Moreover, as the English language evolved, many of the stately, formal constructions of the Renaissance had become archaic. In 1870 the Convocation of Canterbury called for a revision strictly limited to correcting textual errors and improving language which had become obscure. The project's committees invited participation from Church of Scotland, English and Scottish Free Churches, and even Roman Catholic and Unitarian scholars. Of the thirty-seven scholars who worked on the Hebrew Bible, seven were not members of the Church of England. Eventually, American biblical scholars were invited to participate. As the American and British worked independently in parallel committees, regularly exchanging their alternative readings, the Americans decided to publish their own edition. In 1881 the British Revised Version of the New Testament appeared, followed four years later by the Revised Version of the Hebrew Bible. The Americans agreed to withhold publication of their version, on which they continued work, for fourteen years; and the American Standard Version finally appeared in 1901.[12]

With far better original texts and a far better understanding of the nature of Hebrew poetry than their predecessors had enjoyed, the Revised Version's translators offered significant improvements, especially in the more textually challenging books like *Job*. In the opening of the Hymn to Wisdom, the widely debated Chapter 28, the Revised Version's shifts from prose to poetry and from Renaissance English to Victorian English, have significant aesthetic, literary, and semantic effects. The ways in which the lines' parallelism helps to communicate the complex sets of relationships of the worlds beneath the physical and spiritual surfaces transform a set of vivid images into a powerful reflection on the essential harmony and integration

King James

Surely there is a veine for the silver, and a place for golde *where* they fine *it*.

Iron is taken out of the earth, and brasse is molten *out of* the stone.

Hee setteth an ende to darknesse, and searcheth out all perfection: the stones of darknesse, and the shadow of death.

The floud breaketh out from the inhabitant; *even the waters* forgotten of the foote: they are dried up, they are gone away from men.

As for the earth, out of it cometh bread: and under it is turned up as it were fire.

The stones of it *are* the places of sapphires; and it hath dust of golde.

Revised Version

Surely there is a mine for silver,
And a place for gold which they refine.
Iron is taken out of the earth,
And brass is molten out of the stone.
Man setteth an end to darkness,
And searcheth out to the furthest bound
The stones of thick darkness and of the shadow of death.
He breaketh open a shaft away from where men sojourn;
They are forgotten of the foot *that passeth by*;
They hang afar from men, they swing to and fro.
As for the earth, out of it cometh bread:
And underneath it is turned up as it were by fire.
The stones thereof are the place of sapphires
And it hath dust of gold.[13]

In 1893 a translator identified only as Talmid used blank verse for a highly untraditional version. By inverting normal English syntax, relying on singular forms where plurals would be expected, developing unusual constructions, and eliminating some of the articles, Talmid appears to be trying to evoke a sense of the text as a product of an alien culture. Unlike Young and Halsted, his translation creates an exotic rather than confusing effect. In his interpretation of 24:12-14, for example, Talmid is clearly defamiliarizing traditional English rhythms, in contrast to Clarke, Malet, and White:

12 Out from the city mortal men will groan,
And soul of wounded men will cry for help;
Yet God will not be laying heedlessness,--
13 They, they have been with rebels against light;
They have not recognised the ways of it,
Nor have been sitting in the paths of it.
14 At light-time will arise a murderer,
Will kill the suffering and needy one,
And in the night will he be as a thief.

(48)

Although a majority of those discussing *Job* continued to regard it as some sort of drama, the very distinctiveness of its form continued to fascinate translators. Just as Henry Adams defined it as highest form of lyric only to translate it as an epic, few translators seem completely comfortable with the genres available in the Western canon. Attempting to categorize it eventually led John F. Genung (1850-1919) in 1891 to find in it parallels to Robert Browning's monologues, Aeschylus' *Prometheus Bound* ("the embodiment of a national epos, albeit in dramatic form" [25]), legend, saga, debate, drama, and lyric. Ultimately, he titled his translation *The Epic of the Inner Life; Being the Book of Job Translated Anew*, concluding, "I regard this ancient book as the record of a sublime epic action, whose scene is not the tumultuous battle-field, nor the arena of rash adventure, but the solitary soul of a righteous man" (20-21). Genung's result uses lines of varying lengths to emphasize the emotional and psychological qualities of the poem, as in the opening of Chapter 3.

> My soul is weary of my life;
> I will let loose my plaint over myself;
> I will speak in the bitterness of my soul.
> I will say unto God, Holfd me not guilty;
> Make me know wherefore Thou contendest with me.

As critics like Matthew Arnold dismissed the didactic and satirical work of the previous century, it was inevitable that translators would adapt lyric forms and assumptions to their translations. In 1839 Thomas Wemyss used a title that suggested a historical piece, *Job and His Times, or a Picture of the Patriarchal Age*. Much more traditional in his vision of form than Genung, Wemyss goes to some lengths to dismiss the idea of the work as dramatic: "there is no *action* in the work and action is essential to the drama. . . . There is a certain kind of division and arrangement in the conferences, but there are no *scenes* in the dramatic sense of that term" (11). His conclusion, that the work is essentially "pathetic" (53), is reflected in his form. In his interpretation of 7.1-4, for example, he establishes an elegaic tone with his opening tetrameter line dominated by melancholic anapests, followed by a variety of catalectic and hypercatalectic lines playing iambs against anapests to achieve his somber effect:

> Hath not man the life of a servant on earth?
> Are not his days as the days of an hireling?
> Like a slave, he pants for the evening shade;
> Like a hireling, he waits for the finishing of his work.
> The seasons of misery are allotted to me,
> And nights of wretchedness are numbered to me.

When I lay me down to rest, I exclaim,
"When shall I arise, and the tedious night be gone?"
I am full of restlessness until the dawn.

(151)[14]

Although recognizing both the epic struggle in *Job* and its resemblance to such classical tragedy as *Prometheus Unbound* and *Oedipus*, the Earl of Winchilsea reached a curious conclusion in 1860: "The reader will scarcely fail to observe the singular felicity with which the text lends itself to the ballad metre" (x). When Ralph Erskine (1685-1752), inspired by Isaac Watts, had used the same form a century earlier, he had consciously selected from and adapted the work for *Job's Hymns: Or, A Book of Songs upon the Book of Job* (1753). Winchilsea's ambition was greater; he not only intended to translate the entire work, he felt his form suited it better than other English forms. Part of his conclusion may result from his antiquarian interests; he even admitted that, like Sir John Cheke whose work on the gospels first appeared in 1843, he preferred using "many quaint old English words" (xi). As odd as his argument may be, his lines become surprisingly effective in their rapid movement through the work.

To integrate his ballad measure into the entire text, Winchilsea needed to establish structural principles to tie what would normally be stanzas into larger units. Seeking simpler effects, Erskine could attempt simpler structures. In his "Song V: Sin the Cause of Trouble," an interpretation of 5:6-7, the eighteenth-century poet uses three stanzas to establish a fairly simple set of parallels:

(1)
Affliction springs not from the earth,
  Nor trouble from the dust;
Yet man are heirs of woe by birth;
  Sad heritage! but just.

(2)
Flames to their element ascend,
  So men, conceiv'd in sin,
To trouble, as their centre tend,
  Like kindred to their kin.

(3)
For sin and woe, twins of the clan,
  By chance were never convey'd,
But propagate from man to man,
  Since Adam disobey'd.

(27)

Erskine's Scots imagery of the clan and his allusion to Adam argue the inevitability of original sin in the family of man. Although this position is consistent with traditional Christian theology, it can be easily argued that *Job* never really makes a case for original sin. In fact, God himself describes Job as "perfect" and requires atonement for Eliphaz, the speaker of these lines. By tying these verses syntactically together with the following one (5.8), Winchilsea shifts from endorsing Eliphaz's argument to reflecting on the essential mystery of God's actions. The very organization of these twelve lines suggest a logical syllogism, in which the conclusion emphasizes God's marvels rather than man's afflictions:

Although affliction cometh not
  From the dust that flies around,
And trouble is no crop that springs
  Spontaneous from the ground;
Yet the dole of man is trouble;
  Misfortune is his share;
As the sparks of fire fly upwards,
  And lose themselves in air:
Seek unto God I pray thee;
  To Him thy cause commend!
For He doeth things unsearchable,
  And marvels without end.

(18)

In 1869 William Meikle's *The Book of Job in Metre* occasionally used the ballad measure among a variety of primarily tetrameter lines. For Meikle, God speaks in ballad form, as in admonishing Job:

Who over wisdom's boundless works,
  Is he that thus would throw
A covering of imprudent speech,
  And darken counsel so?

38:2

Using a variety of rhyme schemes, Meikle shifts freely between iambic and anapestic lines without any apparent connection between the form and the content. In Job's lament about his life in Chapter 3, for example, he uses interlocking iambic tetrameters, while in his complaint about injustice in the world he uses rhyming anapestic teterameters:

Why was I dandled on the knees,
  Or nurtured on the living breast?
For now should I have lain at ease,
  Then had I slept and been at rest.

3:12-13

The houses of robbers do prosper; and they,
Who provoke the Almighty, are safe from dismay:
Whom God giveth plenty. The beasts will declare
Wouldst thou ask it of them; or the fowl of the air,
And the fulness of earth have a lesson for thee;
Nor mute upon this are the fish of the sea.
12:6-8

Near the end of the century, the Rev. Hiram Mason Sydenstricker showed a similar fascination for tetrameters. Although he titled his translation *The Epic of the Orient: An Original Poetical Rendering of the Book of Job* (1894), his brief "Preface" emphasizes only the originality and poetry rather than the epic quality of both the original and his version. His opening of Chapter 3 introduces a twelve line stanza, beginning and ending with couplets and using interlocking rhyme for the middle eight lines:

With cursings then did Job complain,
And thus began his mournful strain:--
Let perish now my mortal day
In deepest shades of darkest gloom--
May God withhold a single ray,
And from His throne confirm the doom.
In darkness let it 'bide alone,
'Neath gloomy mists and angry cloud,
Let deepest darkness claim his own
And turn its light to blackest shroud.
The king of night, let him possess
That day, and horrid fear oppress.
(11)

The metronomic regularity of these iambs reflects the greatest failing of Sydenstricker's work. His interest in experimenting with meter, especially tetrameter meter, subordinates the text itself. In two of his more interesting metrical experiments, he must wrench his syntax to achieve unrhymed iambic tetrameters at the end of Chapter 40 but he manages to create some rollicking, if not especially appropriate, unrhymed anapestic tetrameters for Elijah at the beginning of Chapter 37:

He trembleth not, nor doth he care
Though Jordan break upon his mouth.
Shall man him trap before his eyes,
Or through his nose a snare project?

(106)

My spirit doth tremble with quaking of fear,
It moveth and leapeth and leaveth its place.
Attentively hear thou the noise of His voice,
The mutterings of thunder that come from His mouth.

(94)

The limits of Sydenstricker's tetrameters become even more apparent in contrast with Thomas Scott's translation into heroic couplets over a century earlier. At times Scott's language is too arcane, reflecting eighteenth-century lexicographical interests at their worst (e.g., "Mean are divine emollients? held for vile,/Friendship's monitions couch'd in friendly style?" 15:11). His version of Job's lament, however suggests the strengths of a poet in command of his form:

At length the suff'ring man, opprest with pain,
Pour'd out his anguish in lamenting strain:
And thus devoted to eternal shame
His natal day, whence all his sorrows came.
Perish the day my hapless years began!
Perish the night, which hail'd the new-born man!
Dark, total darkness, be that day; nor eye
Of God, all viewing from his throne on high,
Its revolution heed: nor orient beam
Revisit, gladd'ning with its golden stream.
Let Death possess it with his dreary shade,
Let storm and thund'ring cloud its heaven invade:
Let boding signs, for all the quarter'd sphere,
Trouble its brow, and terrify the year.

(10-12)

At its best, Scott's version has a vigorous, colloquial quality that transforms the occasionally archaic Authorized Version, with its frequently confusing pronouns, into vivid, dramatic language:

King James 21:19-21

God layeth up his iniquitie for his children: he rewardeth him, and he shall know *it*.

His eye shall see his destruction, and he shall drinke of the wrath of the Almightie.

For what pleasure *hath* he in his house after him when the number of his moneths is cut of in the middest?

Scott

You'll urge, "God treasures vengeance for their seed."

But he, the criminal, himself should bleed:
Living, himself should his own treasure rue,
And his own eyes his tragedy should view;
While at his lips the wrathful cup he sees,
Compell'd to drain it with its bitter lees:
For when his number'd months their tale have spent,
When to oblivion's land himself is sent;
Are then the fortunes of his house his care?
Feels he its triumphs or its sorrows there?

(162-163)

A far more succesful use of tetrameters than Sydenstricker's occurs in Rossiter Raymond's *The Book of Job* (1878). Raymond (1840-1918), who worked on his translation with the Adult Bible Class of Plymouth Church, Brooklyn, follows Meikle and Sydenstricker in using tetrameters organized into three line strophes, printed in parallel columns with the Revised Version, as in 30:1-4

But now around me mocking creep
Young men, whose sires I scorned to keep
Among the dogs that watched my sheep.

A tribe to useless weakness bred,
In whom old age was well-nigh dead,
By want and hunger famished,

They gnaw in desert solitude
The salt-plant by the thickets rude,
Or gather broom-root for their food.

(129)

Raymond's energetic lines, which strive for "Saxon simplicity" (4), at times become a Procrustean bed which forces him to expand or contract the original to meet the demand of his form.

Emile Joseph Dillon (1854-1933), Professor of Comparative Philology at the Imperial University of Kaharkoff, on the other hand, believed that strophes consisted of four lines and, like John Tattersall, arranged his translation into quatrains with lines of differing lengths in his somewhat heterodox collection *The Sceptics of the Old Testament (Job, Koheleth, Agur)*.

But the most successful lyric approach to *Job* occurs in Henry John Marten's *A Metrical Study of the Book of Job* (1869) in which irregular lines are organized to resemble a Cowleyan ode. In 1661 Arthur Brett had dedicated a similar attempt to celebrating the return of sophistication with the restoration of Charles II, but

Marten offers no explanation for his practice. The effect, as in his interpretation of Chapter 14, is to provide a powerful lyrical voice for Job while allowing him to remain a fairly orthodox Christian:

But
If I die?
Ah!
Shall I live again?
Yea!
Without fear,
I'll wait th'appointed time,
Till,
Death revoked,
My glorious change shall come!
Then,
Thou shalt call,
And I will answer Thee,
For Thou wilt yearn toward Thy handy work!
(46-47)

Marten's effectiveness in relying on monosyllabic lines as dramatic interjections underlines Job's anguish even more effectively than Brett's more stately interpretation of the passage:

If from the body the soul take her flight,
And I in pieces fall,
Wilt thou my limbs together call?
Wilt thou my scatter'd parts unite?
Strong Hope and never weary'd Constancy
Shall carry me through every change and turn
Till my last change come, my urn;
And then this great Experiment I'le try:
Then thou to Glory's feast wilt me invite,
And then up I shall start,
And go and take place next thy heart,
Thy bosom-darling, and thy souls delight,
Always thy Creature, then thy Favourite.
(49)

Despite Marten's attempt to recreate the traditionally orthodox Christian figure with a distinctively Romantic lyric voice, other interpreters foresaw the need for a freshly imagined Job who could speak more effectively to a world about to enter the twentieth century. In 1892 Robert Watson would attempt to define the relevance of *Job* in a culture in which religion appeared increasingly marginalized, in which mankind, like the original author, "has to seek room for faith in a world shadowed and confused" (4). In an essay on *Job* shortly after the turn of the century, Gilbert Keith Chesterton recognizes the human need to recreate God in its own evolving image when he describes the theme of the Hebrew Bible as "the loneliness of God" (x). The solace the *Book of Job* can offer us in confronting such a deity arises from its lesson that "man is most comforted by paradoxes" (xxiii). Within this increasingly puzzling and paradoxical universe, new Jobs needed to emerge to answer both ancient and modern questions.

As the Revised Version and the American Standard Version began competing with the King James, an increased interest in biblical scholarship shifted attention away from aesthetic principles towards academic and theological ones and prepared for the dramatically rich expansion of translations in the twentieth century. At the same time, readers found the ambiguities of Job's dialogues a fuller reflection of their age than the certainties of the epilogue. Job, a figure who had evolved from the devout puritan of Broughton and Abbott through the philosopher king of Quarles and Brett, the epic hero of Blackmore and Baker, the man of sensibility of Young and Thompson, and the Arabic prince of Elizabeth Smith to the romantic rebel of Genung and Marten, continued demonstrating the allure that compelled Carl Jung to answer his questions and Chesterton to proclaim the book not only "the most interesting of ancient books" but "the most interesting of modern books" as well (xii). From Kafka's minor bureaucrat Joseph K. and MacLeish's corporate executive J.B. to *Tender Mercy*'s awkwardly articulate hero and Muriel Spark's delicately confused editor, Job has found an abundance of voices to help him write and rewrite his book. But that book now focuses on neither the theophany's call for submission nor the epilogue's abundant reward. Rather, what has spoken to our century is the very material that the earliest translators often omitted, the dialogues, those Samuel Beckettian explorations of emptiness, loss, and failure, with their unrelenting search for meaning and their unanswered questions.

WORKS CITED

"O that mine enemy had written
A book!" - cried Job; a fearful curse,
If to the Arab, as the Briton,
'Twas galling to be critic-bitten;
The Devil to Peter wished no worse.
Percy Bysshe Shelley, *Peter Bell the Third* (1819), Part the Sixth, I

NB. Bibliographic information for all of the Joban translations between Aelfric and 1900 appears in Part Three.

Agrippa von Nettesheim, Cornelius Heinrich. *De incertitudine et vanitate scientiarum et artium*. Antwerp: Ioan Grapheus, c.1530.

-. *De occulta philosophia*. 1510

[American Standard Version.] *The Holy Bible*. New York: Norwood Press, J.S. Cushing and Company, Berwick, and Smith for Thomas Nelson and Sons, 1901

The Anchor Bible. General Editors: William F. Albright and David Noel Freedman. 1966 -

Aquinas, Thomas. *Expositioi super Iob ad litteram. Exposition on Job*. Trans. Peter Philip Riley, O.P. Typescript. Washington, D.C.: Dominican College Library, 1970.

Arnold, Matthew. "On Translating Homer." *On The Classical Tradition*. Vol. 1 of the *Complete Prose Works*. Ed. R.H. Super. Ann Arbor: University of Michigan Press, 1960.

-. "Isaiah of Jerusalem." *Philistinism in England and America*. Vol. 10 of *Complete Prose Works*. Ann Arbor: University of Michigan, 1974.

Barnstone, Willis. *The Poetics of Translation: History, Theory, Practice*. New Haven: Yale University Press, 1993.

Bassnett, Susan. *Translation Studies*. Rev. ed. New York: Routledge, 1961.

Battestin, Martin C. *The Providence of Wit*. Oxford: Clarendon Press, 1974.

Besserman, Lawrence L. *The Legend of Job in the Middle Ages*. Cambridge, Massachusetts: Harvard University Press, 1979.

Beza, Theodore [Théodore de Bèze]. *Du droit des magistrats sur leur sujets*. 574. Rpt. Paris: Editions d'Histoire Sociale, 1977.

-. *Vezelii poemata juvenilia*. Lutetiae: C. Badij, 1548.

Blackmore, Sir Richard. *Alfred. An Epick Poem*. London: J. Knapton, 1723.

-. *The Creation: A Philosophical Poem*. London: S. Buckley, 1712.

-. *Eliza, an Epick Poem*. London: A. and J. Churchill, 1705.

-. *The Nature of Man*. London: S. Buckley, 1711.

-. *Prince Arthur, an Heroick Poem*. London: Awnsham and J. Churchill, 1695.

-. *Satyr against Wit*. London: S. Crouch, 1700.

Bloch, Ariel and Chana. *Song of Songs*. New York: Random House, 1995.

Bradley, George Granville. *Lectures on the Book of Job*. Oxford: Clarendon Press, 1887.

Brett, Arthur. *The Restauration. Or, A Poem on the Return of the Most Mighty and Ever Glorious Prince, Charles II, to His Kingdom.* London: J.H. for Samuel Thomson, 1660.

Broughton, Hugh. *A Censure of the Late Translation for Our Church: Sent unto a Right Worshipfull Knight, Attendant upon the King.* Middelburg: R. Schilders, 1612.

- *An Epistle to the Learned Nobilitie of England Touching Translating the Bible from the Original, with Ancient Warrant for Euerie Worde, unto the Full Satisfaction of Any that Be of Hart.* Middelburgh: Richard Schilders, 1597.

Brown, John. *The Self-Interpreting Bible.* 2 vols. Edinburgh: G. Alston, 1778

Brown, John. *The Swan Song or the Second Part of the Life of Faith in Times of Trial & Affliction.* 1680

Bruce, F.F. *The English Bible: A History of Translations.* New York: Oxford University Press, 1961.

Bunyan, John. *Pilgrim's Progress.* London: Nath. Ponder, 1678.

Burgess, Anthony. "Will and Testament." In *Shakespeare: Patterns of Excelling Nature.* Eds. David Bevington and Jay L. Halio. Newark, Delaware: University of Delaware Press, 1978. Pp. 142-60.

Byron, George Gordon (Lord). *Hebrew Melodies. Works of the Right Honourable Lord Byron.* London: John Murray, 1813.

Calvin, John. *Sermons of Master Iohn Calvin, upon the Booke of Iob.* Trans. Arthur Golding. London: Lucas Harison and George Byshop, 1574.

Carlyle, Thomas. *On Heroes, Hero Worship, and the Heroic in History.* Vol. 5 of the *Works* (Edinburgh Edition). New York: Charles Scribner's Sons, 1903.

Chaloner, Thomas. *A Speech containing a Plea for Monarchy.* London, 1659

Chapman, George. *Euthymiae Raptus; or the Teares of Peace.* London: H.L. for Rich Bonian and H. Waller, 1609

-. *The Iliad of Homer.* London: I. Windet, 1598.

-. "To the Reader." *Chapman's Homer.* Vol. 1. *The Iliad.* Ed. Allardyce Nicoll. Bollingen Series XLI. New York. Pantheon Books,1956.

Carlyle, Thomas. *On Heroes: Hero-Worship, & The Heroic in History.* London: James Fraser, 1841.

Chaucer, Geoffrey. *Works*, ed. F.N. Robinson. 2nd. ed. Boston: Houghton Mifflin Company, 1961.

Cheke, Sir John. *The Gospel According to Saint Matthew and Part of the First Chapter of the Gospel According to Saint Mark.* Cambridge: J. and J.J. Deighton, 1843.

Chesterton, Gilbert Keith. "Introduction." *The Book of Job.* London: Wellwood, 1907.

Cibber, Theophilus. *Lives of the Poets.* 5 vols. London: R. Griffiths, 1753.

Cicero. *De optimo genere oratorum.* In *De Inventione, De Optimo Genere Oratorum.* London: William Heinemann, 1949.

Collier, Jeremy. *A Short View of the Immorality and Profaneness f the English Stage together with the Sense of Antiquity upon this Argument.* London: S. Kebie, R. Save, and H. Hindmarch, 1698.

[Complutensian Polyglot.] *Vetus testimentii multiplici lingua*. 6 vols. Ed. Antonio de Lebrixa et al. Academia Complutensi [Alcala de Henares]: Industria de Bocario, 1514-17.

Croly, George. *The Book of Job*. Edinburgh and London: William Blackwood and Sons, 1863.

Darlow, T.H. and H.F. Moule. *Historical Catalogue of Printed Editions of the English Bible. 1525-1961, revised and expanded by A.S. Herbert*. London: British and Foreign Bible Society, 1968.

Denham, Sir John. *Poetical Works*. Ed. Theodore Howard Banks. New Haven: Yale University Press, 1928.

-. "Preface" to *The Destruction of Troy*. London: Humphrey Moseley, 1656

Dennis, John. *The Grounds of Criticism in Poetry*. London: Geo. Strahan & Bernard Lintot, 1704.

Derham, William. *Physico-Theology*. London: W. Innys, 1713.

Dolet, Estienne. *La manière de bien traduire d'une langue en aultre*. Anvers: Jehan Loe, 1542.

Donne, John. Vol. 3 of *The Sermons of John Donne*. Ed. George R. Potter and Evelyn M. Simpson. Berkeley: University of California. 1957.

Dowglass, Thomas. *The Book of Job: An Allegorical History of the Christian Church*. London: C. Goodall, 1853.

Dryden, John. *Absalom and Achitophel. Poems 1681-1684*. Vol. 2 of *Works*. Ed. H.T. Swedenberg, Jr. Berkeley and Los Angeles: University of California Press, 1972.

-. "Dedication" to the Aeneis." *The Works of Virgil in English*. Vol. 5 of *Works*. Ed. William Frost. Berkeley and Los Angeles: University of California Press, 1987.

-. *The Spanish Fryar. Plays*. Vol. 14 of *Works*. Ed. Vinton A. Dearing. Berkeley and Los Angeles: University of California Press, 1992.

-. *Fables Ancient and Modern*. London: J. Tonson, 1700.

-. "Preface" to *Ovid's Epistles. Poems 1649-1680*. Vol. I of *Works*. Ed. Edward Niles Hooker and H. T. Sweedenberg, Jr. Berkeley and Los Angeles: University of California Press, 1961.

Edwards, John. *A Discourse concerning the Authority, Stile, & Perfection of the Books of the Old and New Testament*. London: Richard Wilkin, 1694.

The English Hexapla. London: S. Bagster and Sons, 1841.

Erasmus, Desiderius. *Novum Instrumentum*. Basle: Joannes Frobenii Hammelburgensis, 1516.

Evans, C.F., G.W.H. Lampe, and S.L. Greenslade, eds. *The Cambridge History of the Bible*. 3 vols. Cambridge: Cambridge University Press, 1963-70.

Fanshawe, Sir Richard. *Il Pastor Fido; or the Faithful Shepheard*. London: William Cademan, 1647.

Fenton, Farrar. *The Holy Bible in Modern English*. London: Bradbury, Agnew for S.W. Partridge, 1903.

Fielding, Henry. *The History of Tom Jones, a Foundling*. 1749. 4 vols. Intro. Martin C. Battestin. Text ed. Fredson Bowers. London: Oxford University Press/ Wesleyan University Press, 1975.

-. *The Voyages of Mr. Job Vinegar. The Champion*, 1740. Ed. S.J. Sackett. Los Angeles: William Andrews Clark Memorial Library/ University of California, 1958.

Fitzgerald, Edward. *Letters*. Ed. Alfred McKinley Terhune and Annabelle Burdick Terhune. Vol 2. Princeton: Princeton University Press, 1980.

Fox, Everett. *The Five Books of Moses*. New York: Schocken, 1995.

Frost, Robert. *A Masque of Reason*. New York: Henry Holt, 1945.

Frost, William. *Dryden and the Art of Translation*. New Haven: Yale University Press, 1955.

Garnett, John. *A Dissertation on the Book of Job*. London: M. Cooper, 1749.

[Gauden, John.] *Eikon Basilike: The Pourtraicture of His Sacred Majestie in His Solitudes and Sufferings*. Reprint of Edition of 1648. London: Elliot Stock, 1880.

Gell, Robert. *An Essay toward the Amendment of the Last English Translation of the Bible*. London: R. Norton for Andrew Crook, 1659.

A Godly Ballad of the Just Man Job. London: Printed for F. Coles, J. Wright, Tho, Vere, & W. Gilbertson [?1645].

Goldsmith, Oliver. *The Vicar of Wakefield*. London: James Blackwood, 1750.

Goldstein, Laurence. *Ruins and Empire: The Evolution of a Theme in Augustan and Romantic Literature*. Pittsburgh: University of Pittsburgh Press, 1977.

(Good News Bible) The Holy Bible, Today's English Version. New York: American Bible Society, 1976.

Goodspeed, Edgar J. *The New Testament: An American Translation*. Chicago: University of Chicago Press, 1923.

Gordis, Robert. *The Book of God and Man: A Study of Job*. Chicago: University of Chicago, 1965. Phoenix Edition, 1978.

Gray, Richard. *An Answer to Mr. Warburton's Remarks on the Book of Job*. London, 1744.

Gray, Thomas. *Elegy Wrote in a Country Churchyard*. London: R. Dodsley, 1751.

Greenberg, Moshe et al. *The Book of Job*. Philadelphia: The Jewish Publication Society of America, 5740/1980.

Greenslade, S.L., ed. *The Cambridge History of the Bible, vol 3: The West from the Reformation to the Present Day*. Cambridge: Cambridge University Press, 1970.

Gregory. *Morals on the Book of Job*. 3 vols. Oxford: John Henry Parker; London: J.G.F. and J. Rivington, 1844-50.

Grove, Henry. "The Reasonableness of Religion." In *The English Preacher*, Vol. 2. London: J. Johnson, 1773.

Gutiérrez, Gustavo. *Hablar de Dios desde el sufrimiento del inocente*. Lima, Peru: Centro de Estudios y Publicaciones, 1986. (English translation by Matthew J. O'Connell. *On Job: God-Talk and the Suffering of the Innocent*. Maryknoll, N.Y.: Orbis Books, 1987.)

Habel, Norman C. *The Book of Job. The Cambridge Bible Commentary.* Cambridge: Cambridge University Press, 1975.

Handel, George Frederick. *Israel in Egypt: An Oratorio, Or Sacred Drama, As It Is Performed at the King's Theatre in the Hay-Market.* London: King's Theatre, 1739.

Hardy, Nathaniel. *A Sad Prognostick of Approaching Judgment.* London: A,M. for J. Cranford, 1658.

Harriss, Charles. *A Scriptural Chronicle of Satans Incendiaries: or the Happy Misery of Good Men in Bad Times, viz. Hard-Hearted Persecutors, and Malicious Informers*. [London], 1670.

Heinlein, Robert A. *Job, A Comedy of Justice*. New York: Ballantine Books, 1984.

Herbert, A.S. *Historical Catalogue of Printed Editions of the English Bible 1525 -1961: Revised and Expanded from the Edition of T. H. Darlow and H. F. Moule, 1903*. London: The British and Foreign Bible Society, 1968.

Hervey, James. *Meditations and Contemplations*. Boston: Phillips, Sampson, 1746.

Hills, Margaret T., ed. *The English Bible in America: A Bibliography of Editions of the Bible & the New Testament Published in America 1777 to 1957*. New York: American Bible Society and the New York Public Library, 1962.

Hobbes, Thomas. *Leviathan: or the Matter, Form, & Power of a Common-Wealth Ecclesiastical and Civil*. London: Andrew Crooke, 1651.

Hooke, William. *New Englands Teares for Old Englands Feares*. London: T.P. for I. Rothwell and Henry Overton, 1641

Horace. *Ars Poetica*. Cambridge, MA: Harvard University Press, 1932.

Hutcheson, James. *An Exposition of the Book of Job: Being the Sum of CCCXVI Lectures Preached in the City of Edenburgh*. London: Ralph Smith, 1669.

Jackson, Arthur. *Annotations upon the Five Books immediately following the historicall Part of the old Testament*. Part 3 London: Roger David, 1658.

Jerome. *Lettres*. Tome III. Paris: Societe d'edition Les Belles Lettres, 1953.

-. "Preface to the Chronicles of Eusebius." *Nicene and Post Nicene Fathers*. Vol. 6. *Jerome: Letters and Select Works*. Ed. Philip Schaff and Henry Wace. Rpt. of edition of 1892. Peabody, Massachusetts: Hendrickson Publishers, 1994.

The Jerusalem Bible. Garden City, New York: Doubleday, 1966.

[Jewish Publication Society.] *The Holy Scriptures according to the Masoretic Text*. Philadelphia: Jewish Publication Society, 1917/5677.

Johnson, Samuel. *Lives of the English Poets*. Ed. Geoge Birkbeck Hill. 3 vols. Oxford: Clarendon Press, 1905. Rptd. New York: Octagon Books, 1967.

Jung, Carl. *An Answer to Job*. Cleveland: World Publishing, 1954. (*Antwort auf Hiob*. Zurich: Rascher, 1952.)

Kallen, Horace Meyer. *The Book of Job as a Greek Tragedy, Restored*. New York: Moffat, Yard, 1918.

Kipling, Rudyard. "Proofs of Holy Writ." (1932). In *Uncollected Prose*. Vol XXIII of *The Burwash Edition of the Complete Works in Prose and Verse*. 1941. Rptd. New York: AMS. 1970. Pp. 663-78.

Knox, Ronald. *The New Testament*. London: Burns Oates & Washbourne, 1944.

-. *The Old Testament*. London: Burns Oates & Washbourne, 1949.
Lamb, Jonathan. "The Job Controversy, Sterne and the Question of Allegory." *Eighteenth Century Studies*, 24 (1990), 1-19.
-. *The Rhetoric of Suffering: Reading the Book of Job in the Eighteenth Century*. Oxford: Clarendon Press, 1995.
Leigh, Edward. *Annotations on Five Poetical Books of the Old Testament*. London: A.M. for T. Pierpoint, E. Brewster, and M. Keinton, 1657.
Letsome, Sampson. *The Preacher's Assistant*. London, 1753.
Lewis, Jack P. *The English Bible from KJV to NIV: A History and Evaluation*. Grand Rapids, Michigan: Baker Book House, 1981.
Lightfoot, John. *The Whole Works of the Rev. John Lightfoot*. Ed. J.R. Pitman. London: J.F. Dove, 1823.
The Living Bible, Paraphrased. Paraphrased by Kenneth Taylor. London: Hodder and Stoughton/Coverdale House, 1971.
Lloyd, William, ed. *The Holy Bible*. London: Bell and Executrix of Newcomb, 1701.
Long, Thomas. *A Sermon against Murmuring*. London: Richard Royston, 1680.
Longfellow, Henry Wadsworth. *Letters*. *The Life of Henry Wadsworth Longfellow*. Vol 3. Boston: Houghton Mifflin (Riverside Press), 1891.
Lowth, Robert. *De sacra poesi Hebraeorum: Praelectiones Academiae Oxonii*. Oxonii, 1753.
-. *Lectures on the Sacred Poetry of the Hebrews*, trans. G. Gregory, 2 vols. London: J. Johnson, 1787.
Luther, Martin. "On Translating: An Open Letter" (1530) and "Preface to the Book of Job" (1545, 1524). Trans. Charles M. Jacobs and revised by E. Theodore Bachmann. *Word and Sacrament*. Vol. 1. Ed. E. Theodore Bachmann. Vol. 35 of *Luther's Works*. Ed. Helmut T. Lehmann. Philadelphia: Fortress Press, 1960. Pp. 181-202, 251-253.
MacGregor, Geddes. *A Literary History of the Bible*. Nashville: Abingdon Press, 1968.
Macaulay, Thomas Babington. *History of England*. *Complete Works* (University Edition). Vols. 1-5. New York: Sully and Kleinteich, 1899.
MacLeish, Archibald. *J.B.* Cambridge, Massachusetts: Riverside Press, 1958.
Mandeville, Bernard. *The Fable of the Bees*. London: J. Roberts, 1714.
Manley, Thomas. *Veni; Vidi; Vici: The Triumphs of the Most Excellent & Illustrious Oliver Cromwell*. London: Iohn Tey, 1652.
Marsh, Richard. *The Vanity and Danger of Modern Theories*. Cambridge: Printed at the University Press for Edmund Jeffrey, 1699.
Masoretic Text of Bible. Soncino. 1488.
Milton, John. *Eikonoklastes*. *Complete Prose Works*. Vol 3. New Haven: Yale University Press, 1962.
-. *Paradise Regain'd*. *Poetical Works*. Vol. 2. Ed. Helen Darbishire. Oxford: Clarendon Press, 1955.
-. *Reason of Church Government*. *Complete Prose Works*. Vol. 1. Ed. Don M. Wolfe. New Haven: Yale University Press, 1953.

Mitchell, Stephen. *The Book of Job*. New York: Harper, 1979. Rev.ed. 1987.
Moffatt, James. *The Historical New Testament*. Edinburgh: T. and T. Clark, 1901.
-. *The Holy Bible* London: Hodder and Staughton, 1926.
Moore, John. *Of Patience and Submission to Authority*. London: R. Royston and Walter Kettilby, 1684.
More, Hannah. *Bible Rhymes on the Names of all the Books of the Old and New Testament*. London: A. & R. Spottiswoode, 1821.
Moulton, William F. *The History of the English Bible*. New Revised Edition. London: Charles H. Kelley, 1911.
The New American Bible. New York: P.J. Kennedy and Sons, 1970. Revised, New York: Catholic Publishers, 1978.
The New American Standard Bible. 1971, Updated 1995.
The New English Bible. Oxford and Cambridge: Oxford and Cambridge University Presses, 1970.
The *New International Version*. Grand Rapids, Michigan: Zondervan, 1978. Rev. 1985.
The New Jerusalem Bible. New York: Doubleday, 1985.
The New King James Version. Nashville: Nelson, 1982.
The New Living Translation. Tyndale House, 1996.
The New Revised Standard Version. New York: American Bible Society, 1990, 1995.
Norton, David. *A History of the Bible as Literature*. 2 vols. Cambridge: Cambridge University Press, 1993.
O'Sullivan, Maurice. "Running Division on the Groundwork: Dryden's Theory of Translation." *Neophilologus*, 64.1 (1980), 144-159.
Partridge, A.C. *English Biblical Translation*. London: Andre Deutsch, 1963.
Patrick, Simon. *Two Sermons: One against Murmuring, the Other against Censuring*. London: Richard Chiswell, 1689.
Penchansky, David. *The Betrayal of God: Ideological Conflict in Job*. Louisville, Kentucky: Westminster/John Knox, 1990.
Pollard, Alfred W. *Records of the English Bible*. London: Oxford University Press, 1911.
Pope, Alexander. *Eloisa to Abelard. Poems*. Twickenham Edition. Vol. 2. Ed. Geoffrey Tillotson. 3rd. ed. New Haven: Yale University Press, 1962.
-. *The Iliad of Homer: Books I-IX. Poems*. Twickenham Edition. Vol 7. Ed. Maynard Mack. New Haven: Yale University Press, 1967.
-. *Peri Bathous: or, Martinus Scriblerus His Treatise of the Art of Sinking in Poetry. Miscellanies*. London: B. Motte, 1727.
-. *Verses to the Memory of an Unfortunate Lady. Poems.* Twickenham Edition. Vol 2. Ed. Geoffrey Tillotson. 3rd. ed. New Haven: Yale University Press, 1962.
Pope, Marvin H. *Job: A New Translation with Introduction and Commentary*. Vol. 15 of *The Anchor Bible*. Garden City, N.Y.: Doubleday, 1973.
Purvey, John. "On Translating the Bible." *An English Garner: Fifteenth Century Prose and Verse.* Ed. Alfred W. Pollard. Rev. ed. Edinburgh: T. and A. Constable, 1903.

Quarles, Francis. *Complete Works in Prose and Verse*. Ed. Alexander B. Grosart. 3 vols. Edinburgh: Edinburgh University Press, 1880-81.
The Revised English Bible. (Rev. of *The New English Bible*), Ed. W.D. McHardy. Oxford and Cambridge: Oxford and Cambridge University Presses, 1989.
(Revised Standard Version) *The Holy Bible. Revised Standard Version*. London: Thomas Nelson and Sons, 1952.
Quiller-Couch, Arthur. *On the Art of Reading*. New York: G.P. Putnam's Sons, 1920.
Richardson, Samuel. *Clarissa*, or the *History of a Young Lady*. 7 vols. London: Samuel Richardson, 1748.
Rider, Henry. *A Sermon Preached in Christ's Church, Dublin, 23 October 1695 . . . before the House of Lords*. Dublin: J. Ray, 1695.
Rosenberg, David. *The Book of J*. New York: Grove Wedenfeld, 1990.
-. *Job Speaks*. New York: Harper & Row, 1977.
Rossetti, Dante Gabriel. *The Early Italian Poets. Poems and Translations 1850-1870*. London: Oxford University Press, 1913.
-. *Letters*. Ed. Oswald Doughty and J. R. Wahl. Vol 1. Oxford: Clarendon Press, 1965.
Rowe, Elizabeth. *Friendship in Death*. London: T. Worrall, 1728.
Rowley, H.H. *The Book of Job. The New Century Bible Commentary*, Grand Rapids, Michigan: Wm. B. Eerdmans, 1970. Rev. ed. 1976.
Safire, William. *The First Dissident: The Book of Job in Today's Politics*. New York: Random House, 1992.
Saintsbury, George. *Dryden*. London: Macmillan, 1881.
Sandys, George. *Ovid's Metamorphosis*. London: W. Stansby, 1626.
Scattergood, Samuel. *A Sermon Preached before the King at Newmarket*, April 2, 1676. Cambridge: John Hayes, 1676.
Schleirmacher, Friedrich. *Ueber die verschiedenen Methoden des Uebersetzens*. 1813.
Schreiner, Susan E. *Where Shall Wisdom Be Found? Calvin's Exegesis of Job from Medieval and Modern Perspectives*. Chicago: University of Chicago Press, 1994.
Scott, Sir Walter. "The Life of John Dryden." *The Works of John Dryden*. Ed. Sir Walter Scott and George Sainsbury. Vol. 1. Edinburgh: W. Patterson, 1882.
Shelley, Percy Bysshe. *Peter Bell the Third; A Facsimile of the Press-Copy Transcript*. Ed. Donald H. Reiman. Garland, 1986.
Sherlock, Thomas. *An Impartial Examination of the Bishop of London's Late Appendix to a Dissertation*. London: C. Corbet, 1750.
Sherlock, William. *A Discourse concerning the Divine Providence*. London: William Rogers, 1694.
Smalley, Beryl. *The Study of the Bible in the Middle Ages*. Notre Dame, Indiana: University of Notre Dame Press, 1964.
Smart, Christopher. *Song to David*. 1763.
Smith, Elizabeth. *The Book of Job*. Ed. with an introduction by Maurice O'Sullivan. Delmar, N.Y.: Scholars' Facsimiles & Reprints, 1996.
-. *Fragments, in Prose and Verse*. Bath: Richard Cruttwell, 1808

-. *Memoirs of Frederick and Margaret Klopstock*. Bath: R. Cruttwell, 1808.

-. *A Vocabulary, Hebrew, Arabic, and Persian*. London, 1814.

Smith, Lemuel. *The History of Job: With Reflections affording Comfort to the Disconsolate*. Utica, 1806.

The Souldiers Pocket Bible. London: G.B. and R.W. for G.C., 1643.

Spark, Muriel. *The Only Problem*. New York: G.P. Putnam, 1984.

Spence, Joseph. *Observations, Anecdotes, and Characters of Books and Men*. Ed. James M. Osborn. 2 vols. Oxford: Clarendon Press, 1966.

Stanton, Elizabeth Cady. *The Woman's Bible*. New York: European Publishing Company, 1895-98.

Steiner, George. *After Babel: Aspects of Language and Translation*. New York: Oxford University Press, 1975.

-. *Homer in English*. London: Penguin, 1996.

Steiner, Thomas R. "English and French Theories of Translation in the Seventeenth Century." *Comparative Literature Studies*, 7 (1970), 50-81.

-. *English Translation Theory 1650-1800*. Assen: Van Gorcum, 1975.

-. *Homer in English*. London: Penguin, 1996.

Stephens, Leslie and Sidney Lee. *The Dictionary of National Biography*. Oxford: Oxford University Press, 1917. Rpt. 1921-22.

Stillingfleet, Edward. *A Sermon Preached before the King*. London: J.M. for Henry Mortlock, 1684

Sylvester, Josuah. *Divine Weeks and Works* (trans of Guillaume Salluste Du Bartas). London, 1592-99.

Tanakh. Philadelphia: Jewish Publication Society, 1985. Rev.ed. 1999.

Tender Mercies. Dir. Bruce Beresford. 1983.

Thuesen, Peter J. *In Disobedience with the Scriptures*. New York: Oxford University Press, 1999.

Thomas, David. *Problemata Mundi: The Book of Job Exigetically and Practically Considered*. London: Smith, Elder, 1878.

Tillotson, John. *Works*. 3rd. ed. London: B. Aylmer & W. Rogers, 1701.

Tindal, Matthew. *Christianity As Old As Creation or the Gospel, a Republication of the Religion of Nature*. London: Thomas Astley, 1730.

Toland, John. *Christianity Not Mysterious; a Treatise Showing There Is Nothing in the Gospel Contrary to Reason Nor above It and That No Christian Doctrine Can Be Properly Called a Mystery*. London: Sam. Buckley, 1696.

Trapp, John. *A Commentary or Exposition upon the Books of Ezra,Nehemiah, Esther, Job, and Psalms*. London: T.R. and E.M. for T. Newberry and J. Barber, 1657.

Tur-Sinai, N[aphtali] H[enry]. *The Book of Job*. Jerusalem: Kiryath Sepher, 1957.

The Twentieth Century New Testament A New Translation into Modern English Made from the Original Greek. 3 vols. New York: F.H. Revell [1898-1901].

Tyndale, William. *The Obedience of a Christen Man: and How Christen Rulers Ought to Governe*. [?Antwerp], 1528.

-. Translation of Erasmus *Novum Instrumentum*. Basle: Froben, 1516.

Ussher, James. *Annales Veteris et Novi Testamenti*. 1635

von Goethe, Johann Wolfgang. *Autobiography [Dichtung und Wahrheit]*. Trans. John Oxenford. Vol. 2. Chicago: University of Chicago Press, 1975.

Walls, Alfred. *The Oldest Drama in the World*. New York: Hunt & Eaton, 1891.

Walpole, Horace. *Correspondence with George Montagu*, ed. W.S. Lewis and Ralph S. Brown, Jr. New Haven: Yale University Press, 1941.

Warburton, William. *The Divine Legation of Moses Demonstrated*. 2 vol. London: F. Gyles, 1738-41.

Warner, James. *The Surest Way to the Safest Peace, in Troublous Times*. London: Thomas Parkhurst, 1688.

Watson, Robert A.. *The Book of Job*. London: Hodder and Stoughton, 1892.

Watts, Isaac. *Hymns and Spiritual Songs*. London: John Lawrence, 1707.

-. *Psalms of David Imitated in the Language of the New Testament and Applyd to the Christian State*. London: J. Clark, R. Ford, and R. Cruttenden, 1719.

Weinbrot, Howard. *Britannia's Issue: The Rise of British Literature from Dryden to Ossian*. New York: Cambridge University Press, 1993.

Wells, H.G. *The Undying Fire*. New York: Macmillan, 1917.

Weymouth, Richard Francis. *The New Testament in Modern Speech; an Idiomatic Translation into Everyday English from the Text of the Resultant Greek Testament*. London: Butler and Tanner for J. Clarke, 1903.

Wheatly, Charles. *The Lawfulness of Feasting, with the Danger of Abusing It*. Oxford: Anthony Peisley, 1714.

Wiesel, Eli. *The Trial of God*. Trans. Marion Weisel. New York: Schocken Books, 1979.

Wolfers, David. *Deep Things out of Darkness: The Book of Job*. Grand Rapids, Michigan: Pharos/William B. Eerdmans, 1995.

Woodhouselee, Alexander Fraser Tytler (Lord). *Essay on the Principles of Translation*. London: T. Cadell, 1791.

Wordsworth, William. *Poetical Works*. Ed. E. de Selincourt. 2nd ed. Oxford: Clarendon, 1952.

Wright, Richard. *Native Son*. New York: Harper and Brothers, 1939.

Young, Edward. *Correspondence*, ed. Henry Pettit. Oxford: Clarendon Press, 1971

-. *The Complaint, or Night-Thoughts on Life, Death, and Immortality*. London: J. Dodsley, 1742.

-. *Conjectures on Original Composition*. Dublin: P. Wilson, 1759.

PART TWO
The Books of Job:
A composite translation

Varietie of Translation is profitable
for the finding out of the sense of the
Scriptures.

Preface, King James Bible (1611)

For the following section I have chosen translations based on a combination of historical importance, aesthetic value, and literary curiosity to suggest the range of possibilities in form and interpretation that English translators have explored.[2] Although the chapters are generally chronological, I have shifted a few texts when necessary or appropriate. While William Thompson's 1726 version and the 1779 anonymous paraphrase of Chapter 38, for example, only address portions of the work, Ralph Sadler's eccentric Victorian interpretations of Arabic spelling reveal themselves most clearly in the final chapter. On a number of occasions I have juxtaposed two very different versions of a single chapter for comparison and contrast. Chapter Nine includes both the original Douai version and Bishop Challoner's 1750 revision, and Chapter Ten brings together both the King James Version and that of its strongest critic, Hugh Broughton. In addition, I have included Charles Thomson's 1808 Septuagint addendum to Chapter Two, Henry Tattam's 1846 Coptic conclusion, and the final section of the first English translation of the pseudigraphical *Testament of Job*.

CHAPTER ONE

John Wyclif (1382)

Incipit liber Job

Ther was a man in the lond of Hus, Job by name; and that man was simple, and ri3t, and dredende God, and goende awei fro euel. And ther ben born to hym seue sones, and thre dou3tris; and his possessioun was seuen thousend of shep, and thre thousend of camailis, also fiue hundrid 3okis of oxen, and fiue hundryd assis, and ful myche meyne; and that man was gret among alle the men of the est. And his sones wenten, and maden festis bi housis, eche in his day; and sendende thei clepeden ther thre sistris, that thei shulden ete, and drinke win with hem. And whan the da3es of the feste hadden passid aboute, Job sente to them, and haliwide them, and risende erli, offride brent sacrifise bi alle. Forsothe he seide, Lest perauenture my sonys synnen, and blisse to God in ther hertis. So Job dide alle da3is. On a dai forsothe, whan the sones of God wer come, that thei shulde stonde nee3 before God, was nee3 among hem and Sathan. To whom seide the Lord, Whennus comest thou? The whiche answerende seith, I haue enuyround the erthe, and thur3 gon it. And the Lord seide to hym, Whether hast thou not beholde my seruaunt Job, that ther be not lic to hym in the erthe, a man simple, and ri3t, and dredende God, and goende awei fro euel. To whom answerde Sathan, Whether in vein Job dredith God? Whether hast thou not strengthid hym, and his hous, and al his substaunce bi enuyroun? To the werkis of his hondis thou hast blissid, and his possessioun wex in the erthe. But strecche out a litil thin hond, and touche alle thingus that he weldeth; but in the face he blesse to thee. Thanne the Lord seide to Sathan, Lo! alle thingus, that he hath, in thin hond ben; onli in hym ne strecche thou out thin hond. And Sathan is gon out fro the face of the Lord. Whan forsothe on a dai the sones and his dog3tris shulden ete, and drinke win in the hous of ther firste gote brother, a messager cam to Job, that shulde sein, Oxen ereden, and she assis weren fed beside them; and Sabeis feerly fellen to, and token alle thingis, and smyte the childer with swerd; and I alone scapide that I shulde telle to thee. And whan 3it he spac, cam an other, and seide, The fyr of God cam doun fro heuene, and the shep touchid, and the childer wastide; and I alone flei3 awei that I telle to thee. But 3it hym spekende, cam and an other, and seide, Caldeis maden thre cumpanyes, and asailiden the camailis, and token hem, also and the childer thei smyten with swerd; and I alone flei3 awei that I telle to thee. And 3it he spac, and lo! an other cam inne, and seide, Thi sones and do3tris etende, and drinkende win in the hous of ther firste goten brother, feerli an hidous wind fel in fro the regioun of desert, and smot togidere the foure corneres of the hous, the whiche fallende opresside thi fre childer, and ben deade; and I alone flei3 awei that I telle to thee. Thanne Job ros, and kutte his clothis, and his hed shauen fel in to the erthe, and honourede, and seide, Nakid I wente out fro the wombe of my moder, and nakid I shal gon a3een thider; the Lord 3af, the Lord toc awei; as to the Lord pleside, so it is do; be the name of the Lord blissid. In alle thes thingus Job synnede not with his lippis, ne any foli thing a3en God spac.

CHAPTER TWO

John Purvey (1388)

Forsothe it was doon, whanne in sum dai the sones of God weren comun, and stoden bifor the Lord, and Sathan was comun among hem, and stood in his si3ght, that the Lord seide to Sathan, Fro whennus comest thou? Which answeride, and seide, Y haue cumpassid the erthe, and Y haue go thur3 it. And the Lord seide to Sathan, Whethir thou hast biholde my seruaunt Joob, that noon in erthe is lijk hym; *he is* a symple man, an ri3tful, and dredynge God, and goynge awei fro yuel, and 3it holdynge innocence? But thou hast moued me agens him, that Y schulde turmente hym in veyn. To whom Sathan answeride, and seide, A man schal 3yue skyn for skyn, and alle thingis that he hath for his lijf; ellis sende thin hond, and touche his boon and fleisch, and thanne thou schalt se, that he schal curse thee in the face. Therfor the Lord seide to Sathan, Lo! he is in thin hond; netheles kepe thou his lijf. Therfor Sathan 3ede out fro the face of the Lord, and smoot Joob with a ful wickid botche fro the sole of the foot til to his top; which *Joob* schauyde the quytere with a schelle, and sat in the dunghil. Forsothe his wijf seide to hym, Dwellist thou 3it in thi symplenesse? Curse thou God, and die. And Joob seide, Thou hast spoke as oon of the fonned wymmen; if we han take goodis of the hond of the Lord, whi forsothe suffren we not yuels? In alle these thingis Joob synnede not in hise lippis. Therfor thre frendis of Joob herden al the yuel, that hadde bifelde to hym, and camen ech man fro his place, Eliphath Temanytes, and Baldach Suythes, and Sophar Naamathites; for thei hadden seide togidere to hem silf, that thei wolden come togidere, and visite hym, and coumforte. And whanne thei hadden reisid afer her i3en, thei knewen not hym; and thei crieden, and wepten, and to-renten her clothis, and spreynten dust on her heed in to heuene. And thei saten with hym in the erthe seuene daies and seuene ny3tis, and no man spak a word to hym; for thei sien, that his sorewe was greet.

SEPTUAGINT ADDENDUM

Charles Thomson (Philadelphia, 1808)

And much time having elapsed, his wife said to him, How long wilt thou persist saying, Behold I will wait yet a little longer, in hope and expectation of my deliverance? For behold the memorial of thee--those sons and daughters, whom I brought forth with pangs and sorrow--, and for whom I toiled in vain, are vanished from the earth; and thou thyself sittest among the putrefaction of worms, all night long in the open air, while I am wandering about, or working for wages, from place to place and from house to house, wishing for the setting of the sun, that I may rest from the labours and sorrows I endure. Do but say something for the Lord and die.

CHAPTER THREE

Miles Coverdale (?Cologne, 1535)

After this opened Job his mouth, and cursed his daye, and sayde: lost be that daye, wherin I was borne: and the night, in the which it was sayde: there is a manchilde conceaved. The same daye be turned to darcknesse, and not regarded of God from aboue, nether be shyned upon with light: but be couered with darcknesse, and the shadowe of death. Let the dymme cloude fall upon it, and let it be lapped in with sorowe. Let the darck storme overcome ye night, let it not be reckened amonge the dayes off the yeare, ner counted in the monethes. Despysed be that night, and discommended: let them that curse the daye, geve it their curse also, euen those that be ready to rayse up Leuiathan. Let the starres be dymme thorow darcknesse of it. Let it loke for light, but let it se none, nether the rysinge up of the fayre mornynge: because it shut not up the wombe that bare me, ner hyd these sorowes fro myne eyes.

Alas, why dyed I not in ye byrth? Why dyd not I perysh, as soone as I came out of my mothers wombe? Why set they me upon yeir knees? Why gaue they me suck with their brestes? Then shulde I now have lyen still, I shulde haue slepte, and bene at rest: like as the kynges and lordes of ye earth, which buylde them selues speciall places: as the prynces that haue great substaunce of golde, & their houses full of sylver. O that I utterly had no beynge, or were, as a thinge borne out of tyme (that is putr asyde) ether as yonge chilsdren, which neuer sawe the light. There must the wicked ceasse from their tyranny, there soch as are ouerlaboured, be at rest: there are those letten out fre which haue bene in preson, so that they heare nomore the voyce of the oppressoure: There are small and greate: the bonde man, and he that is fre from his master.

Wherefore is the light geuen, to him that is in mysery? and life unto them that haue heuy hertes? (Whych longe for death, and it commeth not: for yf they might fynde their graue, they wolde be maruelous glad, as those that dygge up treasure) To the man whose waye is hyd which God kepeth backe from him.

This is the cause, that I syghe before I eate, and my roaringes fall out like a water floude. For the thynge that I feared, is come upon me: and the thynge that I was afrayed of, is happened unto me. Was I not happy? Had I not quyetnesse? Was I not in rest? And now commeth soch mystery upon me.

CHAPTER FOUR

Thomas Matthew [John Rogers]

(?Antwerp, 1537)

Then answered Elihphas a Themanyte and said unto him: If we beginne to commen with the peraduenture thou wilt be dyscontent, but who can withhold him self from speakynge. Behold, thou hast bene a teacher of many, and hast comforted the weery handes.

Thy wordes have set up those that were fallen, thou hast refreshed the weake knees. But now that the plage is come upon the thou shrenkest away. Enow that it hath touched thy self, thou arte faynt harted. Is not this thy feare, thy stedfastnesse, thy pacience, and the perfectnesse of thy wayes. Consydre (I praye the) whoever peryshed beynge an innocent. Or when were the godly destroied? As I have sene them that plowe vanyty and sowe malicie reape the same. With the blast of God hyh they perysh & with the breth of hys anger consumed they awaye the roarynge of the lyon, the voyce of the lyonesse and the teeth of the lyons whelpes are broke. The lyon perisheth for lacke of praye & the lyons whelpes are scatered abrode.

And unto me was the worde hydde, and myne eare hathe receyved a lytell therof. In the phantasyes and thoughtes of the vysyons of the nyght, when slepe cometh on men: feare came upon me and drede made my bones to shake. And when the wynd passed by before my presence it make the heates of my fleshe stande up. He stode there and I knew not his face, in yonage there was before me & there was stylnes so that I heard thys voyce.

Shall man be moare iust then God? Or shall man be purer then this maker. Behold there is no trust to his seruantes, and in his aungelles hath he founde trowardnes. How moche moare in them that dwell in houses of claye whose foundacion is but earth, which shalbe consumed by the Moth. They shalbe smytten from mornynge unto the evenyng yee they shall perysh everlastynglye, and no man thincke theron. Is not their dignitie taken awaye with them, they shall dye and not in wysdome.

CHAPTER FIVE

Richard Taverner (London, 1539)

Call me one els, yf thou canst fynde any: yee loke about the, upon any of the holy men. As for the folysh man, displeasure kylleth him, and anger slayeth the ignoraunte. I have sene my selfe, when the folysshe was depe rooted, that his bewtye was sodenly destroyed, that his chyldren were with out prosperite or helth: that they were slayne in the dore, and no man to delyver them: that his harvest was eaten up of the hungry: that the weapened man had spoyled it, and that ye thurstye had dronke up his riches. It is not the earth that bringeth forthe travayle, neyther commeth sorowe out of the grounde: but it is man, that is borne unto myserye, lyke as the byrde to flyght

But nowe wyll I speake of the Lorde, & talke of God: whiche bothe thynges, that are unsearcheable, and marveles without nombre: which gyueth rayne upon the earth, and poureth water upon all thinges: whiche settes up them of lowe degre, and sendeth prosperite, to those that are in hevynesse: Whiche destroyeth the thoughtes of the wycked, so that they are not hable to performe the thinges that they take in hande: which compaseth the wyse in their owne craftynesse, and overthroweth the counsell of the wycked. In so moche that they run into darckenesse by fayre daye, and grope about them at the none daye, lyke as in the nyght.

And so he delyvereth the poore frome the swearde, frome the mouth, and from the hand of the cruel, that the pore maye have hope, & that the mouthe of the oppressoure maye be stopped.

Beholde, happy is the man, whom God punyssheth: therfore, despyse not thou the chastening of the almyghty. For though he make a wounde, he gyveth a medicine agayn: though he smyte, his hande maketh hole agayne.

He delyvereth the out of sixe troubles, so that in the seventh there can no harme touche the. In the myddest of honger he saveth the frome death: and when it is warre, from the power of the swerde.

He shall kepe the frome the scourge of the tongue, so that when trouble commeth, thou shalt not nede to feare. In havocke and derth thou shalt be mery, and shalte not be afrayed of the beastes of the earth: But the stones in the lande shall be confederate with the, & the beastes of the felde shall gyve the peax.

Yea thou shalt know, that thy dwellynge place shalbe in rest: thou shalt behold thy substaunce, and be no more punysshed for synne. Thou shalt se also, that thy sede shal encrease and that thy progenye shalbe as ye grasse

CHAPTER SIX

The Great Bible (London, 1539)

Job answered also, and sayde, O that the dyspleasure which I have were truely weyed, and my punysshment layde in the balaunces togyther: for now is it heuver then the sande of the see. And this is the cause that my wordes are so sorowfull. For the arowes of the almyghtie are rounde about me, whose indignacyon hath dronke up my spirite, and the terrible feares of God are set agaynst me.

Doth the wylde Asse rore when he hathe grasse? Or cryeth the Oxe, when he hath fodder ynough? That whiche is unsaverye, shall it be eaten without salte, or is there any taste in the whyte of an egge? The thyngs that some tyme I myght not awaye withall, are nowe my meate for very sorowe.

O that I myght have my desyre: and that God wolde graunte me the thynge, that I longe for: O that God wolde begynne and smyte me: that he wolde let his hande go, and take me cleane awaye.

Then shuld I have some comforte: yea I wolde desyre hym in my payne, that he shulde not spare, for I wyl not be agaynst the wordes of the holy one. For what power have I to endure? And what is myne ende, that my soule myght be pacient?

Is my strengthe the strengthe of stones? Or is my flesshe make of brasse? Is it not so that there is in me no helpe: and that my substaunce is taken from me. He that is in tribulacyon ought to be conforted of his neygh hour: but the feare of the Lord is cleane away. Myne owne brethren passe over by me as the water broke, and as the ryver of water doth hastely go away. But they that fere the horye frost, the snowe shall fall upon them. When theyr tyme cometh, they shalbe destroyed and perysshe: when they be set on fyre, they shall be removed out of theyr place, for the pathes that they go in, are croked: they haste after vayne thyngs, and shal perysshe. They turne them to the pathes of Theman and to the wayes of Saba, wherin they have put theyr trust. Confounded are they, that put any confidence in them: For when they come to obteyne the thynges that they loke for, they are brought to confuyson.

Even so are ye also come unto me: but now that ye se my miserye, ye are afrayde. Dyd I desyre you, to brynge unto me, or to gyve me any of your substaunce: To delyver me from the enemyes hande, or to save me frome the hande of tyrauntes? Teachs me, and I wyll holde my tongue: And when I do arre, shewe me wherin. Howe stedfast are the wordes of trueth? And whiche of you can rebuke and reprove them? Do ye take deliberacyon to checke mennes sayenges, and judge a poore worde spoken in vayne? Ye fall upon the fatherlesse and go aboute to overthrowe youre owne frende. And therfore be content, and look now upon me, and I wyl not lye before your face. Turne (I pray you) be indifferent judges turne agayne, and ye shall se myne ungyltynesse: whyther there be any unryghteousnesse in my tongue, or vayn wordes in my mouth.

CHAPTER SEVEN

The Geneva Bible (Geneva, 1560)

Iob sheweth the shortenes and miserie of mans life

1. Is there not an appointed time to man upon earth? and (are not) hys dayes as the dayes of an hyreling.

2. As a seruaunt longeth for the shadowe, and as an hyrelyng loketh for (the end) of hys worke.

3. So have I had as an inheritance the moneths of vanitie, and peinefull nyghts haue bene appointed vnto me.

4. If I laied me downe, I sayd, When shall I arise? and measuring the euening I am euen full with tossing to and fro vnto the dawnyng of the day.

5. My flesh is clothed with wormes and filthines of the dust: my skin is rent, and become horrible.

6. My dayes are swifter than a weauers shittle, and they are spent without hope.

7. Remember that my life is but a winde, (and that) myne eye shall not returne to se pleasure.

8. The eye that hathe sene me, shall se me no more: thine eyes are vpon me, and I shalbe no longer.

9. (As) the cloude vanisheth and goeth away. so he that goeth downe to the grave, shall come up nomore.

10. He shal returne nomore to his house, nether shal his place knowe him any more.

11. Therefore I wil not spare my mouth, (but) wil speake in the troubles of my spirit, (and) muse in the bitternes of my minde.

12. Am I a sea or a whalefish, that thou kepest me in warde.

13. When I saye, My couche shall relieve me, (and) my bed shall bring (comfort) in my meditation.

14. Then fearest thou me with dreames, and astonishest me with visions.

15. Therefore my soule choseth rather to be stangled (and) to dye, then (to be in) my bones,

16. I abhorre it, I shall not liue alway: spare me then, for my dayes (are) but vanitie.

17. What is man, that thou doest magnifie hym, and that thou settest thyne heart upon hym?

18. And doest visit him euerie mornyng, and tryest him euerie moment?

19. How long wil it be (yet) thou departe from me? thou wilt not let me alone whiles I may swallowe my spetle.

20. I have sinned, what shall I do vnto thee? o thou preseruer of men, why hast thou set me (as a marke) against thee, so that I am a burden vnto my self?

21. And why doest thou not pardone my trespas? and take away mine iniquitie? for nowe shal I slepe in the dust, and if thou sekest me in the morning, I shal not be (founde).

CHAPTER EIGHT

The Bishops Bible (London, 1568)

Bildad sheweth that Job is a sinner because God punisheth the wicked and preserueth the good.

1. Then answered Bildad the Suhite, & said: howe long wilt thou talke of such thinges:

2. Howe long shall the wordes of thy mouth be as a mightie wind:

3 Doth God paruert the thing that is lawfull: or doth the almightie destroy the thing that is right:

4. For seyng that thy sonnes sinned against him, did not he send them into the place of their iniquitie:

5. If thou wouldest nowe resorte unto God betimes, and make thy prayer to the almightie,

6. If thou wouldest liue a pure and godly life: shoulde he not awake up unto thee immediatly, and make the habitation of thy righteousnesse prosperous:

7. In so much that wherin so ever thou haddest litle afore, thou shouldest have nowe great aboundaunce.

8. Enquire I pray thee of the former age, and search diligently among their fathers:

9. (For we are but of yesterday, and consider not that our dayes upon earth are but a shadowe.)

10. Shall not they shew thee, and tel thee, yea and gladly confesse the same, and utter the words of their heart?

11. May a rushe be greene without moystnesse: or may the grasse grow without water:

12. No, but whilste it is nowe in his greennesse, though it be not cut downe, yet withereth it before any other hearbe:

13. So are the pathes of al that forget God, and the hypocrites hope shall come to naught.

14. His confidence shalbe destroyed, and his trust shalbe a spiders webbe.

15. He shal leane upon his house, but it shal not stande: he shall holde him fast by it, yet shall it not endure.

16. It is a greene tree before the sunne, & shooteth foorth the braunches ouer his garden.

17. The rootes thereof are wrapped about the fountayne, and are folden about the house of stones.

18. If any plucke it from his place, and it dente, saying, I have not seene thee:

19. Behold it will reioyce by this meanes, if it may growe in another mould.

20. Beholde, God will not cast away a vertuous man, neither wil he helpe the ungodly.

21. Thy mouth shall he fill with laughing and thy lippes with gladnesse.

22. They also that hate thee shalbe clothed with shame, & the dwelling of the ungodly shall come to naught.

CHAPTER NINE

The Doway Bible (Douai, 1609)

Iob approueth that no man avouching his owne iustice before God is iustified.

22. Teacheth that affliction of the innocent standeth wel with Gods iustice, wisdom, and powre.

And Iob answering, said: + In deede I know it is so, & that man can not be
iustified compared with God + If he wil contend with him, he can not answer him
one for a thousand. + He is wise of hart, and strong of force: who hath resisted
him, and hath had peace? + He that transported mountaynes, and they whom he
subuerted in his furie, knew not. + He that remoueth the earth out of her place,

and the pillers therof are shaken. + He that commandeth the sunne, & it riseth not: and shutteth up the starres as it were vnder a seale: + He that alone spreadeth the heauens, and goeth upon the waues of the sea. + He that maketh Arcturus, and Orion, and Hyades, and the inner partes of the south. + He that doth great thinges, and incomprehensible, and meruelous of the which there is no number. + If he come to me, I shal not see him: if he depart, I shall not understand. + If sodenly he aske, who shal answer him? or who can say: Why doest thou so? + God whose wrath no man can resist, and under whom they stoope that carie the world. + How great am I then, that I may answer him, and speake in my wordes with him? + Who although I haue iust thing, wil not answer, but wil besech my iudge. + And when he shal heare me invocating, I do not beleve that he hath heard my voice. + For in a hurlewinde shal he breake me, and shal multiplie my woundes yea without cause. + He graunteth not my spirit to rest, and he filleth me with bitternesse. + If strength be demaunded, he is most strong: if equitie of iudgement, not man dare geve testimonie for me. + If I wil iustifie my self, mine owne mouth shal condemne me, if I wil shew my self innocent, he shal prove me wicked. + Although I shal be simple, the self same shall my soul be ignorant of, and I shal be wearie of my life. One thing there is that I have spoken, both the innocent and the impious he consumeth. + If he scourge, let him kil at once, and not laugh at the paynes of innocentes. The earth is geven into the handes of the impious, he covereth the face of the iudges therof: and if it be not he, who is it then? + My dayes have bene swifter then a poste: they have fled and have not sene good. + They have passed by as shippes carying fruites, as an eagle flying to meate, + When I shal say: I wil not speake so, I change my face, and am tormented with sorow. + I feared al my workes, knowing that thou didst not spare the offender. + But if so also I am impious, why have I laboured in vayne? + If I be washed as it were with snow waters, and my handes shal shine as most cleane: + Yet shal thou dippe me in filth, and my garmentes shal abhorre me. + For neither I wil answer a man that is like my self: nor that may be heard with me equally in iudgement. + There is none that may be able to reproue both, and to put his hand betwen both. + Let him take his rod from me, and let not his dread terrifie me. + I wil speake, and wil not feare him: for I can not answer fearing.

CHALLONER'S REVISION

Richard Challoner (London, 1750)

Job acknowledges God's justice: although he often afflicts the innocent.

And Job answered and, said:

2. Indeed I know it is so, and that man cannot be justified compared with God.

3. If he will contend with him, he cannot answer him one for a thousand.

4. He is wise in heart, and mighty in strength: who hath resisted him, and hath had peace?

5. Who hath removed mountains, and they whom he overthrew in his wrath, knew it not.

6. Who shaketh the earth out of her place, and the pillars thereof tremble.

7. Who commandeth the sun, and it riseth not: and shutteth up the stars as it were under a seal:

8. Who alone spreadeth out the heavens, and walketh upon the waves of the sea.

9. Who maketh Arcturus, and Orion, and Hyades, and the inner parts of the south.

10. Who doth things great and incomprehensible, and wonderful, of which there is no number.

11. If he come to me, I shall not see him: if he depart, I shall not understand.

12. If he examine on a sudden, who shall answer him? or who can say: Why dost thou so?

13. God, whose wrath no man can resist, and under whom they stoop that bear up the world.

14. What am I then, that I should answer him, and have words with him?

15. I, who although I should have any just thing, would not answer, but would make supplication to my judge.

16. And if he should hear me when I call, I should not believe that he had heard my voice.

17. For he shall crush me in a whirlwind, and multiply my wounds even without cause.

18. He alloweth not my spirits to rest, and he fitteth me with bitterness.

19. If strength be demanded, he is most strong: if equity of judgment, no man dare bear witness for me.

20. If I would justify myself, my own mouth shall condemn me: if I would shew myself, innocent, he shall prove me wicked.

21. Although I should be simple, even this my soul shall be ignorant of, and I shall be weary of my life.
22. One thing there is that I have spoken, both the innocent and the wicked he consumeth.
23. If he scourge, let him kill at once, and not laugh at the pains of the innocent.
24. The earth is given into the hand of the wicked, he covereth the face of the judges thereof: and if it be not he, who is it then?
25. My days have been swifter than a post: they have fled away and have not seen good.
26. They have passed by as ships carrying fruits, as an eagle flying to the prey.
27. If I say: I will not speak so: I change my face, and am tormented with sorrow.
28. I feared all my works, knowing that thou didst not spare the offender.
29. But if so also I am wicked, why have I laboured in vain?
30. If I be washed as it were with snow-waters, and my hands shall shine never so clean:
31. Yet shall thou plunge me in filth, and my garments shall abhor me.
32. For I shall not answer a man that is like myself: nor one that may be heard with me equally in judgment.
33. There is none that may be able to reprove me both, and to put his hand between both.
34. Let him take his rod away from me, and let not his fear terrify me.
35. I will speak, and will not fear him: for I cannot answer while I am in fear.

CHAPTER TEN

Hugh Broughton (London, 1610)

My soule is weary of my life: when I leave my sighing for my self: I will speak in the bitternes of my soule.

2. I will say unto the Puissant: condemne me not: Let me know wherefore thou pleadest with me.

3. Doth it please thee to oppresse: that thou dost loth the labour of thyne owne hands: and shinest upon the counsel of the wicked.

4. Are thine eyes of flesh? dost thou see as sorowfull-man?

5. Are thy dayes as sorrowful-mans? are thy yeares as earthly wightes yeres?

6. That thou seekest out my iniquity: and inquirest of my sinne.

7. Thou knowest that I am not wicked: yet none can save me from thyne hand.

8. Thy hands have fashioned me: and have made me in every poinct: and wilt thou destroy me?

9. Remember now, That as the clay thou hast made me: and unto dust wilt returne me:

10. Has thou now powred me as milk: & crudded me like unto cheese.

11. Thou hast clothed me with skinne and flesh: and thou hast covered me with bones and sinewes.

12. Life and louing-kindnes hast thou dealt with me: and thy providence praeserveth my spirit.

13. And these things thou hast layd up in thine heart: I do know that this is with thee.

14. When I do syn thou doest watch me: and wilt not cleare me from my iniquitie.

15. If I be wicked, wo is me: if I be iust, I dare not lift up myne head: Be satisfyed with confusion, and behold my affliction.

16. How it fleeth up: as the ramping-Schachal thou huntest me: and stil art wonderful against me.

17. Thou bringest new witnesses against me: and augmentest thine ire upon me: changes & stayed-army have I.

18. Why broughtest thou me out of the wombe: Oh that I had dyed and no ey had seen me.

19. I should be as if I had not been: brought from the belly unto the grave.

20. Wil not he leave off a little in my dayes: ceasse from me for some refreshing:

21. Before I go whence I cannot returne: to the earth of darknes and shadow of death:

22. Earth obscures as myrknes it self: shadow of death voyd of order: (when light shineth) myrknes it self.

CHAPTER TEN

The King James Version (London, 1611)

1. Iob, taking libertie of complaint, expostulateth with God about his afflictions. 18 Hee complaineth of life, and craveth a little ease before death.

My soule is weary of my life, I will leave my complaint upon my selfe; I will speake in the bitternesse of my soule.

2 I will say unto God, Doe not condemne mee; shewe me wherefore thou contendest with me.

3 *Is* it good unto thee, that thou shouldest oppresse: that thou shouldest despise the worke of thine hands: and shine upon the counsell of the wicked:

4 Hast thou eyes of flesh: or seest thou as man seeth:

5 *Are* thy dayes as the dayes of man: *are* thy years as mans dayes,

6 That thou enquirest after mine iniquitie, and searchest after my sinne:

7 Thou knowest that I am not wicked, and *there is* none that can deliver out of thine hand.

8 Thine hands have made me and fashioned me together round about; yet thou doest destroy me.

9 Remember, I beseech thee, that thou hast made me as the clay, and wilt thou bring me into dust againe:

10 Hast thou not powred me out as milke, and cruddled me like cheese:

11 Thou hast clothed me with skin and flesh, and hast fenced me with bones and sinewes.

12 Thou hast granted me life and favour, and thy visitation hath preserved my spirit.

13 And these *things* hast thou hid in thine heart; I know that this *is* with thee.

14 If I sinne, then thou markest me, and thou wilt not acquite me from mine iniquitie.

15 If I be wicked, woe unto me; and *if* I be righteous, *yet* will I not lift up my head: I *am* full of confusion, therefore see thou mine affliction:

16 For it increaseth, & thou huntest me as a fierce Lion: and againe thou shewest thy selfe marveilous upon me.

17 Thou renuest thy witnesses against me, and increasest thine indignation upon me; Changes and warre *are* against me.

18 Wherfore then hast thou brought me forth out of the wombe: Oh that I had given up the ghost, and no eye had seene me!

19 I should have bene as though I had not bene, I should have bene
caried from the wombe to the grave.
20 *Are* not my dayes few: cease then, *and* let me alone, that I may take
comfort a little,
21 Before I goe *whence* I shall not returne, *even* to the land of darknes
and the shadow of death,
22 A land of darknes, as darknes it selfe, *and* of the shadow of death,
without any order, and *where* the light *is* as darknes.

CHAPTER ELEVEN

Joshua Sylvester (London, 1614)

Then answered *Zophar*, the *Naamathite*;
Should words preuail? Shal prating pass for right?
Should all be mute? Shall no man dare reply?
To mock thy Mocks, and giue thy Lie the Lie?
For, Thou hast said (and that, too vehement)
My Words, and Deeds, and thoughts are innocent;
Pure in Thine eyes. But O! that God would speak;
That He would once His sacred Silence break;
To shew thee Wisdome's Secrets: Thou might'st see,
Thou merit'st double what he lays on Thee;
And surely know that (in his *Iustice* strict)
After thy Sins, He does not Sores inflict:
But seems to haue forgoten, or forgiuen
Thy Trespasses against Him Selve and heauen.
Canst Thou, by searching, GOD's deep Counsel find?
Conceaue th'Almighty? Comprehend His mind?
Reach His perfection? It doth Heauen excell
In Height; in Depth exceeds the lowest Hell:
Longer then Earth: larger then all the Seas.
O! What? When? Where? How wilt Thou measure These?
If He cut-off, shut-up, collect, reiect;
Who can diuert Him? Who his Course correct?
He knows vain Men: He sees their harts that hard them

In Guiles and Wiles; and will not He regard them?
That foolish man, made wise, may be reclaimed:
Borne bruit and dull, as an Ass Colt, untamed.
 If therefore, by Repentance, thou prepare
Thine humbled heart: if that, in hearty Prayer,
Thou stretch thine hands vnto his Throne aboue:
Though thou haue sinn'd, if Thou thy Sin remoue:
If Thou remoue it, and permit no more
Iniquity to dwell within thy Doore:
Then shalt Thou, doubtlesse, free from Fault & Fear,
Settled and safe, thy Face againe uprear:
Then shalt thou sure forget thy Misery;
Or, but esteem it as a Streame past by:
Then shall thy Daies be, then the Noon more bright;
And Thou shalt shine, as Morning after Night:
Then shalt thou rest secure and confident,
Hopefull, and Happy, in thy proper Tent,
In thine owne Dwelling: where, for Eminence,
Sutors shall flock, with seemly Reuerence.
 But, as for stubborne, wilfull Wicked-ones,
That still run-on in their Rebellions,
Their Helps shall faile, and all their Hap shall fall;
And as a Ghasp, their Hopes shall vanish all.

CHAPTER TWELVE

Francis Quarles (London, 1624)

 But *Iob*, euen as a Ball, against the ground
Banded with violence, did thus rebound:
 You are the only Wisemen, in your brests,
The hidden Magazen of true Wisdome rests,
Yet (though astunn'd with sorrowes) doe I know
A little, and (perchance) as much as you;
I'm scorned of my Friends, whose prosprous state,
Surmises me (that haue expyr'd the Date,
Of Earths faire Fortunes) to be cast away,

From Heauens regard, thinke none belou'd, but they;
I am despised, like a Torch, that's spent,
Whil'st that the wicked blazes in his Tent:
What haue your wisdoms taught me, more then that,
Which Birds and Beasts (could they but speak) would chat?
Digests the Stomake, 'ere the Pallat tastes?
O weigh my Words, before you iudge my Case.
But you referre me to our Fathers dayes,
To be instructed in their wiser Layes.
True, length of dayes brings Wisdome; but, I say,
I haue a Wiser teacheth me, then they:
For I am taught, and tutor'd by that Hand
Whose unresisted power doth command
The limits of the Earth, whose Wisdome schooles
And traines the Simple, makes the learned, Fooles:
His hand doth rayse the poor, deposes Kings:
On him, both Order, and the Change of things
Depend, he searches, and brings forth the light,
From out the shaddowes, and the depth of night.

CHAPTER THIRTEEN

George Sandys (London, 1638)

Thus by mine Eyes and eares have I convay'd
Downe to my heart: and in that Closet laid.
Need I in depth of knowledge yeild to you?
Is not as much to my discretion due?
Oh that th'All-seeing Judge, who cannot erre,
Would heare me plead; and with a wretch conferre!
You Corrasives into my wounds distill:
And ignorant Artists, with your physick kill.
Ah! shame you not to vent such forgeries?
Seale up your lips and be in silence wise.
And since you are by farre more fit to heare,
Then to instruct; afford my tongue an eare.

Oh will you wickedly for God dispute?
And by deceitfull wayes strive to confute?
Are you, in favour of his person, bent
Thus to prejudicate the Innocent?
Need's he be an Advocate to plead his Cause?
To justifie the untruth's against his Lawes?
Can you on him such falsities obtrude?
And as a Mortall the most wise delude?
Will it availe you, when he shall remove
Your painted vizors? will not he reprove,
And sharply punish; if in secret you,
For favour, or reward, Injustice doe?
Shall not his Excellence your Soules affright?
His Horrors on your heads like Thunder light?
Your memories to Ashes must decay:
And your fraile bodies are but built of claye.
Forbeare to speake, till my Conceptions shall
Discharge their Birth; then let what will befall.
Why should I teare my flesh? cast of the care
Of future life? and languish in despaire?
Though God should kill me, I my confidence
On him would fixe; nor quit my owne defence.
He shall restore me by his saving might:
Nor shall the Hypocrite approach his sight.
Give me your eares, Oh you who were my Friends;
While injur'd Innocence it selfe defends,
I am prepar'd, and with my Cause were try'd:
In full assurance to be justifi'd.
Begin; who will accuse? should I not speake
In such a truth, my heart with griefe would breake.
Just Judge, two lets remove: that free from dread,
I may before thy high Tribunall plead.
Oh let these torrents from my flesh depart;
Nor with thy terrors daunt my trembling heart:
Then charge: so I my life may justifie:
And to my just complaint doe thou reply.
What sinnes are those that so pollute my brest:
Oh shew how oft I have thy Lawes transgrest?
Wilt thou thy Servant of thy sight deprive,
And as an Enemy to Ruine drive?

Wilt thou a withered leafe to powder grind?
Tost by the aire by every breath of wind:
Or with thy Lightning into Ashes turne
Such worthlesse Stubble? only dry'd to burne.
Thou hast indited me of bitter Crimes:
Now punisht, for the faults of former times.
Lo! my restrained feet thy fetters wound;
Watcht with a Guard, and rooted in the ground.
Like rotten fruit I fall: worne like a cloth
Gnawne into rags by the devouring Moth.

CHAPTER FOURTEEN

Thomas Manley (London, 1652)

1 Man that is borne of woman hath a life
Though short of daies, yet full of troublous strife.
2 He as a flower springeth forth and blossomes,
But cropt before the time of ripenes comes.
And as a shadow he does flye away,
Either without continuance or stay.
3 And dost thou such an one behold and see,
And into judgement bringest me with thee?
4 Will nature changed be? a cleaner thing
Out of an uncleane masse what man can bring,
5 Seeing his daies appointed are, and thou
The number of his months and bounds dost know?
6 Turne but thine hand from him, that rest he may,
Till as an hireling he make up his day.
7 For of a tree some hope doth yet remaine,
Although cut down, that it will sprout againe;
And that its tender branch yet will not cease,
But budding first, further at length encrease.
8 Although its root grow old within the ground,
And in the earth its stock decay'd be found:
9 Yet through the tent of water will it sprout,

And like a plant, greene boughs afresh shoot out.
10 But man, poore man, does die, and waste, and flee;
He giveth up the Ghost, and where is he?
11 As Rivers faile to run into the Sea,
And so the floud doth dry up and decay;
12 So man lies down and rises not againe,
Untill the heavens no more be, or remaine:
They shall not waken, but shall silence keep,
Nor shall they raised be out of their sleep.
13 Oh that the grave might be a hiding place,
Wherein to hide me till thy wrath do pass:
And that thou wouldst appoint a time wherein
Thou wouldst thinke on me, and forgive my sin.
14 If once man faile by stroke of look'd-for death,
Shall he yet live againe and draw his breath?
The daies of my appointed time Ile waite,
Untill my change my paines abreviate.
15 Thou shalt call me, and I will answer make,
Thou in thy workmanship wilt pleasure take.
16 For now my steps thou numbrest, and dost note;
Dost thou not watch over my acted fault?
17 My sin, as in a bag, is sealed fast,
And my transgression sewed up thou hast.
18 The mountains falling come to nought, sure 'tis,
And from his place the rock removed is:
19 The waters weare the stones: the things that grow
Thou spoilest, and mans hope dost overthrow.
20 Thou dost prevaile against him, and he's gone,
His countenance thou changest, and he's done.
21 His sons though great, unknown to him's their lot,
They are dejected, but he knows it not.
22 His flesh upon him shall be payned sore,
And's soul within him shall for anguish roar.

CHAPTER FIFTEEN

Arthur Brett (London, 1661)

1. The Noble Temanite replies,
2. This is not handsom (Sir) for one so wise
To give himself to Not'ons such as these,
This is to feed upon an Eastern breeze;
3. Such a one should not this day Method take
Or such unprofitable speeches make:
4. Thou has so little of the Orator,
Thy Auditors thou car'st not for;
But boldly carry'st on thy speech begun,
Subtracting what
Thou add'st too much to that
From thy unperfected Devotion;
Thy Prayer-incense, which of late
Arab'as perfumes did perfume,
Like those gross odours now is taught
To spend with using and consume:
5. That Mouth wherewith thou used'st heav'n to greet
Now speaks not ought
But what is nought,
Thy Tongue has prov'd of late an arrant Cheat:
6. I would thee willingly acquit,
But thou by talking thus wilt not permit,
Thou thy own Dirge do'st sing.
No witness need against thee rise,
It will abundantly suffice
Thy self against thy self to bring:
7. Why, *Job*! art thou the *Protoplast*
Or (prithee say)
Wert thou molded out of clay
E'er this ruff-superficies ball was cast?
8. Has heav'n acquainted you with that Decree
Which had lain hid from all Eternity?
Doth wisdom only appertain to thee?
Hast thou a grant of the Monopoly?
9. What knowest thou that we ne'r knew?
What do'st perceive that we perceive not too?
10. The rev'rend White upon our heads appears,

Thy father, liv'd he, would want of our years:
11. We'd have you only owne your fault,
And upon true Contrit'ons feet
Step and fetch Comfort from the mercy-feat;
And is this Comfort profer'd ye worth naught?
Have you in Divinity
More skill than we?
And can you e'en into Gods closset see?
12. Whither away by thy proud heart art born?
Why read we in thy winking art such scorn?
13. Why d'*you* (one man) oppose our Common Lord?
Why can't you better words at least afford?
14. Alas! what is discursive dust
That he should be accounted just?
Where is there now the *Eve*
A *Right'ous Abel* to conceive?
15. His greatest Saints God dares not trust;
They and the Heav'n they're heirs unto
Are both impore as to his view,
Who in his Saints sees vice, in th'heav'nly Spangles rust.
16. Much filthy'r's Man who quaffs Iniquity
17. As doth *Leviathan* the Sea:
Hearken, and I shall let you understand
(What I my self have seen and understood;)
18. What Volumes treat of writ before the flood,
And thence derived down from hand to hand;
And what was held by men as Great as Good,
19. Who had the world at their command;
Whose neighbours ne'r incroach't upon their land;
20. How that the Sinner doth in torment live,
And *travail* with the plots he doth devise,
Not knowing how long he has to tyrannise;
21. He hears strange tones and frighting cries;
And when they cease, and he in quiet lies,
He's set upon by Enemies
Which quarter neither use to take nor give:
22. He quite despairs of scaping those black foes,
Of getting out of those eternal woes
To which, the sword now sending him, he goes:
23. Hungry he grows

And then to ev'ry one he shows
His meager face, his hollow eye,
And *Oh, some bread, some Bread*'s his cry;
The terrible Night-day is nigh,
And that he knows:
24. His sin shall trouble, trouble sorrow bring,
The pangs of both which he already feels;
Fear charges him like some puissant King
With a great Army at his heels:
25. For he has gi'n his Maker the first blow,
And thinks to deal with an Almighty foe;
26. Whom he doth therefore fur'ously assail,
Whose very throat he maketh at,
Ready but he will come at that
To cut through's thick-boss't Shields and Coats of Mail:
27. Large level vallies of Fat smooth his face,
Mountains thereof his pamper'd sides do grace;
28. Such to Mankind is his antipathy,
He dwells in towns and rooms from concourse free,
Towns where no man lives but he,
And houses which e'r long will rubbish be:
29. His bags, when most, they shall be quickly told,
In their enjoyment he shall not grow old;
H'has got him an estate, but that shan't hold:
30. He shall be cast on that Blind rock the Grave,
Never from thence to launch;
And there the flame no light shall have,
But heat enough to quite dry up his branch;
He shall be blown by the Almighty's breath
Below the Center, beyond Hell and Death:
31. It is not meet
Men on themselves should put so great a cheat
As to expect high things from *being Vain*,
Alas! a Golden Nothing's all they gain;
32. The emolument for which they do so strive
Like an Abortive birth shall thrive;
The *Auto-focus* shall about 'um move,
But ne'r their branches into green improve:
33. Look at the Sinner as a Vine,

His raw grapes make but sowre wine;
Look on him as an Olive-tree,
His flow'r as soon as such shall cease to be:
34. Death and destruction shall exercise
New tricks, new fallacies
On the Grand Masters of the same;
Bribes sha'nt stave off the raging flame
From Palaces which by their heaps did rise:
35. Fond hypocrites believe
They something really conceive,
But this conception at last we find
To be a Tympany and caus'd by wind;
They do with Sin
(As 'twere) lie in,
And therefore that which they bring forth
Accordingly must be little worth.

CHAPTER SIXTEEN

Simon Patrick (London, 1679)

Argument: Job reproves the vanity and obstinacy of Eliphaz, in repeating the same things over again, and still persisting in his Inhumanity, though he saw his Case so pitiable. Which he again describes, to make him sensible how unworthily he was treated by him and the rest of his Friends: who, in effect, joyned with his Enemies; who took this opportunity to rail at him. Whereas there was no Crime of his appeared to justifie their Accusations, and to make good Eliphaz his Argument: which signified nothing, unless he meant to say, that Job was like that wicked Tyrant of whom he had discoursed. Which was so far from any shew of truth, that he protests he never hurt any-body, and was always a sincere lover of God., i.e. V. 17,18. The truth of which God knew; to whose Bar he appeals from their unjust Sentence.

1. Here Job interrupted him, and said,

2. Thou dost but repeat what hath been often said already: Such Comforters as you, are as troublesome as my Sufferings.

3. May not one endlessly pour out such empty Discourses? (as I may more reasonably call thine, then thou didst mine XV.3.) I wonder at thy confidence, that, having so little to say, thou shouldst take upon thee to answer.

4. I could insult as well as you; and, if we could change conditions, let you see how easy it would be to oppress you with such words as these, and in a grave fashion to mock at your Calamities.

5. But I abhor the thought of such a guilt: I would not fail to fortify you, in that case, with the best Arguments I could invent; and carefully abstain from the least word that should augment your Grief.

6. Though, as for my self, I find my Misery admits of no Consolation: For whether I defend my Innocence, or silently suffer you to condemn me, it makes no difference.

7. God hath long since quite tired me with one Trouble upon another. Thou hast not ceased, O God, till Thou hast left me neither Goods, nor Children, no nor a Friend to comfort me.

8. The furrows in my face (which is not old) show the greatness of my Affliction: which is extreamly augmented by him, who rises up with false Accusations to take away mine honour, as this Consumption will do my Life.

9. He rends my Good name in pieces with a passion equal to his hatred: my Enemy is inraged against me, and cruelly sets himself to spy out the least occasion to calumniate me.

10. There is no small number of such as these, who look like so many wild beasts coming to devour me: having already most shamefully abused me, and joyned themselves together to give full satisfaction to their wrath wherewith they are fill'd against me.

11. So God will have it; who hath abandoned the protection of me and delivered me bound into the hands of the ungodly, to use me at their pleasure.

12. How happy was I heretofore! and now I am crushed in pieces: From an eminent condition He hath thrown me down into the most despicable; and there I am exposed (as a Butt to the Arrow) to all manner of Indignities and Miseries.

13. He is not content to take away all my Goods, and destroy my Family; but, to the reproach of my Friends, (which strike like so many darts to my very heart,) He hath added Ulcers in every part of my Body, with inward pains which rack me without intermission; and, in one word, hath so mortally wounded me, as if my bowels were already shed upon the ground.

14. Before one Wound be closed, He makes another; and in so violent a manner, that I can make no more resistance than a Dwarf can do against a Giant.

15. The Sackcloth which I put on at the first, now cleaves so fast to me, as if I had sewed it to my skin: and all my Authority and Honour is changed into Contempt.

16. My Face is dirty, and mine Eyes, in a manner, quite put out, by the very Tears which have faln from thence.

17. And yet I must still say, I never offered such a violence as this to any man; and was always (so false is Eliphaz his Accusation XV.4.) a sincere Worshipper of God.

18. If this be not true, let my Bloud be left to the Dogs to lick, when I am dead; and let neither God nor man regard my Complaint while I am alive.

19. But what need these imprecations? The great God who rules over all is my Witness; and can testify how just I have been toward my Neighbours, and how pious toward Himself.

20. From your judgment therefore (who, in stead of comforting my innocence, scornfully set your selves to defame me) I appeal to His; and beseech Him with perpetual tears to vindicate me.

21. I am so assured of the goodness of my Cause, (as well as of his Justice,) that I wish for nothing more, then to have it speedily heard and tried by Him, in the same manner that pleas are held before earthly Judges.

22. For my Life cannot last long; and I know that when I am gone, I cannot return hither again, for Him to doe me justice.

Charles Garden (Oxford, 1796)

1. Then Job answered thus:
2. I have heard of many such things as these;
Ye are all miserable comforters.
3. What! shall there be an end to vain words?
Or what emboldenest thee, that thou shouldst answer?
4. I also could speak as well as you,
If my body were in the place of yours:
Would I join words against you?
And shake my head often at you?
5. I would embolden you with my mouth;
And my vehement speech would be restrained.
6. Though I speak, my grief is not abated;
And though I cease, does it go away from me?
7. Truly now my grief hath made me weary:

Thou hast made thin all my company.
8. Also thou hast apprehended me with publick evidence;
He that belieth me riseth up against me,
And accuseth me to my face.
9. His fury teareth me, and he hateth me;
He gnasheth on me with his teeth:
My afflicter sharpeneth his eyes on me.
10. They have opened wide on me with their mouths;
With reproach they have struck me on my cheek;
Together they glut themselves on me.
11. God hath shut me up to the unjust.
And turned me over into the hands of the wicked.
12. I was quiet, but he has broken me into pieces;
Yea, he hath taken hold of my neck, and he shattered me exceedingly;
And he hath placed me up to be for a mark.
13. His multitude encompass me round about;
He cutteth my reins asunder, and does not pity;
And poureth out my gall on the ground.
14. He breaketh me up with wound upon wound;
He runneth on me like a giant.
15. I have sewed sackcloth together on my skin;
And my head I have covered with dust.
16. My face is exceedingly disordered with weeping;
And on my eye-lids is the shadow of death.
17. Not because of injustice in my hands;
And my prayer is pure.
18. O earth, cover thou not my blood!
And let there be no place for my cry.
19. Also now behold my witness is in the heavens;
And my eye-witness is on high.
20. My friends deride me:
My eye droppeth out tears to God.
21. O! that one might plead with God,
As a man does for his neighbour.
22. For the few years shall come to an end;
And I go the way whence I shall not return.

CHAPTER SEVENTEEN

Richard Blackmore (London, 1700)

Corruption my consuming Flesh devours,
And Time has almost paid my number'd hours.
The opening Grave invites me to her Womb,
And in the Dust prepares to give me Room.
But clear, before I dye, just God, my Fame,
And cover my pervidious Friends with Shame:
For do not pious Scoffers here abide,
Who mock for God, and all my Groans deride?
Their sharp Reproaches vex my Soul by Day,
And chase by Night my wish'd-for Sleep away.
Would God on high would suffer me to state
My Case aright, and hear the whole Debate.
For these my Friends against th'Assaults of Sense
Have rais'd a strong impenetrable Fence.
Such Gates of Darkness ne'er to be unbarr'd,
Such Forts of gloomy Shades the Passes guard,
That Reason's strongest Forces they repel,
Entrench't in Errors inaccessible.
But sure the Righteous God will ne'er permit,
That Men so blinded should to judge me sit.
Those, who to flatter Heav'n their Neighbour wrong,
Shall not their Power and prosp'rous days prolong.
Destructive Suff'rings shall their Sons assail,
Whose Eyes in looking after Aid shall fail.
I was the People's Darling and Delight
In former times; for when I came in sight,
Thro' crowded Streets loud Acclamations rung,
They to the Tabret my loud Praises sung;
And on my Chariot Wheels transported hung.
A waving Sea of heads was round me spred,
And still fresh Streams the gazing Deluge fed.
As I advanc'd, the eager, wond'ring Throng
Their Eye-balls strain'd, to see me pass along;
They feasted on me with their greedy Eyes,
And with Applauses fill'd th'ecchoing Skies.
Now, for as sad an Object I am shown;
My wondrous Troubles are Proverbial grown.

The Men who curse their Foes with deadly spite,
With *Job*'s Affliction on their heads may light.
My Neighbours cry, when they my Suff'rings see;
Is *Job* thus chang'd? Good Heav'ns! it cannot be.
My Eyes with Sorrow sunk within my Head,
Of Light defrauded, seem already dead.
So much my Flesh and Vigour I have lost,
I seem an empty Shade, or groaning Ghost.
But the Good Man will pity, not arraign
Afflicted *Job*, to aggravate his Pain
He will revere this Providential Turn,
Nor judge my Person, but my Suff'rings mourn.
Tho' he with wonder shall observe the Just,
Are by th'Almighty trodden in the Dust,
Yet he with sacred Indignation prest,
Shall shun the Wicked, and his way detest.
He for afflicted Vertue shall declare,
And Innocence to prosp'rous Sin prefer.
He shall the Heav'nly Path of Justice keep,
However rough, embarast, dark and steep.
Let him by bloody Out-laws be opprest,
And Robbers, who the Way to heav'n infest.
Let Persecution's blackest storm arise,
And with a dismal Night deform the Skies;
Let stern Affliction muster in the Air
Her fiercest Troops, to drive him to despair;
Let bitter Tongues their sharp Reproaches spend,
And impious Scoffers galling Arrows send;
The God-like Trav'ller shall his Path pursue,
Whose very Suff'rings shall his hopes renew.
He'll with undaunted Courage make his Way;
Danger his heart shall strengthen, not dismay.
    But you my Friends, to my Discourse attend,
And weigh my Words your Errors to amend.
For hitherto I can't among you find,
One of a clear, judicious, equal Mind.
You would in vain my Expectations raise,
(If I repent) of future prosp'rous Days.
For my appointed Hours are almost past,
My Hopes and Projects Death will quickly blast.

The Lamp of Life burns dimly in my Breast,
Soon from its beating toil my weary Heart will rest.
If for a happy Change you lay a Scheme,
You but amuse me with an empty Dream,
Terrestrial Joys are but an idle Theme.
With my Designs and anxious Thoughts I part,
Farewel ye Cares, that once possest my Heart.
I to my Sorrows only can attend,
In groans the Day, in groans the Night I spend.
If Grief or Woe denominate the Night,
I ne'er enjoy the Day, or see the Light.
The gloomy Terrors that my Soul surround,
Efface its marks, and Day with Night confound.
Alas 'tis madness to expect that Rest
And Restoration, which my Friends suggest;
For by a fixt, irrevocable Doom,
My Grave's prepar'd, my everlasting Home:
Where friendly Death has laid my easy Bed,
With Dust beneath, around with Darkness spread.
I to the Grave have said, O Parent Grave,
Me of thy Dust, a wretched Offspring save.
To take me in, thy gloomy Arms extend,
Thou art my Father, O be now my Friend;
And me from hostile Life and Light defend!
I to the Worm have said, my Brother Worm,
From whom I differ but in Shape and Form;
Submitted to thy Powers, I soon must lay
This loathsome Heap of putrifying Clay.
Where's then the Hope which you pretend to give,
That I may yet in Peace and Pleasure live?
If I repent, to see it you must go
Down to the Grave, and the Cold Shades below.
There you may see how all my hopes and I,
In the same Grave together lye.

CHAPTER EIGHTEEN

Thomas Heath (London, 1756)

1., 2. * And Bildad the Shuhite answered and said, * How long will you hunt after
cavils against established maxims? speak your meaning plainly, and
3. afterwards we will reply. * Why are we accounted as beasts, why are we vile
4. in your eyes? * Let him tear himself in his fury; what? shall the earth be
5. forsaken for thee? or shall the rock be removed from its place? * Rather let
6. the light of the wicked be put out, and let not the flame of his fire shine. * Let
the fire in his tabernacle be darkened, let his lamp which is before him be
7. extinguished. * Let the steps of his strength be straitned, and let his own
8. counsel cast him down. * Surely he is cast into the net by his own feet, he
9. runneth to and fro in the toils; * The gin taketh him by the heel, the noose
10. fasteneth close upon him; * The snare is lain secretly for him in the ground,
11. and a trap is set for him in his path. * Terrors affright him on every side, and
12. drive him to his wit's end. * Consternation shall be his substance, and

Elizabeth Smith (Bath, 1810)

1. And Bildad the Shuhite spake and said,

2. How long will you set snares of words
Understand us, and then we will speak.

3. Why are we considered as beasts?
Why are we unclean in your eyes?

4. O thou that tearest himself, in his fury!
Will the earth be left desolate because of thee?
Will the rock be torn from its place?

5. Yea, the light of the wicked shall go out,
And the flame of his fire shall not shine:

6. The light shall be darkened, in his tent,
And his lamp before him shall go out:

7. The stress of his activity shall be confined,
And his own strength shall throw him down:

8. For he is cast into the net, by his won feet,
And he walketh on the meshes:

9. The snare shall catch him by the heel,
The starvelings shall prevail against him:

10. The toil is hid for him in the earth,
And the trap on the path:

11. All around, destructions terrify him,
And his deliverance is only in his feet:

12. The fruit of his labour shall be famine,
And ruin prepared at his side:

13. The first-born of death shall feed on the fulness of his skin
Shall consume his plumpness:

14. He shall be plucked up from his tent, his security,
And devastation, like a king, shall march against him:

15. It shall dwell in his tent, because he is not,
Brimstone shall be shattered on his abode:

16. From beneath, his roots shall dry up,
And above, his young branches cut off:

17. His remembrance is perished from the earth,
And there is no name for him on the face of the field:

18. He is thrust from light to darkness,
He is banished from the world.

19. He has no son, nor grandson, among his people,
There is no remnant in his habitation:

20. Posterity shall be astonished at his life,
And the elders shall be seized with horror.

21. Surely such are the dwellings of the perverse,
And such the place of him who knoweth not God.

CHAPTER NINETEEN

William Langhorne (London, 1760)

How long, ye Friends, shall sharp Invective try
The last Resource of Sorrow to destroy?
The Patriarch said.--Be these Reproaches true,
Yet to myself I err'd, not injur'd you.
Need ye add Sharpness to the Sword Divine,
Or with Omnipotence in humbling join?
To Rocks, to Hills, to Friends I pour my Woe--
Nor Rocks, nor Hills, nor Friends Compassion show.
Lo, angry Heav'n hath pull'd my Glories down,
And from these Temples torn the princely Crown,
As at some furious Dragon speeds the Dart,

And the swift Vengeance rankles in this Heart.
Strong Bands, by heav'n impell'd, my House surround:
Fast fly my Friends, astonish't at each Wound.
Estrang'd my Brethren like Infection shun
The Fortune low deprest, the Soul undone.
Slaves of my Wealth desert the joyless Hour,
Attracted by the Glare of other Pow'r.
My Wife's imperious Words my Wrongs upbraid,
By each slain Son tho' I besought her Aid.
Nay, each young Minion, Imitation's Child,
Hiss'd at my Moan, or at my Mis'ries smil'd,
Forbidding Mis'ries of abhorr'd Disease,
That each untender Eye with cold Aversion seize.
Ye Friends that yet remain, if Friends ye be,
This Wretch with Pity--Oh! with Pity see!
But if yur ruthless Souls no Tear afford,
I fly, I seek my ever-gracious Lord.
Oh that some Pen of Steel these Words would grave
On yon tall Rocks that bound the threatening Wave!
This Prophecy, which, Heav'n-illum'd, I pour,
Shall reach the hoary World's declining Hour.
--My blest Redeemer lives--His Beams divine
On Earth new-form'd in latter Days shall shine.
Tho' Worms destroy this animated Clod,
Again, embodied, I shall see my GOD.
An Eye, acknowledg'd mine, the King shall view
To each just Hope of this his Servant true.--

CHAPTER TWENTY

Anthony Purver (London, 1764)

Again Zophar the Naamathite made answer:

2. Therefore my Sentiments make me reply, because they hasten me in my self.

3. I hear the Correction of my Shame, and the Spirit causes me to answer from

my Understanding.

3. Dost thou know this was for ever, since Man was placed upon the Earth?

5. That the Mirth of the Wicked is soon over, and the Joy of the Hypocrite for a Moment?

6. If his Excellency ascend to the Heavens, and his head reach to the Clouds:

7. He perishes eternally like his own Dung; those who have seen him say, Where is he?

8. He flies away as a Dream, so that they do not find him, and is fled like a Vision of the Night.

9. The Eye that has looked on him does so no more, nor observes him any more in his Place.

10. His Children please the Poor, and his Hands restore his Substance.

11. His Bones being full of his youthful Things, they lie down with him in the Mould.

12. Though Wickedness be sweet in his Mouth, *though* he conceal it under his Tongue;

13. Should he spare it, so that he will not forsake it, but with-hold it within his Palate:

14. His Bread in his Bowels is turned, it is the Gall of Asps within him.

15. He having swallowed down Wealth, vomits it up; God expels it out of his Belly.

16. He sucks the Poison of Asps; the Tongue of the Viper slays.

17. He does not see the Streams, the Rivers, the Floods of Honey and Butter.

18. He restores *what* he laboured for, and swallows not down; according to the Wealth his Retribution is, and he does not rejoice.

19. Because he has oppressed, forsaken the Poor, has taken away a House, which he did not build.

20. For he knows no Quiet in his inside, does not escape by what is pleasing in him.

21. There is Nothing left of his Food; therefore, his Welfare cannot remain.

22. When his Sufficiency is fullest, he is straightened; every Hand of the Troublesome comes on him.

23. Being about to fill his Belly, *God sends on him his fervent Anger; and rains it* upon him at his Meat.

24. He fleeing from the Armour of Iron, the Bow of Steel strikes him through.

25. It is drawn forth, and comes out of the Body, as the glittering Thing does out of his Gall: Terrors are upon him.

26. All Darkness is hid at his secret Places, a Fire not blown consumes him: it is ill with him who is remaining in his Tent.

27. The Heaven reveals his Iniquity, and the Earth raises up it self at him.

28. He discovers the Increase of his House, the Things that flew away in the Days of his Anger.

29. This is the Portion of a wicked Man from God, and what his Sayings possess from him.

Rev. John Fry (London, 1827)

Zophar's Second Address.

1. Then answered Zophar the Naamathite, and said:
2. Therefore would my agitated thoughts make me reply,
And because 'of this' is my hurry within me.
3. I would hear the reproof of my shame!
And the spirit of my understanding shall answer for me.
4. This surely thou hast known from of old,
From the time that man was placed upon earth.
5. That[3] "the triumphing of the wicked is short,
"And the joy of the profane but for a moment.
6. "Though his exaltation mount up to the heavens,
"And his head touch the clouds:
7. "In his evolution altogether shall he perish,
"They who saw him shall say, Where is he?
8. "He shall fly away like a dream, and cannot be found,
"And he shall vanish as a vision of the night.
9. "The eye had caught a glimpse of him, but cannot
repeat it,
"And never again shall his place behold him.
10. "His children shall seek to please the poor,
"And their hands make restitution from his labour.
11. "His bones were filled with his secret sin,
"And with him in the dust it shall lie down.
12. "Though wickedness should be sweet in his mouth,
"And he conceal it under his tongue:
13. "He be tender of it, and will not let it go,
"But retain it still on his palate;

14. "His food shall turn on his stomach!
"It shall be the gall of asps within him!
15. "Though he glut himself with riches, yet shall he vomit
them up.
"El shall cast them forth from his bowels.
16. "He shall suck the poison of asps,
"And the tongue of a viper shall kill him.
17. "He shall not see the rills of the streams,
"The torrents of honey and butter.
18. "'Though' he return to labour, yet shall he not eat;
"Sterility 'shall be' his recompense, and nothing
shall he taste.
19. "Because he hath violently handled the orphan of the poor,
"Ransacking the house, instead of building it up.
20. "Because he knew no rest to his appetite,
"Nor could the object of his desire be extorted from him.
21. "There was no remnant of his food,
"Therefore could none expect his bounty..
22. "With both his hands full, shall he be in want;
"Every lot of calamity shall befal him.
23. "It shall be, that, while he is filling his belly,
"He shall send against him the fierceness of his wrath,
"And rain it upon him while he is eating.
24. "'Though' he shall flee from the clashing steel,
"The brazen bow shall transfix him.
25. "Let him draw it out, and it shall come from his entrails;
"Ay, the crimsoned shaft from his gall!
"Terrors shall come upon him.
26. "All darkness treasured in reserve for him:
"A fire, not blown, shall consume him,
"And shall destroy what is left in his tent.
27. "The heavens shall declare his wickedness,
"And the earth shall rise up against him.
28. "The increase of his house shall go into captivity,
"Dispersed abroad in the day of His wrath.
29. "Such is the lot of the wicked man from Elohim,
"And the portion ordained him from El."

CHAPTER TWENTY-ONE

Thomas Scott (London, 1771)

1,2. Then Job: Give audience, audience I implore,
Be that your charity; I ask no more:
3. Indulge me utt'rance--then insult again.
4. Shall I of man, censorious man, complain?
The cruel slanders which my fame defile,
Would justify rensentment's sharpest style.
5. Observe me, wonder, and in silent fear
The mystic ways of Providence revere.
6. Astonish'd, trembling, I the scene review;
Which truth displays and mem'ry wakes anew.
7. Why live the wicked, and wax old in pow'r,
Their wealth augmenting to the mortal hour;
8. Live, while the children of their children rise,
And the strong nurslings shoot before their eyes?
9. They dwell securely, all is peace sincere,
The rod of heav'n knows no commission there:
10. Whose trusty bull, ne'er butts his amorous spouse,
But full of genial fire, absolves his vows:
Whose heifer calves, with no untimely throe,
And lively births in all their pastures low:
11. Fruitful their fold; alike in fruitful pains,
Their wives with yung succession fill their plains;
A fry undisciplin'd, that skips around,
Like wanton kids, upon the houshold ground.
12. Meanwhile the fires, with music's lightest airs,
Flute, harp, and timbrel, laugh at human cares;
13. A long, long life in sensual bliss consume,
Then instant drop, full mellow'd for the tomb.
14,15.Bold therefore to blaspheme, "Away (they cry)
Thou phantom of weak fear, call'd Deity;
Our necks the burden of thy yoke disdain,
Vain is our incense, and our vows are vain."
16. Not their own hand their blessings could bestow,
Their blessings from a higher fount must flow:
But, O my soul, from their assembly flee,
Far be their counsels and their lot from me.
17. Oft mourn these miscreants their high-sparkling light

Extinguish'd? Often in tempestuous night
Are they involv'd? For them hath vengeance stor'd,
Of plagues enormous a peculiar hoard?
18. Are they like stubble, when the tempest roars?
Like chaff, when sweepy whirlwinds cleanse the floors?
19,20. You'll urge, "God treasures vengeance for their seed."
But he, the criminal, himself, should bleed:
Living, himself should his own treason rue,
And his own eyes his tragedy should view;
While at his lips the wrathfuyl cup he sees,
Compell'd to drain it with its bitter lees:
21. For when his number'd months their tale have spent,
When to oblivion's land himself is sent;
Are then the fortunes of his house his care?
Feels he its triumph or its sorrow there?
22. Shall man instruct, in his presuming school,
The Lord of heav'n this petty orb to rule?
23. Here one prolongs voluptuous life in ease,
Deflow'r'd by no misfortune or disease:
24. Sweet in his veins his fatt'ning dairy flows,
And death's soft dews his slumb'ring eyelids close.
25. Another, comfortless, and hard bested,
With sorrow worn, with sighing eats his bread;
Long while in pain and pining sickness lies,
Then with deep groans and violent struggle dies:
26. Both equal in the grave; on both is spread
The worm for covering, and the clay their bed.
27. I penetrate your thoughts; resolv'd in wrong
Harsh answer still springs forward in your tongue;
28. "His own sad story will his cause disgrace,
Why mourns our Emir his extinguish'd race?
Where is th'encampment of the wicked Great,
The circling clan, the roomy tent of state?"
29,30. Hath trav'lling wisdom never won your ear,
With foreign histories imported here?
Scorn you their allegations? "That the day
Whose vengeance sweeps the sick'ning tribes away,
Spares the lewd tyrant? With carousal high
His riots the destroying scourge defy.
31. Who dares reprove his crimes? what hand presume

To sign the mighty malefactor's doom?
32. With pomp he's carry'd to the grave; his name
There lives afresh, in monumental fame:
33. There he enjoys, in some delicious vale,
Turf ever green and springs that never fail;
Preceded, follow'd, to his dusty bed,
By all the former, all the future dead."
34. Cease then; nor falsities for comforts vend,
Alike to truth unfaithful and your friend.

CHAPTER TWENTY-TWO

Thomas Wemyss (London, 1839)

1. Then Eliphaz the Temanite addressed Job, and said:
2. "Can a man, then, be profitable to God,
As one who is prudent profits himself?
3. Is it an advantage to the Almighty, that thou art rightous?
Or again, that thou canst justify thy ways?
4. Will he enter into a controversy through fear of thee?
Will he come to a trial with thee?
5. Is not thy wickedness sufficiently great?
Yea, there is no bound to thine iniquities.
6. Thou hast unjustly taken a pledge from thy brethren,
Thou hast stripped the destitute of their garments.
7. Thou hast not refreshed with water the weary,
Thou hast refused bread to the hungry.
8. Thou hast suffered the man of power to seize the land,
And the man of authority to take possession of it.
9. Thou hast sent widows empty away,
And hast bruised the orphans' arms.
10. Therefore thou art surrounded with snares,
And sudden ruin alarms thee.
11. Thy light is changed into darkness,
And a flood of waters covers thee.
12. Truly, God is higher than the heavens,

And sees the topmost stars, however lofty:
13. How then dost thou say, 'Can God know?
Can he discern those things which are transacted in
darkness?
14. Thick clouds enclose him, that he cannot see;
He walks on the convexity of the heavens.'
15. "Hast thou observed the ancient tract,
Which was trodden by wicked mortals;
16. Who perished by a sudden death,
Whose foundation is a molten flood?
17. Who said to God, 'Depart from us,--
What can the Almighty do to us?'
18. Though he had filled their houses with wealth.
(Far from me be their wicked conduct!)
19. The righteous beheld and rejoiced;
The innocent derided them, saying,
20. 'Surely their substance was carried away,
And a fire consumed their riches.'
21. "Turn therefore to Him, and be an upright man;
So shalt thou have abundant produce.
22. Receive the law from his mouth,
And store up his sayings in thy mind.
23. If thou return to the Almighty, thou shalt be restored,
If thou put away all iniquity from thy tent.
24. Then shalt thou reckon treasure as dust;
Then shall he make fountains to rush forth amidst rocks.
25. For the Almighty himself shall be thy treasure,
And be reckoned by thee as heaps of silver.
26. Then thou shalt delight in the Almighty,
And shalt lift up thy face to God.
27. Thou shalt pray to him, and he will hear thee,
And thou shalt perform thy vows.
28. What thou purposest shall be fulfilled,
And on thy goings light shall shine.
29. For he humbleth the proud,
But the lowly he bringeth into a spacious place.
30. He rescueth the innocent man;
So thou, too, shalt escape by the purity of thy hands."

CHAPTER TWENTY-THREE

George Hunt (Bath, 1825)

1. And Job answered and said,
2. "Yea, my complaint is grievous this day;
My hand is oppressive on my sighs.
3. Oh! that I knew where I might find Him,
I would go to His seat;
4. I would lay open my cause before Him,
And fill my mouth with argument:
5. Then should I know the words He would answer me,
And understand what He would say unto me,
6. Would He plead against me in the greatness of His strength?
No, surely, He would interpose for me.
7. There the upright may plead with Him;
And I should clear myself for ever from my judge.
8. Behold! I go forward, but He is not there;
And backward, but I cannot perceive Him.
9. In his operations on the left, I cannot grasp Him;
And upon the right He hides Himself,
And I see Him not.
10. But He knoweth my way;
And when He hath tried me,
I shall come forth as gold.
11. My foot hath taken hold of His steps;

I have kept His way, and have not turned aside.
12. I have not shrunk from the commandment of His lips:
I have treasured up the words of His mouth
More than my daily bread.
13. But He is immutable, and who can turn Him?
What His soul desireth, He doeth.
14. Therefore He will accomplish on me His decree,
And many such are with Him.
15. Wherefore I am troubled at His presence,
And when I reflect, I am afraid of Him.
16. God hath caused my heart to sink,
And the Almighty hath terrified me.
17. For I have not been severed from the face of darkness,

Nor from the face of thick darkness been concealed."

The Whole Book of Ayub

Henry Tattam (London, 1846)

1. Job answered

2. Verily I know that my reproach is from him, and his hand has been heavy upon my groaning.

3. For who would know that I might find him, and come to the end of the matter?

4. And I would plead the cause with him, and my
mouth should be filled with arguments.

5. And I would know the remedies which he would tell me, and I would perceive the things which he would declare to me.

6. Though he should come upon me with great power, then he will not handle me in wrath.

7. For truth and reproof are from him; and he will bring forth my judgement to an end.

8. And I shall go with the first, and am no more and what do I know of the last things?

9. He hath wrought on the left, and I apprehended it not: he will hide himself on the reght, and I shall not see him.

10. For he knows already my way; and he hath tried me as gold.

11. And I will go forth in his commandments, for I have kept his ways; and I shall not turn aside from his commands.

12. Neither have I despised his words; but I have hid them in my bosom.

13. If he hath judged thus, who hath contradicted him? For he who hath willed it, is he who hath done it.

14. Therefore I have hastened to him, and he will instruct me; I have been afraid of him.

15. Therefore I will hasten before his face, I will consider, and be afraid of him.

16. But the Lord has softened my heart, and the Almighty hath troubled me.

17. For I thought not that darkness would come upon me, and thick darkness, which hath covered me before my face.

CHAPTER TWENTY-FOUR

John Hamilton Gray (Edinburgh, 1836,37)

1. Wherefore are not evil times hoarded up by the Almighty?
And wherefore do those that honour him not behold his
days of revenge?
2. They displace boundaries, they plunder herds,
And feed themselves.
3. They lead away the ass of the orphan,
And take the widow's ox for a pledge.
4. They drive the poor out of the way;
The oppressed of the land hide themselves together.
5. Lo! like wild asses they go forth into the desert
to their work,
Seeking for prey;
The desert giveth them bread for their children.
6. On the field they reap their piled-up harvest,
And gather gleanings in the vineyard of the wicked.
7. They lie naked at night without clothing,
And uncovered to the cold.
8. They are made wet by the rain of the mountains,
And they embrace the rocks without refuge.
9. They rob the orphan from the mother's breast,
And they bring destruction on the needy.
10. They lead them in naked without clothing,
And hungring they bear sheaves.
11. Between their walls they must press the oil,
Tread the grapes, and suffer thirst.
12. Out of the city come the groans of the dying,
And the soul of those who are wounded unto death call aloud;
Yet God regardeth not their supplication!
13. There are those who have wandered from the light;
They knew not its rays, and dwell not in its paths.
14. When light dawns, the murderer departs,
Who slays the needy and the poor;
Yet in the night he is like a thief.
15. The eye of the adulterer watcheth for the twilight;
No eye, saith he, shall recognize me;
And he covers his face with a veil.
16. In the darkness they break into houses;

They shut themselves up by the day,
They know not the light!
17. Yea, morning is to them darkness;
Yea, they know well the horror of darkness.
18. May he lie light on the surface of the water,
May his heritage by accursed upon earth,
May he not turn to the way of the vineyards!
19. As dryness and heat draw to them snow-water,
So shall the realms of the dead draw to them the sinner!
20. The mother's womb shall forget him,
The worm shall devour him,
He shall no more be remembered.
May wickedness break like a staff!
21. He who plundered the barren that bore not,
And who did not shew favour to the widow!
22. Yet the mighty man long retaineth his strength;
He raiseth himself anew, and yet believeth no more in life.
23. He (God) bestoweth on him security, so that he may
support himself;
And yet his eyes take knowledge of his ways.
24. They stand on high--a moment--and they are no more;--
They are laid low, like those who are gathered together,
And they are cut off like the ears of corn.
25. And even when it is not so with them,
who can reprove me for lies?
Or make my speech nothing worth?

CANTO TWENTY-FIVE

Isaac Leeser (Philadelphia, 1854)

1. Then answered Bildad the Shuchite, and said:

2. Dominion and terror are with him; he maketh peace in his high places.

3. Can the number of his host be given? and over whom riseth not his light?

4. How then can man be justified with God? or how can be pure one that is born of woman?

5. Behold, even as regardeth the moon, that is not bright; yea, the stars are not pure in his eyes.

6. How much less the mortal, the mere worm? and the son of earth, the mere maggot?

CHAPTER TWENTY-SIX

The Earl of Winchilsea (London, 1860)

Then answer'd Eliphaz the Temanite and said:--
"Should a man utter vanity
And in folly solace find?
Or fill his belly with the blast
Of the bitter eastern wind?
Should his arguments be profitless,
His talk absurd, or should
He deal in speeches wherewithal
He never can do good?
Yea, thou castest off the fear of God,
And thou restrainest prayer.
Thy tongue is crafty, and thy mouth
Doth thine own sin declare:
For the witness that condemneth thee
Is thine own mouth--not I!
Yea, against thee and thy wickedness
Thine own lips testify.
Art thou the first man that was born?
Before the hills, wast made?
Hast thou heard God's secret? and alone
Comes wisdom to thine aid?
What knowest thou that we know not?
What cunning is with thee?
What understandest thou which is
To us a mystery?
With us are now the grey-headed
And very aged men,
Much elder than thy father:--
Are all mistaken then?
Are consolations small with thee?
Is any secret place

With thee? Why do thine heartstrings fail?
        What dost thou fear to face?
That thou turnest in thy naughtiness
        Against the God of right,
And lettest go out of thy mouth
        Such words of deadly spite?

CHAPTER TWENTY-SEVEN

J. M. Rodwell (London, 1864)

Then Job again took up his strain and said:

As El lives, who has deprived me of my *fair* judgment,
And Shaddai, who has embittered my soul,

All the while my breath is in me,
And Eloah's spirit in my nostrils,

My lips shall not speak iniquity,
And my tongue shall not utter deceit.

Far be it from me to pronounce you right;
Till I breathe my last, I will not part with my integrity;

I hold fast my righteousness, and will not let it go;
My conscience reproaches not one of my days.

May my foe be like the wicked,
And he that rises up against me like the impious!

For what can the hypocrite hope for, though he get him gain,
When Eloah shall take his soul?

Will El hear his cry,
When distress comes upon him?

Can he delight himself in Shaddai,--
Invoke Eloah at all times?

I will teach you of the hand of El,
I will not conceal how Shaddai deals.

Lo, all of you have seen it:
Why then speak ye thus vainly?

This is the portion of a wicked man with El,
And this the lot, which oppressors shall receive from Shaddai.

If his children be multiplied, the sword awaits them,
And his offspring shall not have their fill of bread:

His survivors shall be buried at their death,
But their widows shall not bewail them:

Though he heap up silver like dust,
And get together clothing as the clay,

That which he has gotten together shall the righteous wear,
And the innocent shall divide the silver.

He builds his house as a moth,
And like a booth which a vineyard-keeper makes:

The rich man lies down, but it is for the last time;--
When *a man* opens his eyes, he is no more.

Terrors invade him like a flood,
A whirlwind carries him off by night;

And east-wind catches him up and he is gone,
And like a storm sweeps him from his place:

God casts evils upon him, and spares not,
Though he strive to escape His hand.

Men clap their hands at him,
And hiss him from his place.

CHAPTER TWENTY-EIGHT

Francis Bolton (Edinburgh, 1866)

1. For there is a mine for the silver,
   And a place for gold which they fine.
2. Iron is taken out of the dust,
   And he poureth forth stone as copper.
3. He hath made an end of darkness,
   And he searcheth all extremities
   For the stone of darkness and of the shadow of death.
4. He breaketh away a shaft from those who tarry above:
   There, forgotten by every foot,
   They hang and swing far from men.
5. The earth--from it cometh forth bread,
   And beneath it is turned up like fire.
6. The place of the sapphire are its stones,
   And it containeth gold ore.
7. The way, that no bird of prey knoweth,
   And the eye of the hawk hath not gazed at,
8. Which the proud beast of prey hath not trodden,
   Over which the lion hath not walked.
9. He layeth his hand upon the pebbles;
   He turneth up the mountains from the root.
10. He cutteth canals through the rocks;
    And his eye seeth all kinds of precious things.
11. That they may not lead, he dammeth up rivers;
    And that which is hidden he bringeth to light.
12. But wisdom, whence is it obtained?
    And where is the place of understanding?
13. A mortal knoweth not its price,
    And it is not found in the land of the living.

14. The abyss saith: It is not in me,
And the sea saith: It is not with me.
15. Pure gold cannot be given for it,
And silver cannot be weighed as its price;
16. And it is not outweighed with the fine gold of Ophir,
With the precious onyx and the sapphire.
17. Gold and glass are not equal to it,
Nor is it exchanged for jewels of gold.
18. Pearls and crystal are not to be mentioned,
And the acquisition of wisdom is beyond corals.
19. The topaz of Ethiopia is not equal to it,
It is not outweighed by pure fine gold.
20. Whence, then, cometh wisdom,
And which is the place of understanding?
21. It is veiled from the eyes of all living,
And concealed from the fowls of heaven.
22. Destruction and death say:
With our ears we heard a report of it.--
23. Elohim understandeth the way to it,
And He--He knoweth its place.
24. For He looketh to the ends of the earth,
Under the whole heaven He seeth.
25. When He appointed to the wind its weight,
And weighed the water according to a measure,
26. When He appointed to the rain its law,
And the course to the lightning of the thunder:
27. Then He saw it and declared it,
Took it as a pattern and tested it also,
28. And said to man: Behold, the fear of the Lord is wisdom,
And to depart from evil is understanding.

CHAPTER TWENTY-NINE

John Noble Coleman (London, 1869)

At the conclusion of Chapter XXVIII Job paused a second time, waiting to see whether any one of his three friends would continue their argumentation. All three remained silent. Job then continued his self-vindication.

Job contrasts his past prosperity with his present degradation and misery, prays to God to answer his supplications and vindicate his cause, and makes this solemn appeal to the Searcher of hearts

:

WHAT IS MY PORTION? GOD MOST HIGH.
WHAT IS MINE INHERITANCE? THE ALMIGHTY SUPREME.

1. Then again Job resumed his discourse, and said:
2. O that I were as in former months!
As in days when God protected me!

3. When he caused his lamp to shine over my head,
By his light I walked through darkness.

4. As I was in my autumn days,
When the counsel of God was over my tabernacle.

5. While yet the Almighty was with me,
My children were round about me.

6. When my footsteps were bathed in cream,
And the rock poured out by me rivers of oil

7. When I went forth to the gate of the city,
And placed my seat at the forum.

8. The young men saw me and retired,
And the elders rose up and stood.

9. The rulers refrained from speaking,
And laid their hands on their mouths.

10. The chiefs suppressed their voice,
And their tongue cleaved to the roof of their mouth.

11. When the ear heard me, then it blessed me;
And when the eye saw me, than it witnessed for me.

12. Because I delivered the poor that cried,

The orphan, and him that had no helper.

13. The blessing of him that was ready to perish
came upon me,
And I caused the widow's heart to sing for joy.

14. I put on righteousness, and it clothed me,
My rectitude was to me for mantle and turban.

15. I was eyes to the blind,
And feet was I to the lame.

16. I was a father to the indigent,
And the cause which I understood not I searched out.

17. And I broke the grinders of the wicked,
And plucked the spoil from his teeth.

18. Then said I: "I shall die in my nest,
And shall multiply days as the sand.

19. My roots are outspread by the waters,
And the dew lodges all night on my branches.

20. My glory is unfading around me,
And my bow shall be renewed in my hand."

21. To me men gave ear and waited,
Yea, they silently awaited my counsel.

22. After my words they replied not,
And my speech distilled upon them as dew.

23. Yea, they waited for me as for the rain,
And opened their mouths wide, as for the latter
rain.

24. Smiled I upon them? they were incredulous,
And the light of my countenance they could
not cast down.

25. I directed their course, and presided as chief,
And dwelt as monarch over the host,
As comforter of the grief-oppressed.

CHAPTER THIRTY

William Meikle (Falkirk, 1869)

1. But they who are younger than I, even they
Now mock me, whose fathers did witness the day,
2. When I had disdained to have set such a folk,
To share it in one with the dogs of my flock.

3. Yea, what would their labour to me have availed,
Who were wretched and old, and so utterly failed,
4. For want they, and famine, to solitudes flew,
The first whom the waste and the wilderness knew,
5. They mallows cut up by the bushes to eat,
And fed upon juniper roots for their meat!

6. Forth from among men they were driven abhorred,
(As after a thief, they after him roared,)
7. In cliffs of the valleys remotely to dwell,
Where earth had a cave, or the mountain a cell.

8. They were heard in the bushes to clamour and bray,
Hid under the nettles, they herded and lay;
9. The children of fools, the refuse of mankind,
Who left every creature in vileness behind!

10. Now I am their song, and their byword and jest;
They flee far from me, as a thing they detest;
11. And spare not to spit in my face. Since he drew
Away the restraint which around me he threw,

12. And afflicted me thus, they have also let loose
Before me the wildest unbridled abuse.

13. All decent respect is withheld by the youth,
Who push me aside in a manner uncouth;
14. Against me a tumult of mischief they raise,
And vex me in all of their most singular ways,

15. They came, like the whole of my plagues, with a rush;
In the great desolation they on me did gush.

16. Thus terrors are turned upon me: my mind
They pursue as a thing that is borne in the wind;
17. And my welfare and comfort are speedily driven
Away like a cloud in the tempests of heaven.

18. To sadness and sorrow myself I resign;
The lot of affliction hath surely been mine.

19. In the night with my pains I am pierced to the bone;
For a season of resting my sinews have none;
20. My garment is changed, and tormenteth me sore;
Like the neck of my coat it is hardened with gore.
21. Me down in the mire He hath angrily thrown,
And the likeness of dust and ashes I'm grown.

22. I cry unto Thee, and Thou hear'st not my cries;
Thou regardest me not, when I plead and arise;
23. So cruel to me Thou art turned, and in fight
Unequal against me opposest Thy might.

24. Thou liftest me up to the wind; and a play
Of me making, dissolvest my substance away;
25. For I know Thou wilt bring me to death, and the doom
For all living appointed, me bring to the tomb.
26. A hand to the grave yet He will not extend,
Though now they their shouts with His thunders would blend.

27. Wept I not for him who did trouble endure?
Was my soul not in pain for the woes of the poor?

28. Yet evil came on me, when looking for good;
When I waited for light, did the darkness intrude.
29. For me, I was even in ferment and fear,
But wist not my day of affliction so near.

30. I sorrowing went, to all pleasure denied;
In the midst of the people I stood up and cried.
31. A brother to dragons am I in their sight,
A companion more meet for the owls of the night.

32. Most odious and black is the look of my skin,
And I'm withered with heat that is burning within.
33. To mourning my harp, and the exquisite flow
Of my organ is turned to the meltings of woe.

CHAPTER THIRTY-ONE

Rossiter W. Raymond (New York, 1878)

1. I made a law mine eyes obeyed.
How should I look upon a maid
With thoughts of lawless wrong? I said

2. For what hath God on high decreed
3. *But ruin as the sinner's meed?*
4. *And he discerneth every deed.*

5. If I have walked in falsehood--nay,
6. Let God in scales of justice weigh,
And know me guiltless, as I say!

7. If from the path of honour plain
Mine eyes have led my heart, for gain,
And on my hands be any stain,

8. Then may I plant, and other hands

Reap food from off my harvest lands,
Uprooting all that on them stands!

9. If I for lust have lain in wait
10. To wrong my neighbor, let that fate
Make my own household desolate!

11. For this is wickedness indeed;
A crime by human laws decreed,
12. A fire, destroying all my seed.

13. If I despised a servant's right,
Or man or maiden, in my spite,
14. How should I answer in His sight,

When God ariseth, He who doth
15. Visit, inquire--who made us both,
Yea, fashioned us and gave us growth?

16. If I withheld what beggars prayed,
Or caused the widow's eyes to fade,
17. Or no place at my table made

18. For orphans (Rather, by my side
He like a son did always bide
And she hath found in me a guide);

19. If e'er the naked met mine eye
20. And did not bless me speedily,
Warmed with the fleece my lambs supply;

21. If I have raised my hand to offend
The fatherless, nor feared the end,
Becuase I knew the judge my friend,

22. Then may that arm drop out and break!
23. Yea, as before God's wrath I quake,
Nor dare to Him resistance make!

24. If e'er I put my trust in gold,

25. Or worshipped, as I proudly told
With joy my treasures manifold;

26. Or if to sun or moon on high
27. I paid mine homage secretly,
Kissing my hand when none was nigh,

28. This too were crime: nor gold nor sun
And moon are gods; and this being done
Were treason to the Almighty One.

29. If I rejoice to see my foe
By any evil fate laid low,
And thriumph'd o'er him, falling so;

30. Nay, I forbade my lips to speak
With curses, my revenge to wreak
(Or with a wish his life to seek!);

31. If any in my tent can say
I sent one man unfilled away
32. (My doors were open night and day);

33. Or if, like Adam, I have tried
Within my breast to seal and hide
Any iniquity beside;

34. Then let me hide in silent shame,
Nor dare to come where once I came,
And meet the great assembly's blame!

35. O that there were a judge to hear!
Behold my sign; let God appear,
Answer, and make indictment clear!

36. Upon my shoulders as a gown,
Or round my temples like a crown,
I'd bind the charge, to make it known,

And fearless to His presence bring,

37. To give account of everything,
Advancing upright, like a king!

38. If against me my land complain,
Its furrows wet with tears for rain,
39. Of slaves unpaid who toiled in vain,

40. And died thorugh me, in cruel pain;
Let thorns spring up in place of grain,
And poisonous weeds alone remain!

CHAPTER THIRTY-TWO

Henry John Marten (London, 1869)

So these three men, they ceased to answer Job,
Because in his own eyes, he was so just.

Then was aroused the wrath of Elihu,
The son of Barachel, a man of Buz,
And of the tribe of Ram.
His wrath was roused e'en against Job,
Because he justified himself to God, as right;
'Twas roused as well 'gainst Job's three friends,
Because
Though they could not refute,
They yet condemn'd poor Job.

Now, Elihu had waited patiently,
Till Job had finished speaking,
For they were all older than himself;
But when he saw,
Not one of the three could answer Job,
His wrath was roused;
And so, thus answ'ring, spake,
Elihu,
Son of Barachel of Buz;--

"I am but young, and ye are very old!
Hence, fill'd with awe, I durst not shew my mind:
I said;--
'Lo, days should speak,
And multitude of years should wisdom teach!'
But lo, in man there is a Spirit;
Yea!
Inspired by God,
The gift of understanding dwells in him!
Old men, alone, are not at all times wise,
Nor do the aged, only, grasp the truth!
'Twas hence I said;--
'Now hearken to my words,
Whilst mine opinion I unfold to you!'

Behold!
I waited whilst you argued on;
Mine ear attentive conn'd your reasons o'er;
Whilst ye were searching up and down for words,
I gave close heed to you;
And yet, behold,
There was not one of you could answer Job,
Nor any able to refute his words!
So,
Do not vaunt that you have found the truth;
'Tis God alone, not man, has thrust him down!

Now, I'm not prejudiced by what he's said,
Nor will I answer him as you have done!"

They were all amazed, nor answered more;
They ceased to speak;
So,
Having paused awhile,
(For still they stood, and answer'd not, nor spake,)
He said;--

"I now will answer on my part myself;
Yea!
My opinion I'll unfold to you.

My burthen'd spirit is full charged with words;
My soul within,
(Like newly bottled wine that hath no vent)
Is ready to burst forth;
Yea! I will speak;
Yea! now, with parting lips, I'll answer you,
So I may breathe once more.
This sole, I pray you, let me flatter none,
Nor pay undue respect to any man;
For were I prone to flatter,
(Which I'm not)
My Maker soon would move me from my pace!

CHAPTER THIRTY-THREE

William Kelly (London, 1879)

Notwithstanding, Job, I pray thee, hear my speech,
And hearken to my every word.
Behold, I pray thee, I opened my mouth,
My tongue speaketh in my palate
My words [shall be] the uprightness of my heart,
And my knowledge shall my lips utter purely.
The Spirit of God [El] hath made me,
And the breath of Shaddai gave me life.
If thou canst, answer me;
Draw up before me, take thy stand.
Lo! I am God's [El], as thou;
Out of clay was I also formed.
Behold, my terror will not affright thee,
And my hand shall not be heavy on thee.
Surely thou hast said in mine ears,
And I heard the voice of the words:
I am pure, without transgression,
I [am] clean and have no iniquity:
Lo! He findeth hostilities against me,
He counteth me as His enemy;

He putteth my feet into the stocks;
He watcheth all my ways.
Behold, in this thou art not right, I answer thee;
For God [Eloah] is greater than a mortal.
Why hast thou contended against Him?
For He answereth not fall His matters.
When God [El] speaketh once, and twice,--
[Man] regardeth it not--
In a dream, in a vision of the night,
When deep sleep falleth on mortals,
And sealeth up their instruction,
To withdraw man [from] doing;
And pride from man he concealeth .
He keepeth back his soul from corruption,
And his life from passing away by the dart.
He is also chastised with pains on his bed,
And the strife of his bones [is] lasting.
And his life loatheth bread,
And his soul meat of desire.
His flesh wasteth out of sight,
And his bones that were not seen stand out,
And his soul draweth near to corruption,
And his life to the destroyers.
If there be by him a messenger,
An interpreter, one of a thousand,
To declare to man His uprightness;
And He is gracious to him, and saith,
Deliver him from going down to corruption:
I have found a ransom.
His flesh [is] fresher than childhood,
He returneth to the days of his youth.
He supplicateth [Eloah] God,
And he accepteth him.
And he shall see His fare with rejoicing,
And He requiteth to mortal man His righteousness.
He sinneth before mortals, and saith,
I sinned and perverted right, and it satisfied
me not.
He ransomed my soul from passing to corruption,
And my life looketh on the light.

Lo! all there worketh God [El] twice, thrice
with man,
To bring back his soul from corruption,
That he may be enlightened with the light of life.
Attend, O Job, hearken to me;
Be silent, and I shall speak.
If thou hast words, answer me--
Speak, for I have a desire to justify thee.
If not, hearken thou unto me;
Keep silence, and I will teach thee wisdom.

CHAPTER THIRTY-FOUR

Henry James Clarke (London, 1880)

1. Then Elihu proceeded, and said:
2. Hear ye my words, ye wise men; and give ear
To me, ye who have ripe experience.
3. Because the ear is critical in words,
Just as the palate notes the taste of food
By eating.
4. Let us ascertain that which
Is right; let us distinguish what is good,
5. Among ourselves. For Job said, "I have right
On my side; and yet God hath overruled
6. My claims. Shall I belie my cause? The wound
God's arrow hath inflicted on me still
Remains unhealed, although by no misdeed
7. Envenomed." What man is there who, as Job,
8. Drinks in like water impious rant, and thus
Associates himself with those who work
Iniquity, nor scruples to affect
9. The company of wicked men; in that
He hath affirmed, "In nothing is a man
Befriended through affecting intercourse
10. With God?" Therefore, ye men of thoughtful minds,
Give ear to me. Far be't from God to do
A wicked deed, and the Almighty to

11. Act wrongfully! Nay surely, each man's work
He pays him back, and, whatsoe'er one's course
May be, ordains that what befalls him shall
12. Accord with it. Yea verily, God acts
Not wickedly, nor does the Mightiest
13. Wrest justice. Who committed to His charge
The earth? Or who establiched the whole world?
14. Were He to give attention to Himself
Alone, were He to draw back to Himself
15. His spirit and His breath, then would all flesh
Expire together, and mankind return
16. To dust. But oh now, understand: hear this:
17. Lend to my words a listening ear. Could He
Who is a foe to law and order rule?
Then wilt thou the Supremely Just condemn?
18. Is licence given for saying to a king,
"Thou worthless one!" or to a nobleman,
19. "Thou villain!" How much less to Him who shews
No partiality to princes, nor
Bestows regard upon the wealthy man
In preference to the poor, since they are both
20. His handiwork! In but a moment's time
They die,--yea, at the middle hour of night
A people, reeling 'neath a sudden stroke
Of doom, are overthrown and perish: then
Are swept away the mighty by no hand.
21. For His eyes are intent upon the ways
Of every one, and all his steps He notes.
22. There is no darkness, wherein
The workers of iniqiuty may hide
23. Themselves. For no necessity does He
Impose on man a second time to meet
24. With God in judgment. He the mighty slays
With havoc indiscriminate, and in
25. Their place sets other men. So then their works
He sees through, and o'erthrows them in the night;
26. And they are crushed. As wicked men He smites
27. Them openly: since to this issue they
Fell off from Him, and no attention gave
28. To any of His ways, that they might cause

The outcry of the helpless poor to come
Before Him, and that He might hear the plaint
29. Of the oppressed. For once let *Him* give peace,
And who shall stir up bitter turmoil? But
If He should hide His face, who is there can
Behold Him? Whether He is dealing with
A nation, or with but a single man,
30. He deals out equal measure; to dethrone
The impious man, that such may cease to be
31. The snare of the community. Howe'er,
If one should say to God, "I have been made
To suffer; I will cease to do amiss.
32. What yet I see not, do Thou show to me.
If I have acted wrongly, I will not
33. Repeat what I have done," must we suppose
That He will recompense these good resolves
According to *thy* view? For thou hast raised
Objections, and so now 'tis by thyself
This question must be solved, not me. Then speak
34. Thine own opinion. Men of common sense
Will say to me, and any wise man who
35. Is listening to me, "Job speaks foolishly,
And his assertions are but random words."
36. May Job be tested to the uttermost,
Because of his replies, the counterpart
37. Of those of worthless men. For now he adds
Rebellion to his sin. Disdainfully
He strikes his hands among us, and still swells
The number of his speeches against God.

CHAPTER THIRTY-FIVE

Samuel Cox (London, 1880)

Then Elihu took up his discourse and said:
2. Thinkest thou this to be right, that thou shouldest say,
"My righteousness is greater than God's?"

3. Yet thou saidst, "What profit shall it be to me,
And what shall I gain from it more than from sinning?"
4. I will answer thee
And thy friends with thee.
5. *Look up to the heavens and see,*
And behold the clouds, how high they be!
6. *What canst thou do against Him, if thou sinnest?*
Though thine offences be many, yet what canst thou do against Him?
7. *If thou art righteous, what dost thou confer on Him,*
And what will He take at thy hand?
8. *Thy wickedness can but affect a man like thyself,*
And thy righteousness a son of man.
9. *If men groan at the multitude of oppressions,*
And cry out under the arm of the mighty.
10. *Yet none saith, "Where is God my Maker,*
Giver of songs in the night,
11. *Who teacheth us more than the beasts of the earth,*
And maketh us wiser than the birds of the air?
12. *They cry out indeed--but He answereth not--*
Because of the tyranny of the wicked,
13. *For God will not hear vain outcries,*
Neither will the Almighty regard them.
14. *Even when thou sayest thou shalt never see Him,*
Thy cause is before Him: wait therefore for Him
15. *But now, because his anger hath visited thee lightly,*
And He ignoreth many of thy faults,
16. *Job openeth his mouth with vanity;*
He multiplieth words without sense.

CHAPTER THIRTY-SIX

G. H. Bateson Wright (London, 1883)

1. And Elihu proceeded to say,
2. Wait a little for me and I will show thee,
That there are still arguments for God.
3. I will bring my knowledge from afar,
And I will establish my Maker's justice.

4. For surely my words are not false.
5. Perfect in knowledge, lo God is almighty,
And mighty in power he despises not understanding.
6. He preserves not the life of the wicked,
But gives sentence for the afflicted.
7. He withdraws not his eyes from the righteous;
But with kings on the throne,
He sets them and they are firmly established.
8. And if they are bound with chains,
Being seized with the cords of affliction;
9. Then he tells them their deeds,
And their crime how arrogant they are.
10. He uncovers their ear to reproof,
And bids them renounce iniquity.
11. If they hear and obey;
Their days shall end in prosperity,
And their years in pleasure.
12. But if they do not hear;
They pass away by the weapon,
And expire in ignorance.

13. The proud ungodly indulge in wrath,
They will not cry for help when he binds them.
14. Their soul dies while they are young,
And their life ends as that of the unclean.
15. He delivers the poor in trouble,
And by affliction he makes them listen.
16. And thee also will he bring out of distress,
To freedom without any restraint in it.
And thy table shall remain full of fatness,
17. Full even with the sentence of the wicked;
Sentence and justice shall be united.
18. But beware lest in plenty anger incite thee,
And lest the size of the ransom turn thee aside.
19. Should thy wealth equal it?
No not gold nor all accumulated riches.
20. Thou wilt not long for the night,
When peoples are removed from their place.
21. Beware lest thou turn to iniquity,
For on this very account hast thou been proved by

suffering.
22. Lo God towers aloft in his might;
Who is a teacher like him?
23. Who can correct him for his way,
Or who can say "Thou hast done wrong"?
24. Remember how great is his work;
Which men have beheld.
25. Which all men see,
And mortals view from afar.
26. Lo God is exalted beyond our knowledge,
The number of his years is beyond research.
27. When he withholds the drops of water,
They are resolved from rain into mist;
28. And what the skies distil,
Drops upon men as showers.
29. Can any understand the spreading of the clouds,
The rumblings of his pavilion?

30. Lo he spreads the light above,
While he covers the depths of the sea.
31. For thus he both judges nations,
And gives food in abundance.
32. With both hands he covers the light,
Or brings it forth when one prays for it;
33. Therewith he indicates his friend,
Whose anger is zealous against iniquity.

CHAPTER THIRTY-SEVEN

Henry Frederick Gibbons and
William M. Thompson,
Translation of Ernest Renan
(London, 1889)

Listen! Listen! to the noise of His voice;

The rumbling which proceeds from His mouth.

He fill with it all the vault of heaven
His lightnings reach to the ends of the earth.

After the lightning comes the roar of His voice;
He thunders loudly with a stately sound;
His voice is heard; the dart is then in hand.

God thunders with a voice wondrous to hear;
He does great things we cannot understand:

He says to the snows, Fall ye to the earth;
He commands the waves and the heavy rains,

He thus puts seals upon the hands of man,
So that he may learn to know his Maker.

Then the wild beast goes into his shelter
And lays himself down in his den.

The storm rushes from its hidden retreat;
And the northerly breezes bring the cold.

At the breathing of God the ice is formed,
The water contracts and is pressed close together,

He fills the cloud with watery vapour:
He thrusts before him thunder-bearing clouds.

Under His direction they go here and there,
To carry out commands as He ordains
Upon the face of the earth inhabited.

It may be He will punish His creatures,
Or He may make them instruments of mercy.

Job! lend thine ear to all this:
Listen to the wonders of God.

Dost thou know the chief end of His wonders,
And why He makes fire shine out of the clouds?

Dost thou know the equal law of the clouds?
The secret of him whom we know is perfect?

Wherefore thy garments are they much too hot
When the earth rests from the blasts of midday?

Wouldest thou beat the clouds with a hammer,
And make them solid as a mirror of metal?

Give us to know what you can answer Him;
Rather let us be silent: we are so ignorant.

Let not my talk be reported to Him.
What man has ever wished to lose his life?

In a moment one sees not the sun
When its light is hidden behind the clouds,
A puff of wind passes and the sky is clear.

A golden ray comes sudden from the north;
Oh! wonderful splendour of God!

We shall never reach near the Almighty,
Great in power, right and justice, answering none.

Let man then go always in fear of Him;
He doth not regard the wise men of earth.

CHAPTER THIRTY-EIGHT

(London, 1779)

VERSE I.

Thick darkness shrouds the troubled air,
The whirlwind's sounding wings declare
The mighty GOD is nigh:
Afflicted Job with prostrate head,
Loud as the tempest, hears with dread
Th'omnific word reply

V. 2

What son of vain, of feeble man,
Eternal counsels dares to scan,
Or from their light to hide?
The child of perishable dust,
Oh let him own those counsels just,
Though dark to human pride.

V. 3

Frail son of man! thy Maker bows!
To hear what boasting science knows,
From heavn's empyreal throne:
Hear, and reply to each demand,
Or own JEHOVAH'S plastic hand
In wisdom rules alone.

V. 4 & 5

How were the world's foundations laid?
From shore to shore whose hand display'd
The circumscribing line?--
Was then the passing flower of morn,
Was murmuring Job co-eval born
To ken the work divine?

V. 6

How balanc'd earth in ambient air
Suspended hung-canst *thou* declare?--
Whose potent word hath join'd
In harmony's attracting chain
The varying aether, earth, and main,
Discordant, yet combin'd?

V. 7

Did then the music of the spheres,

Exulting, strike thy ravish'd ears,
Swell'd by seraphic lays;
When all the lyres of heaven were strung,
When GOD'S unnumber'd offspring sung
Triumphant hymns of praise?

V. 8

Whose power the raging seas restrain'd,
The dark unfathom'd depths contain'd,
When, with tremendous roar,
They swell'd impatient for a birth,
O'erwhelm'd the dun imperfect earth
With floods without a shore?

V. 9 & 10

Then, at my word, the mantling cloud
Did first the new-born waters shroud,
Wrapp'd was their boisterous wave
In misty night's impervious shade;
Hollow'd by me their rocky bed,
I taught them where to rave.-

V. 11

"Thus far, oh deep! thy tides shall flow:
"These shores--thy fated limits--know;--
"The bulwarks heaven hath made
"To chech thy wrath--to guard the land:
"By these huge cliffs--these moles of sand,
"Shall thy proud waves be staid."--

V. 12

Lift up thy prostrate head--and shew
The morning's blushes where to glow
Obsequious to thy sway;--
Or taught by *Thee*, will orient beams
Disperse the night's pale silver gleams,
And rule the varying day?

V. 13

Canst thou command with voice divine
The sun's pervading ray to shine
On all that lives below,
To strike the trembling wretch with dread,
Who wraps in shades his guilty head,
But shrinks from light his foe?

V. 14

True as the yielding clay receives
The forms the graven signet leaves,
Emerging earth displays
True to the gazer's ravish'd fight,
Her forms, illumin'd with the light
Of morning's golden rays.

V. 15

But though her golden rays be spread,
To guide and gless the virtuous head;
The ten-fold glooms of night,
Ev'n in the solar blaze of day
Confound the sinner's devious way,
And check the arm of might.

V. 16

Whence ocean's springs exhaustless flow,
Doth Job's keen eye pretend to know?--
Did e'er its search survey
The green waves deep capacious bed,
Where the Leviathans are bred,
And tempest in their play?
Then, while the briny billows rise
In angry murmurs to the skies,
Go, daring mortal, trace
Where sleep beneath the ocean's roar
In coral groves, on pearly shore,
The glittering finny race.

V. 17

For thee will yawning earth display
Death's murky caverns to the day
Where human pride descends?--
There, view with heav'ns all piercing eye,
Where mouldering millions equal lye,
And boasting science ends.--
Say, where the spirits of the just
Releas'd from erring, toiling dust
From vanity are flown?--
Bid death's black gates, thrown wide display
The realms of everlasting day,
And glory's sapphire throne.

Where, radiant as the beams of morn,
Unfading crowns the just adorn;
Where, with eternal spring,
Reclin'd in amaranthine bowers,
Their golden harps lead on the hours
On pleasure's downy wing.

V. 18

Ev'n o'er the wide-spread plains of earth
The golden compasses stretch forth,
The meted space declare:
Or scale the pendent mountain's side,
Whose tops hybernal horrors hide;--
Will knowledge meet thee *there*?

V. 19

Canst thou describe what glistening way
Leads to the blazing source of day,
When eve illumes her horns?
Or where the star-crown'd night retires,
Whene'er the morning's reddening fires
The dewy world adorns?

V. 20

Put forth thy hand--to grasp the fun,
The earth's diurnal circuit run:
To light's primeval throne
Then speed thy rapid radiant race,
The silver reins of night possess,
And guide the spheres alone.

V. 21

Have rolling ages on thy head
Their silver-streaming honours shed,
And hoar experiennce giv'n,
To trace with sure observing eye
The glittering planets round the sky,
The azure fields of heav'n?

V. 22 & 23

Ought of the snow's exhaustless stores,
The dreadful hail my vengeance pours,
Doth human wisdom know?--
Reserv'd, remote from human ken,
The scourge of contumacious men,

And sinful realms below.

V. 24

Canst thou divide a single ray
Of light; diffusing instant day,
Pure effluence divine?
Say, did that sultry shriveling blast
That over the fervid desart past
Proceed from lips like thine?--

V. 25

Who taught the teeming cluds to flow,
Distil their kindly drops below?--
Or through the lurid air
Give the red lightnings wings to fly,
Attend the thunders from the sky,
Wrapp'd in their forky glare?

V. 26

Far from the haunts of man remov'd,
The lonely wilds my care have prov'd,
In bland prolific rains;
Where roses bend their blushing head,
Where pines their weeping amber shed,
And palms adorn the plains.

V. 27

Where down the bleak rock's rugged way,
I bade refreshing waters stray,
To saturate the vale;
To cheer the savage herds that pant
With parching thirst, to feed the plant
That scents the desart gale.

V. 28 & 29

Hath rain a sire? or dost thou know
From what paternal causes flow
The balmy tears of dew?
Who gave cerulean ice its birth?
Or o'er the dusky, joyless earth
Its sleet hoar mantle threw?

V. 30

Where dwells the cold, whose breath alone
Congeals the floods to solid stone,
Binds up the torrent's roar?--

Whose hand with adamantine chain
Fetters the wild reluctant main,
That sleeps, and raves no more?

V. 31

When rising in their seven-thron'd sphere
The vernal pleiades appear,
Benignant shed their ray;
Will laughing spring at thy command
Forbear to deck the dreary land,
Or gladness cease her lay?

When red Orion wrapp'd in storms
Arises, and the year deforms;
Say, can thy quick'ning voice
Call from the clods the golden grain,
Call labour's hand to toil again,
Or bid the flocks rejoice?

V. 32

Sanded with constellations o'er,
Will heav'ns broad zone respect thy pow'r,
And move his radiant signs,
Harmonious, as the seasons roll,
Submissive, as thy laws controul,
Thy voice their post assigns?--

V. 33

To guide the northern sparkling cars,
Arcturus, with his trail of stars,
Will venturous Job essay?--
Repair each waning orb with light,
Or lead the dazzling files of night
In all their bright array?--

V. 34

Then raise thy voice to reach the sky,
Call down distended clouds that lye
Convolv'd in solemn gloom;
Bid their deep urns around thee pour
Their congregated wat'ry store,
Nor dread the whelming tomb.

V. 35

When rolling storms o'erhang the sky,

Bid the slant lightnings instant fly,
The messengers of heaven:
Hear'st thou their piercing tongues declare,--
"We go"--And through the flaming air
JEHOVAH'S word is given.

V. 36

Who feeds within the human frame
Reason's pure, bright, immortal flame?--
Whose liberal hand imparts
Each vary'd sense that life can bless,
Each light to future happiness,
That glows in human hearts?--

V. 37 & 38

Yet can thy wisdom number o'er
The fleeting clouds? their humid store
Can e'er *thy* dictates sway,
When arid earth no more complains,
But genial moisture swells her veins,
Cements her rifted clay?--

V. 39 & 40

Will the stern lions own thy power,
Seek thee at evening's solemn hour
To guide their midnight chace?
Their wild steps mark'd with smoking gore,
Their dark dens echoing with the roar
Of all their tawny race.

When hunger whets their cruel soul,
With rage their fiery eye-balls roll,
Horrific waves their mane;
Dar'st thou attend their shaggy side,
With reeking food their whelps provide,
And share their desart reign?

V. 41

Even of the raven's new-fledg'd brood
Who stills the clamorous cry with food?--
Driven from the parent-nest,
They wander helpless through the sky;
But GOD'S unfailing hand is nigh,
And life with plenty blest.

Ch. 40. V. 2

Shall then the morning's withering flower
Arraign JEHOVAH'S boundless power?--
Let Job repine no more;
But, humbled to his kindred dust,
Own his Creator's ways are just,
And bid the world *adore*.

CHAPTER THIRTY-NINE

George H. Gilbert (Chicago, 1889)

Dost thou know when the rock-goats bring forth?
The travail of hinds canst thou mark?
Canst thou count the months they fulfill,
And the time when they bear dost thou know?
They crouch, let their young break forth,
Their pangs they cast off.
Their young become strong, they grow up in the field;
They go forth, and return not again.
5 Who has sent the wild ass away free,
And the bands of the fleet one hath loosed?
To whose house I have made the waste place,
And the desert of salt his abode.
He doth laugh at the din of the town,
The noise of the driver he hears not.
The mountains' choice spots are his pasture,
And for every green thing he doth seek.
Is the wild ox willing to serve thee,
Will he pass the night at thy crib?
10 Canst thou bind the wild ox to the ridge with his cord,
Or harrow the valleys behind thee will he?
Dost thou trust him since great is his strength.
And committest thy labor to him?
Dost thou trust him to gather thy seed,

And bring to thy floor?
The wing of the ostrich waves gladly:
Is't a gentle feather and pinion?
Nay, she leaveth her eggs to the earth,
And warmeth them on the dust;
15 She forgets that a foot may crush them,
May trample them beasts of the field.
She treats harshly her young, as not hers;
Is her labor in vain, she cares not;
For wisdom God made her forget,
And gave her no dower in insight.
When she beateth her pinions on high,
She doth laugh at the horse and his rider.
Canst thou give to the charger strength?
Canst thou mantle his neck with trembling?
20 Canst thou cause him to leap as a locust?
A dread is his neighing majestic.
He stamps in the valley, and joys in his might;
To meet the armed host he goes forth.
He laugheth at fear unamazed,
And turneth not back from the sword.
Upon him the quiver doth rattle,
The glittering lance and spear.
With stamping and anger he swallows the earth,
And stays not when soundeth the trumpet.
25 He saith when it soundeth, Aha!
And from far he scenteth the battle,
The princes' shout and the war-cry.
Doth the hawk spread his wings by thine insight,
His pinions stretch out for the south?
Or soars, at thy bidding, the eagle
And buildeth his eyrie on high?
He dwells on the rock, and doth lodge
On the crag of the rock and stronghold.
From thence he doth spy out food,
His eyes can behold from afar.
30 And his brood quaff blood,
And where carcasses are, there is he.

CHAPTER FORTY

Otis Cary (London, 1898)

Shall cavilling man oppose the Mighty One?
He that disputes with God, let him an answer give.

Job. Lo, I am weak; what shall I answer Thee?
Upon my mouth I lay my hand.
Once have I spoken,--I will not reply;
Twice I have spoken,--I will add no more.

The Lord. Gird now thy loins like a man.
I will demand of thee; thy answer give.
Wilt thou my judgment disannul,
And Me condemen that thou mayst clear thyself?
Hast thou an arm like God's,
And canst thou thunder with a voice like His?
Deck now thyself with splendor and with pride,
Array thyself with majesty and pomp;
Pour forth the overflowings of thy worth,
Look thou on every one that's proud and humble him;
Yea, look upon the proud and bring him low,
And trample down the wicked where they stand.
Together hide them in the dust,
Their faces in the darkness bind.
Then even I will make acknowledgment
That thy right hand can save thee by itself.
Behemoth see, whom I have made with thee;
He feedeth on the herbage like an ox;
But in his loins, lo, what strength is there!
His force is in the muscles of his flanks.
As 'twere a cedar moveth he his tail;
The sinews of his thighs are woven firm,
His bones are tubes of brass,
His limbs like bars of iron.
The master-piece is he of all God's works,
And he who made him gave to him a sword.
The mountains yield to him his food,
There all the forest beasts disport themselves.
Beneath the lotus plants he lieth down,

Within the covert of the reedy fen.
The lotus plants protect him with their shade,
The willows of the brook encompass him.
The river overflows,--he trembles not;
Fears not although a Jordan splash his mouth.
Shall any take him while he's on the watch,
On with the binding-cord pierce through his nose?

CHAPTER FORTY-ONE

William Thompson (1726)

Or, say, presumptuous Job!
Canst thou draw out the vast Leviathan,
Huge Monarch of the Deep, and lead him bound
Transfix'd with barbed Spears, in captive State
With sportive Triumphs shewn? Or, part his Bulk
For Merchandise, or Banquet, mighty fund?
Or, will he sue with Supplication bland
And Prayer submiss, for Life? Or, make a League
To do thee Service, mighty as his Strength,
To tame Subjection thrall'd? The fiercest Fall
Astounded at the Sight; who then shall dare
To rouse him into Rage? And is my Hand
That form'd this hideous Terrour of the Deep,
Less dreadful deem'd, that thou shouldst tempt my Wrath
With Vengeance to descend on thy rash Head
Devote to Ruin? View, with narrow Ken,
His scaly Garment, like a Robe of State,
Immeasurably vast, with Regal Pride
Spread o'er his spatious Bulk, of Texture firm,
Contiguous wove, inseparably join'd
In Union strong. Or, say, canst thou unfold
The Doors of his tremendous Face, dilate
With hideous Aperture, and view his Jaws
Fenc'd round with serried Arms, a double Front

Of formidable Teeth, huge massy Bars
In brazen Sockets sunk, firm and unmov'd
By Dint of mightiest Force; his Nostrils wide
Spout Cataracts of Fire, with rolling Smoke
In bikering Conflict wag'd, from hollow Throat
Eructant with deep Thunder, dreadful Sound
To Mariner remote; his glaring Eyes
Sparkle, as when the Eye-lids of the Morn
Opening with ruddy Flame, portend fell Storm
Of Rain or rising Tempest, in his neck
A Fortress huge, the Glory of his Strength
Is seated eminent, of Force to turn
What may oppose, to Flight or foul Defeat,
With dire Discomfit quell'd; his dauntless Heart,
Firm as the nether Milstone, heaves with Pride
And joyous Triumph, scornful of the Foe
However arm'd with Implements of Death,
Fell Sword and pointed Dart and missive Spear,
A Panoply of War; the doubled Blade
Guiltless of Blood, recoils; the shiver'd Lance
Lies scatter'd by his Side with scaly Coat
Of Mail impenetrable arm'd; he deems
Iron as straw, and Brass as rotten Wood;
The barbed Arrow whizzes through the Air
On fruitless Errand sped; and clattering Stones,
With mighty Jaculation hurl'd from Slings,
Are turn'd before him into chaff, which Winds
Scatter with easy Blast; the brandish't Spear
Is with Derision seen; and round him strown
[The] shatter'd Armour; which he spurns with Scorn,
[As] Pebbles in the Mire; when he upheaves
His bulky Vastness o'er the troubled Waves,
Emergent like a Rock, or Isle upthrown
From Bottom of the Sea, the Mighty, chill'd
With Horror and fell Dread, and inly mov'd
To penitence, as in the Jaws of Death
Inevitable deem'd, with Eyes aghast
View the chaf'd Deep boiling with bubbled Foam,
Commotion strange! Behind him shines a Path
Distinct with hoary Light; in Peerless Strength,

Wallowing unweildy, enormous in his Gate
He flounces on, as Need or Pastime leads,
Guiltless of Fear, thro' all the watry Realm,
His Territory large, a mighty King
O'er all the Sons of Pride.

Farrar Fenton (1898)

Why, to try for him would be in vain!
One drops, if but looking at him!
4 I will not relate of his limbs,
His courage, and power, and form!
5 Who dare open his mouth for a bit,
Or bring double bridle to him?
6 Who dare open the doors of his mouth
Surrounded with terrible teeth?
7 His back is the bosses of shields
Pressed close with the print of a seal,
8 Where everyone sticks to his mate,
And the wind cannot go in between!
9 For everyone holds in its place.
They grasp, and they cannot be split!
10 And when he is sneezing, light shines;
And his eyes are the eyelids of dawn!
11 And flashes come out of his mouth,
And sparkles of fire escape;
12 From his nostrils a vapor proceeds
Like flame from a furnace, or straw!
13 His breath is the burning of coals
And flames proceed out of his mouth!
14 His vigor sits down on his neck,
And terror precedes his advance!
15 The flakes of his flesh stick as one
So close that they cannot be moved!

16 His heart is as hard as a stone,--
Yes! as hard as the stone of a mill!
17 When he rises, the brave are dismayed;
They stagger, as tho' in the waves!
18 If the sword reach, it will not pierce him,
Nor the spear, or the stone, or the dart!
19 He fancies that the iron is straw,
And the steel to be mere rotten wood!
20 No arrows can turn him to flight!
Sling-stones he converts into chaff!
21 He thinks that the club is a rush!
And laughs at the shake of a spear!
22 And his sharp-pointed claws are beneath,
Supporting his course on the mud!
23 He makes the deep boil like a pot
And embroiders the water with foam,
24 And after his passage it shines!
It seems that the depths have turned grey!
25 On the dust there is nowhere his match
Who was made so as not to feel fear!
26 He gazes on all that is great;--
He is king over all the wild beasts.

2[4] Who are you, who dare not arouse him,
Yet who dare resist Me to My face?
3 Who has worked for Me?--I will repay.
All under the heavens is Mine!

CHAPTER FORTY-TWO

Ralph Sadler (London, 1897)

And Ayub replied to Jehovah, and said: I see that Thou canst do anything; and craft can withhold Thee no jot. Who will hide counsel thus without knowledge? Therefore my words were mere gush, and I have no discernment. Far be distinction from me; and I know nothing.

Hear, I pray Thee, and I will speak; I will ask of Thee, and do Thou instruct me. I had heard of Thee with my ears, and now my eye has seen Thee; wherefore I abhor myself, and lament in dust and ashes.

And it came to pass, after Jehovah had spoken these words to Ayub, Jehovah spoke also to Eliphaz the Temanite: My anger is kindled against thee and against thy two companions, because they did not utter sincerity to Me like My slave Ayub.

And now, take you seven byllocks and seven rams; and go to my slave Ayub, and offer them as a burnt offerint to testify to you. And Ayub my slave shall make intercession on your behalf--for lo, I lift up his countenance--lest I do you a mischief; for you have not uttered sincerity to Me, like My slave Ayub.

And Eliphaz the Temanite, and Bildad the Shuhite, and Zophar the Naamathite, went and did according as Jehovah said to them. And Jehovah lifted up the face of Ayub, and Jehovah turned the captivity of Ayub, when he made intecession in testimony to his companions.

And Jehovah added all that Ayub had twice over. And there came all his brethren, and all his sisters, and all who had known him before; and all bred with him in his house.

And they condoled with him, and comforted him, over all the evil which Jehovah had brought upon him. And they gave him each, one kesita and one ring of gold.

And Jehovah blessed the after-life of Ayub more than his beginning; and he had fourteen thousand sheep, and six thousand camels, and a thousand yoke of oxen, and a thousand she-asses.

And he had seven sons and three daughters. And he called the name of the first Jemima, and the name of the second Keziah, and the name of the third Keren-Happuch.

And no women were found so fair as the daughters of Ayub in all the land; and their father gave them property among their brothers

And Ayub lived, after this, one hundred and forty years; and saw his sons and his sons' sons, four generations. And Ayub died an old man and full of days.

The Whole Book of Ayub

COPTIC ADDENDUM

Henry Tattam (London, 1846)

17. And Job died, being an old man, and full of days: and it is written again concerning him that he will rise with those whom the Lord shall raise up.

This man hath been described in the Syriac book as having dwelt in the land of Ausis, on the borders of Idumea and Arabia: and his name before was Jobab; and he took an Arabian wife, and she bare him a son whose name was Enon. And his own father was Zara, who was of the sons of Esau, and his mother was Bozora, so that he was the fifth after Abraam. And these were the kings who reigned in Edom, the county which he also ruled over: the first was Balak the son of Beor, and the name of his city was Dennaba: after Balak, Jobab, who is called Job: after him Asom, who was the governor of the country of Thaeman: and after him Adad, the son of Arad, who destroyed Madiam, in the field of Moab; and the name of his city was Keththem. And his friends who came to him, Elisaph, a son of one of the sons of Esau, the king of the Thaemanites, and Baldas, the king of the Sauchaeans, and Sophar, the king of the Minaeans.

TESTAMENT OF JOB
CHAPTER XII (CONCLUSION)

Kaufmann Kohler (Berlin, 1897)

1. After these three had finished singing hymns, did I Nahor (Neros) brother of Job sit down next to him, as he lay down. 2. And I heard the marvelous (great) things of the three daughters of my brother, one always succeeding the other amidst awful silence. 3. And I wrote down this book containing the hymns and signs of the [holy] Word, for these were the great things of God. 4. And Job lay down from sickness on his couch, yet without pain and suffering, because his pain did not take strong hold on him on account of the charm of the girdle which he had wound around himself. 5. But after three days Job saw the holy angels come for his soul, and instantly he rose and took the cithara and gave it to his daughter Day (Yemima). 6. And to Kassia he gave a censer (with perfume = Kassia), and to Almathea's Horn (= music) he gave a timbrel in order that they might bless the holy angels who came for his soul.

7. And they took these, and sang, and played on the psaltery and praised and glorified God in the **holy dialect**.

8. And after this came He who sitteth upon the great chariot and kissed Job, while his three daughters looked on, but the others saw it not. 9. And He took the soul of Job and He soared upward, taking her (the soul) by the arm and carrying her upon the chariot, and He went towards the East. 10. His body, however, was brought to the grave, while the three daughters marched ahead, having put on their girdles and singing hymns in praise of God.

11. Then held Nahor (Nereos) his brother and his seven sons, with the rest of the people and the poor, the orphans and the feeble ones, a great mourning over him, saying:

12. "Woe unto us, for today has been taken from us the strength of the feeble, the light of the blind, the father of the orphans;

13. The receiver of strangers has been taken off, the leader of the erring, the cover of the naked, the shield of the widows. Who would not mourn for the man of God!" 14. And as they were mourning in this and in that form, they would not suffer him to be put into the grave. 15. After three days, however, he was finally put into the grave like one in sweet slumber, and he received the name of the good (beautiful) who will remain renowned throughout all generations of the world.

16. He left seven sons and three daughters, and there were no daughters found on earth as fair as the daughters of Job. 17. The name of Job was formerly Jobab, and he was called Jobab by the Lord. 18. He had lived before his plague

eighty five years, and after the plague he took the double share of all; hence also his years he doubled, which is 170 years. Thus he lived altogether 255 years. 19. And he saw sons of his sons unto the fourth generation. It is written that he will rise up with those whom the Lord will reawaken. To our Lord by glory. Amen.

Endnotes

[1] In the earlier chapters I have preserved the Middle English yogh (3) used to represent the gutteral (a3een = ageen = again). the palatal voiced spirant (3okis = yokis = yokes), and the voiceless spirant (ri3t = right). When authors indicated a letter in some generally accepted form (e.g., the line above a vowel indicating an m or n as in fro = from and paciece = pacience = patience), I have supplied the letter. Because in some texts the consistently inconsistent spellings appear to reflect the author's practice (e.g., Hugh Broughton--or his printer--uses both "yeares" and "yeres" in the same verse), I have retained the original spellings. Achieving a common, consistent spelling was not universally thought a significant achievement until the eighteenth century. One important Renaissance printer, for example, spelled his name variously as John (or Iohn or Jhon) Day, Daye, and Daie.

[2] Fry presents the following lines as a parable of antiquity quoted by Zophar.

[3] "Verses 2 and 3 should come after verse 26 of this 41st chapter. As they are palced by some error of an old copier, they break the sense of the address, and have no meaning. I therefore restore them to their original position at the end of the description of the Leviathan." Fenton's note, p. 46

PART THREE:
A JOB BIBLIOGRAPHY

> In the fulness of his sufficiency he
> shall be in straits: every hand of the
> wicked shall come upon him.
>
> 20.22 (King James Version)

To illustrate the differences among the following translations, I have selected a passage which, although apparently unremarkable, has an essential ambiguity in the King James Version. Despite that ambiguity, the extraordinary influence of the Authorized Version becomes apparent in the persistence of its language, imagery, and rhetoric, despite occasional shifts of syntax, in many subsequent translations. Even those translators who attempt to clarify the passage appear to find themselves locked into that language and imagery, dealing as much with the KJV as with the original sources. In fact, between 1611 and 1900 the King James Version had become not only one of the sources but perhaps the most important one for all translations of *Job* into English. To provide some perspective on these versions, I have also included the Hebrew, Greek, and Latin sources, as well as five contemporary translations.

Unlike such verses as 13.15 and 19.25, *Job* 20.22 has never become the focus of serious doctrinal debate. Part of a passage in which Zophar describes the plight of the sinful, this verse lies among a catalogue of punishments which will visit sinners. Although the King James Version of the first half of the verse, with its contrast between fullness and constriction, offers a nicely rhetorical balance, the second half seems unnecessarily repetitive. And the Authorized Version also appears a bit ambiguous. After all, who are the wicked? And why will they attack the sinner? As early as 1657 Edward Leigh's *Annotations on Five Poetical Books of the Old Testament* recognized the problems with this passage. One of only two verses that Leigh comments on in chapter 20, his attempt at a clarification falls victim to his reliance on the ambiguous phrasing of the King James. After citing various authorities, he concludes, "The Spirit of God speaks according to their apprehension, they lookt for a fulness of sufficiency in the creatures" (13).

Before 1611 translators focused primarily on the sinner. Relying primarily on the language of the Vulgate, they emphasized the sorrow that would befall him. The Great Bible of 1539 added a suggestion of charity to the passage, reinforcing the irony of the contrast between material success and physical trials. With the Geneva Bible (1560) the source of the sorrow appears in an assailant, the hand of the wicked, in a Calvinist image re-emphasized by Thoedore Beza in 1589. Attempts to characterize the wicked (Sylvester's "spightful" in 1614, Purver's "Troublesome" in 1764, Garden's "miserable" in 1796) steadily gave way to attempts to explain the source of the danger. In 1648 the Catholic translation of Senault suggests "heaven" (1648), while in 1853 Ross offered an ambiguously dramatic "unseen hand." Most translators, however, located the source either in the wicked's own evil (e.g., Blackmore's "fellow-sinners" in 1700 and Stather's "miscreant" in 1860) or, especially among Victorians, in an almost Dickensian poetic justice as those whom the sinner has oppressed (20:19) rise to punish him, identifying them as "the poor" (Gray, 1836,37), the "needy" (Bolton, 1866), the "labouring" (Smith, 1876), the "wretched, toil worn" (Clarke, 1880), and the "suffering" (Smith, 1882). Some even make this connection explicit, arguing that the wicked are wicked because he has oppressed them (1716, Presbyter) or that they are "workmen" motivated by "spite" (Wright, 1883). By the end of the nineteenth century, Farrar Fenton even suggested that the sinner's suffering was primarily psychological based on the fear of what might happen.

Hebrew

כב במלאות שפקו יצר לו כל־יד עמל תבאנו

Latin (Vulgate)

Cum satiatis fuerit, arctabitur, aestuabit, et
omnis dolor irruet super eum.

The Jerusalem Bible (1966)

His abundance at its full, want seizes him,
misery descends on him in all its force.

The New English Bible (1970)

with every need satisfied his troubles begin
and the full force of hardship strikes him.

Marvin H. Pope, *Job* (*The Anchor Bible*) 1973)

At the peak of plenty stricken,
Every misery will befall him.

Stephen Mitchell, *The Book of Job* (1979)

At the height of his fortune he falls;
every disaster strikes him.

The Book of Job (Jewish Publication Society (5740/1980)
When he has all he wants, trouble will come
Misfortunes of all kinds will batter him.

BIBLIOGRAPHY

c. 1000 Aelfric. *Forbisne of Job*. Cotton MS. Veesp. D. XIV.

[Aelfric's Homily on Job, offering a paraphrase of the opening and closing of *Job* with occasional commentary, has been included in *Early English Homilies from the Twelfth Century MS. VESP. D. XIV.* ed Rubie D-N. Warner. Early English Text Society, O. S. No. 152. London: Kegan Paul, Trench, Trubner, 1917 (for 1915).]

c. 1388 John Wycliffe (with Nicholas de Hereford). MS.

[Early and late versions of the translations by Wycliffe and his followers appear side by side in Volume II of *The Holy Bible, Containing the Old and New Testaments, with the Apocryphal Books, in the Earliest English Versions Made from the Latin Vulgate by John Wycliffe and His Followers*, edited by the Rev. Josiah Forshall and Sir Frederic Madden (Oxford: University Press, 1850).]

Whan he shal be fulfild, he shal ben streyned, and brenne: and alle sorewe shal falle in to hym.

c. 1395 John Purvey. [The Later Wycliffe.] MS.

Whanne he is fillid, he schal be maad streit; he schal be hoot, and alle sorewe schal falle in on hym.

c. 1400 *Pety Job*. MSS.

[Three English paraphrases exist of the nine passages from *Job* used liturgically in the matins of the Office of the Dead. Douce MS. 322 in the Bodlean Library has a poetic version attributed to Richard of Hampole. It has been printed in *Twenty-Six Political and other Poems (Including "Petty Job)*, ed. Dr. J. Kail, pp. 120-143. Early English Text Society, O.S., No. 124. London: Kegan Paul, Trench, Trubner, 1904. The two prose versions are British Museum ADD. MS. 39574 and MS. Dd. 11, 82, ab 1420-30 AD at the University of Cambridge. The former appears in *The Wheatley Manuscript*, ed. Mabel Day, Early English Text Society, O. S. No. 155, pp. 59-64 (London: Humphrey Milford for Oxford University Press, 1921 for 1917), and the latter in *The Prymer or Lay Folks' Prayer Book*, ed. Henry Littlehales. Early English Text Society, O.S. No. 105 (London: Kegan Paul, Trench, Trubner, 1895).]

c. 1410 [Middle English Metrical Paraphrase of the Old Testament.] MS.

["A Middle English Metrical Paraphrase of the Old Testament," ed. Herbert Kalen and Urban Ohlander in *Goteborgs Hogskolas Arsskrift* 28:5 (1922) and in *Gothenburg Studies in English* 5 (1955), 11 (1960 [1961]), 16 (1963). In the style of the York cycle of plays, this paraphrase is drawn from biblical, apocryphal, and popular sources.]

c. 1473 *The Life of Job*. MS.

[This Middle English emblematic account of Job in rime-royal is based loosely on the biblical original with additional material from apocryphal and popular sources. Henry E. Huntington Library MS HM 140 (ff93b-96b). Reprinted in *Early English and Norse Studies Presented to Hugh Smith in Honour of His Sixtieth Birthday*, ed. Arthur Brown and Peter Foote. London: Methuen, 1963.]

1483 William Caxton. *The Golden Legend or Lives of the Saints.*

Westminster: William Caxton.

[Caxton's translated the prologue and epilogue from the *Legenda Aurea* by Jacobus de Voragine, the Archbishop of Genoa.]

1535 [The first printed Bible in English.] Miles Coverdale. *The Boke of Job* in *Biblia. The Bible: that is, the holy Scripture of the Olde and new Testament, faithfully and truly translated out of Douche and Latyn into Englishe*. ?Marburg: E. Cervicornus and J. Soter. [Coverdale used German {i.e., Douche or Dutch} and Latin sources to translate the poetical and prophetic works of the Hebrew Bible which he published together with William Tyndale's translation of the New Testament, Pentateuch, Jonah, and historical books through 2 Chronicles.]

Though he had plenteousnesse of every thinge, yet was he poore, & therfore he is but a wretch on every syde.

1537 [The Matthews Bible.] (John Rogers.) *The Byble, which is all the holy Scripture: in whych are contayned the Olde and Newe Testament, truly and purely translated into Englysh by Thomas Matthew*. ?Antwerp: for R[ichard] Grafton and E[dward] Whitchurch of London. [Tyndale's translation of the New Testament and *Genesis* to *2 Chronicles* with the remainder of the Hebrew Bible from Coverdale, was revised and edited, probably by John Rogers, often described as Tyndale's secretary.]

Though he had plenteousnesse of every thynge/yet was he poore/and therfore he is but a wretch on every syde.

1539 [The Great Bible or Cranmer's Bible.] *The Byble in Englyshe, that is to saye the content of all the holy scrypture, both of the olde and newe testament, truly translated after the veryte of the Hebrue and Greke textes, by the dylygent studye of dyuerse excellent learned men, expert in the forsayde tonges*. London: Rychard Grafton and Edward Whitchurch. [Despite the title, this was essentially Myles Coverdale's revision of Matthew's Bible.]

Whan he had plenteousnesse of every thyng; yet was he pore though he was helped on every syde.

1539 Richard Taverner. *The Most Sacred Bible, Whiche is the holy scripture, conteyning the old and new testament, translated into English, and newly recognised with great diligence after most faythful exemplars*. London: John Byddell for Thomas Barthlet. [Taverner, a layman admired for his Greek scholarship, revised the Matthews Bible, especially the New Testament.] London: John Byddell for Thomas Barthlet.

Though he hadde foyson of everye thynge, yet was he poore, and therfore he was but a wretche on every syde.

1560 [The Geneva Bible.] *The Bible and Holy Scriptures. conteyned in the Olde and Newe Testament. Translated according to the Ebrue and Greke, and conferred with the best translations in diuers languages*. Geneva: Rouland Hall. [William Whittington, with the help of such associates in Geneva as Anthony Gilby and Thomas Sampson edited this revision of Whittington's New Testament and a complete revision of the Hebrew Bible, especially those books which Tindale had not translated, based on Hebrew sources.]

When he shalbe filled with his abundancew, he shalbe in peine, & the hand of all the wicked shal assaile him.

1568 [The Bishops Bible] *The. holie. Bible. conteyning the olde Testament and the newe.* Jugge. London: R. Jugge. [Archbishop Matthew Parker supervised this complete revision of the Great Bible, based partly on a comparison with Latin Versions of the Hebrew Bible translated directly from the Hebrew by Sancted Pagninus in 1528 and Sebastian Munster in 1539.]

When he had plenteousnesse of every thyng, yet was he poore, though he was helped on every side.

1569 W. Samuel. *An Abridgement of all the Canonical Books of the Olde Testament, written in Sternholds meter.* London: William Seres.

[Each chapter is reduced to eight lines with no exact equivalence. Chapter 20 reads

When Iob had doon, then Suphar spake,
 and telles the wickeds lot:
How that his gain shall home again
 whiche he uniustly got.
And having fore yet raking more,
 still saying he is poore:
He shall not scape the wrath of God,
 when he on him doth loure.]

1589 Theodore Beza. *Job Expounded by Theodore Beza Partly in Manner of a Commentary, Partly in Manner of a Paraphrase. Faithfully Translated out of Latine into English.* Cambridge: John Leggatt.

For after hee hath scratched and scrapt together so much, as might satisfie the most greedie and covetous wretch, that liveth upon the earth, then shall the wicked set upon him on all sides, in so much that he shall be brought into great streites.

1609, 1610 [The Doway Version] *The Holie Bible faithfully translated into English, out of the authentical Latin. Diligently conferred with the Hebrew, Greeke, and other Editions in diuers languages.* Doway [Douai]: Lavrence Kellam. [The Roman Catholic translation of the Hebrew Bible from the vulgate by the English College at Douai, primarily Cardinal Allen, Gregory Martin, and Richard Bristow. Together with the New Testament published at Rheims, this translation became known as the Doway-Rheims Version and, with a major revision by Bishop Richard Challoner in 1750, represented the standard Catholic translation until the twentieth century.]

When he shal be filled, he shal be straytened, he shal burne, and al sorow shal falle upon him.

1610 Hugh Broughton. *IOB. To the King. A Colon-Agrippina Studie of One Moneth, for the Metricall Translation: But of Many Yeres, for Ebrew Difficulties.* London.

When he hath filled him with sufficiency, then he shallbe distrest: ech hand of injuried will come upon him.

1611 [The King James or Authorized Version] *The Holy Bible, Conteyning the Old Testament and the New: Newly Translated out of the Originall tongues: & with the former Translations diligently compared and reuised, by his Maiesties speciall Commandement.* London: Robert Barker.

In the fulnesse of his sufficiencie, he shalbe in straites: every hand of the wicked shall come upon him.

1614 Josuah Sylvester. *A Divine & True Tragi-Comedy; Iob Triumphant in his Triall: or The Historie of His Heroicall Patience, in a Measured Metaphrase*. In The Parliament of Vertues Royal. Second Series. London.

Nay: in his Ruffe, and at his Greatest Height
He shall be stocked in full many a Strait:
Continuall Hazards shall him round enring;
Each spightful hand shall have at him a fling.

1624 R. H. *Iob's Pietie, or the Patience of a Perfect Man*. London.

[A very broad attempt to present "Iobes Conflict by way of Dialogue with a good deal of shifting, adding, and omiting text. No exact parallel.]

1624 Francis Quarles. *Iob Militant: with Meditations Divine and Morall.* London: Felix Kyngston for George Winder.

Soak't with extorted plenty, others shall
Squeeze him, and leave him dispossest of all.

1632 Francis Quarles. *Divine Fancies: Digested into Epigrammes, Meditations, and Observations*. London: M.F. for J. Marriot.

[Poetical paraphrase of selected sections of the text. No exact parallel.]

1638 George Sandys. "A Paraphrase upon Iob." In *A Paraphrase upon the Divine Poems*. London: At the Bell.

He, in the pride of his full Glory, shall
To earth descend; and by the wicked fall.

1640 George Abbott. *The Whole Book of Iob Paraphrased, or Made Easie for Any to Understand.* London: Edward Griffin, for Henry Overton.

Then, when he takes himselfe to be in his prime and hight of happinesse, shall hee be brought to the greatest indigency and want, God shall let loose every wicked unconscionable man to molest and impoverish him, like as aforetime he himselfe hath done to others.

1648 [Anonymous.] *A Paraphrase upon Job written in French by J. F. Senault, Father of the Oratory, and dedicated to the Cardinal of RICHLIEU*. London: Robert Bostock.

Since his good fortune must be so fatall to him, and that he shall be never neerer his ruine, than when he is mounted on the top of his happinesse, I would he were happy that he might be presently miserable, and that heaven might discharge upon him its anger, and stick him with all its thunders.

1652 Thomas Manley Iun, Esq. *The Affliction and Deliverance of the Saints: or, the Whole Booke of Iob Composed into English Heroicall Verse, Metaphrastically.* London: W.H., for John Tey.

In all the fulnesse of his pride, and height
Of his possessions, he shall be in streight:
The wicked shall oppresse him with their force;
And every hand shall vexe him in their course.

1657 *[Anonymous.] The Pattern of Patience, in the Example of Holy Job: A Paraphrase upon the Whole Book.* London: Joseph Cornford.

[A reissue of the 1648 Senault with a new title.]

1657 Theodore Haak. *The Dutch Annotations upon the whole Bible: Or, all the Holy Canonical Scriptures of the Old and New Testament, together with, and according to their own Translation of all the Text: as both the one and the other were ordered and appointed by the Synod of Dort, 1618, and published by Authority, 1637. Now faithfully communicated to the use of Great Britain, in English.* London: Henry Hills for John Rothwell, Joshua Kirton, and Richard Tomlins.

When his sufficiency shall be full. [i.e. when he shall have wealth and riches enough, to live a happy and contented life here.] He shall be afraid: all (or every) hand of the afflicted shall come upon him. [i.e. all the poor which were bereaved and undone by him, shall seek and endeavour to recover their own.]

1661 Arthur Brett. *Patientia Victrix: or the Book of Job, in Lyrick Verse.* London: Richard Gammon

When he shall seem with all things to abound
He destitute of all things shall be found;
And he shall be
An *Axine* Sea
Expos'd to all kinds of storms,
Mater'a prima to all luckless *Forms*:

1679 Symon Patrick. *The Book of Job Paraphras'd*. London: E. Flesher for R. Royston.

The greater fuylness you can suppose him to regain of worldly Goods, the more he shall be distressed; for the hand of every man whom he hath afflicted shall lay hold on him to demand satisfaction.

1685 William Clark. *The Grand Tryal: or Poetical Exercitations upon the Book of Job*. Edinburgh: Heir of Andrew Anderson.

Even in the hight and affluence of all
Worldly delites, and pleasure, in the prime
Of his enjoyments, in the pruning time,
Of all his projects, when his life appears,
Entituled to many happy years,
When he doth triumph in his high-swoln paunch,
Then shall he be destroyed, root and branch:
Then shall his fellow-sinners fall upon him,
Kill him, and so there shall be no more on him.

1700 Sir Richard Blackmore. *A Paraphrase on the Book of Job*. London: Awnsham and John Churchill.

When he shall most with Power and Wealth abound,
With Guards encompass'd, and with Empire crown'd,
Then suddain Mischiefs shall his Seat surround.
Fierce Bands of Spoilers shall his Lands invade,
And far away his Wealth shall be convey'd.

1700 R. P. *The Book of Job in Meeter*. London: Thomas Parkhurst.

[Poetic translation of selected sections, rearranged. R.P. does not include 20:22.]

1706 Daniel Baker. *The History of Job: A Sacred Poem. In Five Books*. London: Robert Clavel.

[No exact parallel.]

1716 [A Presbyter of the Church of England]. *A Short Paraphrase of the*

Book of Job. London: S. Keble.
In the fulnesse of his sufficiency, [and riches] he shall be in streights: every hand of the wicked [he had oppressed,] shall come upon him, [to make him restore their goods.]

1719 Edward Young. *A Paraphrase on Part of the Book of Job*. London: Jacob Tonson.
[Mostly God's speech. No exact parallel.]

1726 William Thompson. *A Poetical Paraphrase of Part of the Book of Job in Imitation of the Style of Milton*. London: Thomas Worrall.
[Chapters 40-42. No exact parallel.]

1727 William Broome. "Parts of the 38th and 39th Chapters of Job: A Paraphrase." In *Poems on Several Occasions*. London: Bernard Lintot.
[Extensively revised for a 1739 edition. No exact parallel.]

1727 Edward Wells. *An Help for the more Easy and Clear Understanding of the Scriptures*. Oxford Theater: William Wells; London: J. Knapton.
In the fulness of his Sufficiency he shall be in Straits: every hand of the Afflicted *by him* shall come upon him *to do themselves what Justice they can*.

1731 John Husbands. "Job, Chap. the 3rd." In *A Miscellany of Poems by Several Hands*. Oxford: Leon Lichfield.
[No exact parallel.]

1734 *[Anonymous.] The Complaint of Job: A Poem*. London: Richard Wellington.
[Portions of Job's speeches. No exact parallel.]

1748 Daniel Bellamy the Younger. *A Paraphrase on the Sacred History, or Book of Job*. London: J. Hart.
Tho' we should suppose him to abound once more with Wealth and Power; yet then he'll be surrounded with unexpected Mischiefs; for every one whom he has oppress'd will seize upon him, and demand Atonement for their Wrongs. In the Midst of all his sensual Enjoyments, God himself will torment him with the most direful Effects of his Divine Vengeance; which, whilst he imagines himself most secure, shall pour down like an impetuous Torrent on his devoted Head.

1750 Richard Challoner, Bishop of Debra. *The Holy Bible, Translated from the Latin Vulgate*. ?Dublin. [Revision of Doway]
When he shall be filled, he shall be straitened, he shall burn, and every sorrow shall fall upon him.

1750 Eugenio [?Thomas Beach]. *Age in Distress: or, Job's Lamentation for his Children*. London.
[A blank verse lament, dedicated to the Rev. Dr. Young, *Age in Distress* incorporates some lines from *Job*, but has only a peripheral connection with the original. No exact parallel.]

1750 Walter Hodge. *Elihu: or, an Enquiry into the principal scope and design of the Book of Job*. London: James Hodges.
[This discussion of Elihu's point of view offers a paraphrase of Chapters 32-37. No exact parallel.]

1752 Leonard Chappelow. *A Commentary on the Book of Job, In Which Is Inserted the Hebrew Text and English Translation: with a Paraphrase*. 2 Volumes.

Cambridge: J. Bentham

When in any of our negotiations we joyn the labour of our hands to our best premeditated counsels: This is the surest method we can take to crown our endeavours with success. These are the most probable means we can pursue, not only to advance our interest in the world, and raise ourselves to the highest eminencies of fortune; but to enjoy likewise the plentiful fruits of our industry. The very reverse appears if you view the man's circumstances. *In the fulness of his sufficiency he shall be in straits*. In the height of his prosperity and affluence; in the multitude of his temporal possessions; his change is so great, and so sudden, as to reduce him to poverty and distress, and to render him extremely miserable. Like a man who *strikes hands with another*, to establish, as he thinks, an advantageous contract: and yet finds all his prudence and sagacity entirely defeated.--He must then cease to triumph. All his state and grandeur fall: His wealth and fortunes decay: His plenty and prosperity disappear. And what is worse, *All the power of sorrow shall come upon him*. The scene of his joy and transport is altered. In their place follows, (like a strong, invading Army) a rapid, quick succession of anxiety. One trouble presses hard upon another. They give him no time for refreshment. his calamities are so various, and of such a complicated nature; the weight of them so grievous and burdensom; that he hath no strength to resist. All that he can do, is, to lament his misfortune, and groan under the heavy yoke, without any hopes of recovery.

1753 Ralph Erskine. *Job's Hymns: Or, A Book of Songs upon the Book of Job*. Glasgow: J. Newland.

[100 songs in common meter. No exact parallel.]

1756 Thomas Heath. *An Essay Towards a New English Version of the Book of Job from the Original Hebrew*. London: A. Millar.

In the fullness of his sufficiency he shall be in straits; all kinds of misery shall come upon him.

1760 William Langhorne. *Job. A Poem in Three Books*. London: R. Griffiths.

This was the Man of Pride, whose Tyrant Pow'r
Rul'd with a Rod of Steel the short-liv'd Hour;
Crush'd with unpitying Rage the friendless Soul,
That Floods of Wealth might in his Channel roll.
Sure the foul Flood with bitter Streams shall flow
    To fill th'envenom'd Cup of ceaseless Woe.
    Their unabating Wrath the Heav'ns shall rain,
    And he shall sink amid the Racks of Pain.
    High-brandish'd, Horror's Sword shall plunge him down,
    And Realms of Night the kindred Spirit own.

1763 Lawrence Holden. *A Paraphrase on the Books of Job, Psalms, Proverbs, and Ecclesiastes*. London: M. Reily for C. Henderson.

In the height of his prosperity he shall meet with the greatest difficulties; and, as in an instant, be unawares croud in upon and thoroughly plunder him.

1764 Anthony Purver. *A New and Literal Translation of All the Books of the Old and New Testament*. London: W. Richardson and S. Clark.

When his Sufficiency is fullest, he is streightened; every Hand of the Troublesome comes on him.

1771 Thomas Scott. *The Book of Job, in English Verse; Translated from the Original Hebrew*. London: W. Strahan.

In the full season of exulting pride,
Distress shall straiten him on every side:

1779 [Anonymous.] *A Paraphrase of the Thirty-Eighth Chapter of the Book of Job*. London: J. Parker

[No exact parallel.]

1782 Christopher Pitt. *Job*, Chap. III; Job, Chap. XXV Paraphrased. *Poetical Works of Christopher Pitt*. Edinburgh: Apollo Press.

[No exact parallel.]

1790 Rev. Job Orton, S.T.P. *A Short and Plain Exposition of the Old Testament*. Vol. IV. Shrewsbury: J. and W. Eddowes. [Edited by Robert Gentleman.]

In the fulness of his sufficiency he shall be in straits; *the greater abundance he has gained, the more shall he be distressed by his own conscience*: every hand of the wicked shall come upon him, *being obliged to restore to some and being plundered by others*.

1795 Richard Devens. *A Paraphrase on Some Parts of the Book of Job in Verse*. Boston: Samuel Hall.

[A poetic version, primarily of Job's and God's speeches.]

1796 Charles Garden. *An Improved Version Attempted of the Book of Job; a Poem*. Oxford: J. Cooke.

In the fulness of his exultation, he shall be distressed;
Every hand of the miserable shall come upon him.

1796 William Carpenter. *A Poetical Paraphrase on the Book of Job*. Chittenden: William Carpenter.

1797 William Mason. *Ode on Wisdom; or, the Twenty-Eight Chapter of the Book of Job Attempted in Lyrical Verse*. Privately printed.

[No exact parallel.]

1799 [John Mead Ray]. *A Revised Translation and Interpretation of the Sacred Scriptures after the Eastern Manner, from concurrent authorities of the critics, interpreters, and commentators, copies and versions: showing the inspired writings contain the seeds of valuable sciences*. London: G. Robinson and Company.

when his sufficiency is fullest he shall be in straits; every hand of the troublesome shall come upon him.

1800 Valentine Lumley Bernard. *A Sacred Poem in Four Books. Being a Paraphrase on the Book of Job*. Norwich: Stevenson & Matchett.

[No exact parallel.]

1805 The Right Rev. Joseph Stock, Bishop of Killalla. *The Book of Job: Metrically Arranged according to the Masora and newly Translated into English*. Bath: Richard Crutwell.

In the fulness of his hand-clapping shall a strait be
on him,
All the powers of mischief shall overtake him.

1808 Charles Thomson. *The Old Covenant commonly called The Old Testament: Translated from the Septuagint.* Philadelphia: Jane Aitkin.
In the fullness of his sufficiency he shall be afflicted, and all manner of distress shall come upon him.

1810 Elizabeth Smith. *The Book of Job; Translated from the Hebrew.* Bath: Richard Cruttwell.
While clapping his hands in the fulness of joy,
tribullation comes on him,
Every hand shall bring him affliction.

1812 John Mason Good. *The Book of Job, Literally Translated from the Original Hebrew, and Restored to Its Natural Arrangement.* London: Black, Parry & Company.
Amidst the fulness of his belly shall he be in straits;
Every branch of misery shall come upon him.

1816 William M'Even. "A Paraphrase on the Book of Job." In John Wilson's *The Polar Star and Centre of Comfort.* New York: James Sharan.
[Primarily the prologue and God's speech. No exact parallel.]

1818 John Bellamy. *The Holy Bible, Newly Translated from the Original Hebrew.* London: Longman, Hurst, Rees, Orme and Brown.
In the fulness of his abundance distress will be before
him: every hand of the wicked shall come upon him.

1825 George Hunt. *The Book of Job. Translated from the Hebrew.* Bath: Wood & Cunningham.
In the plentitude of his abundance,
He shall be straitened;
Every hand of the oppressed shall come upon him.

1825 Abraham Rowley. *Ten Chapters on the Book of Job.* Boston: J. H. A. Frost.
[No exact parallel.]

1827 Rev. John Fry. *A New Translation and Exposition of the Book of Job.* London: James Duncan.
With both his hands full, shall he be in want;
Every lot of calamity shall befal him.

1827 George R. Noyes. *An Amended Version of the Book of Job.* Cambridge, Massachusetts: Hilliard and Brown.
In the fulness of his abundance he shall be brought low;
Every kind of misery shall come upon him.

1833 Noah Webster. *The Holy Bible, Containing the Old and New Testaments, in the Common Version, With Amendments of the Language.* New Haven: Durrie & Peck.
In the fullness of his sufficiency he shall be in straits: every hand of the wicked shall come upon him.

1836, 37 Rev. John Hamilton Gray. *A New Version of the Book of Job.* Edinburgh: Thomas Clark. 2 vols.
In the fulness of his superfluity he feeleth straitened,

And the oppression of the poor weigheth him down.

1837 Samuel Lee. *The Book of the Patriarch Job, Translated from the Original Hebrew*. London: James Duncan.
In the fulness of his sufficiency he shall be distressed;
the whole force of the wretched shall come in upon him.

1838 [Mrs. Walter Birch]. *Job; or the Gospel Preached to the Patriarchs: Being a Paraphrase of the Last Ten Chapters of the Book of Job*. London: J.G. & F. Rivington
[No exact parallel.]

1838 Charles Wellbeloved. *The Holy Bible, A new Translation: Part III*. London: Smallfield and Sons.
In the fulness of his exultation, distress shall
befall him;
The hand of every miserable man shall come upon him.

1839 Thomas Wemyss. *Job and His Times, or a Picture of the Patriarchal Age . . . a New Version of that . . . Poem*. London: Jackson and Walford.
Amidst the fulness of his tyranny he shall be in straits;
All manner of distress shall come upon him.

1841 Rev. Alfred Jenour. *The Books of the Old Testament (Or, Covenant) Translated from the Hebrew and Chaldee*. London
[Volume II, *Job*, was apparently the only section published.]
In the fulness of his exultation he shall be distressed;
trouble of every kind shall come upon him.

1844 Albert Barnes. *Notes, Critical, Illustrative, and Practical on the Book of Job: with a New Translation*. London: Wiley & Putnam. 2 vols.
In the fulness of his abundance he shall be in want;
The whole power of wretchedness shall come upon him.

1844 Sir Lancelot Charles Lee Brenton, Bart. *The Septuagint Version of the Old Testament according to the Vatican Text*. Volume II. London: Samuel Bagster & Sons.
But when he shall seem to be just satisfied, he shall be straitened; and all distress shall come upon him.

1846 Henry Tattam, Archdeacon of Bedford. *The Ancient Coptic Version of the Book of Job the Just*. London: William Straker.
When he thinketh that he is complete, he shall be afflicted; and all distress shall come upon him.

1848 Dr. M. Budinger. *The Way of Faith; or, the Abridged Bible; containing Selections from All the Books of Holy Writ*. Translated by David Asher. London: Samuel Bagster and Sons.
[The prologue, parts of Job's speeches, God's speech, and the epilogue translated from the fifth edition of Budinger's German version for Jewish families.]

1852 [Sarah Hustler Fox.] *A Metrical Version of the Book of Job*. London: C. Gilpin.
In fulness of sufficiency
He even then shall straitened be;--

And wickedness in every form,
On every hand, shall work his harm.

1853 [5614] Isaac Leeser. *The Twenty-Four Books of the Holy Scriptures: Carefully Translated according to the Massoretic Text, on the Basis of the English Version, After the Best Jewish Authorities*. Philadelphia: Stereotyped by L. Johnson.
In the fulness of his abundance will distress assail him:
every hand of (those he) troubled will come against him.

1853 F.W.L. Ross. "The Book of Job." In *The History of Joseph and the Book of Job: Episodical Portions of a Poem, On the Principal Events Contained in the Holy Scriptures, from the Creation to the Ascension*. London: T. Blower.
[Ross abbreviates the friends' comments and expands Job's. The closest passage would be the following:
Surely no rest his troubl'd soul shall know!
An unseen hand shall strike the sinner low!]

1855 Levi M. Arnold. *The History of Job; A Tale Illustrative of the Dispensations of the Almighty; Re-Constructed in the English Language to accord with the Long Lost Original Arabic.* Washington City, D.C.: Samuel Reeve.
In the fulness of his boasting he shall be afflicted,
And every kind of distress shall fall upon him.

1856 James Lillie. *Literal Translation of the First and Second Chapters of Job*. New York.
[No exact parallel.]

1858 Rev. Carteret Priaulx Carey. *The Book of Job*. London: Wertheim, MacIntosh, and Hunt.
In the fulness of his abundance he shall be distressed;
The hand of every wretch shall be upon him.

1858 [Alexander Vance.] *The Authorised Version of the Old Testament Scriptures; Revised, Condensed, Corrected, and Reformed*. London: Holyoake and Company.
[Reorganizes AV into two parts: I (History and Job's Friends); II (Job's Psalms.)]
In the fulness of his sufficiency he shall be in straits: every hand of the wicked shall come upon him.

1859 Francis Patrick Kenrick, Archbishop of Baltimore. *The Book of Job and the Prophets. Translated from the Vulgate.* Baltimore: Kelly, Hedian & Piet.
When he shall be filled he shall be straitened, he shall burn, and
every sorrow shall fall upon him.

1860 Rev. H. Bolton. *Thoughts on Spiritual Impressions, with a Separate Notice of Swedenborgism; To Which Is Added the Book of Job, Epitomised in Blank Verse*. London: Simpkin, Marshall, & Company.
[Selected passages from the text broadly interpreted. The closest passage would be the following:
The wicked's triumph hath been ever short,
The hypocrite's a moment; and his fall
From zenith to the dunghill comes to naught.]

[1860] Lieutenant-Colonel W.C. Stather. *The Book of Job; in English Verse. Translated*

from the original Hebrew. Bath: Binns & Godwin.
'Mid teeming plenty, shall arise distress,
And every miscreant shall lift his hand t'oppress.

1860 The Earl of Winchilsea. *The Poem of the Book of Job Done into English Verse*. London: Smith, Elder and Company.
In the fulness of his confidence
Straitened his line shall be;
The hand of every wicked man
To smite him shall be free.

1861 Abraham Benisch. *Jewish School and Family Bible*. London: Longmans and Company. Vol. 2 [The *Jewish School and Family Bible* was published in four volumes between 1851 and 1861.]
In the fulness of his sufficiency he shall be in straits:
every hand of the wicked shall come upon him.

1861 Rev. John Selby Watson. "Job, or Patience." In *Sons of Strength Wisdom Patience*. London: Longman, Green, Longman, & Roberts.
When he seems to have an abundance, he shall be reduced to want; those whom he has oppressed and ill-treated shall involve him in destruction.

1862 A.B. Davidson. *A Commentary, Grammatical and Exegitical, on the Book of Job; with a Translation*. London: Williams and Norgate. Vol. 1.
[Davidson only published the first volume, chapters 1-14, of his translation. No exact parallel.]

1862 Leicester Ambrose Sawyer. *The Holy Bible: Translated and Arranged, with Notes*. Vol III. The Hebrew Poets. Boston: Walker, Wise, and Company.
in the fulness of his abundance he shall be straitened; every laboring
hand shall come upon him

1863 Robert Young. *The Holy Bible, Containing the Old and new Covenants, Literally and Idiomatically Translated out of the Original Languages*. London: A. Fullarton & Company.
In the fulness of his sufficiency he is straitened,
Every perverse hand meeteth him.

1864 Henry W. Adams. *The Book of Job in Poetry; or, A Song in the Night*. New York: Robert Craighead.
When fulness of abundance on him waits,
Then he shall be reduced to dreadful straits.

1864 Frank Chance. *The Book of Job*. London: Hamilton, Adams. [Translation of Hermann Hedwig Bernard.]
In the fulness of his abundance shall he be put to straits;
Every plague of the wretched shall come upon him.

1864 J. M. Rodwell. *The Book of Job*. London: Williams and Norgate.
In the fulness of his abundance shall he be straitened,
The full force of trouble shall come upon him.

1865 Samuel Sharpe. *The Hebrew Scripture: A Revision of the Authorized English Old Testament*. Vol. II. London: Whitfield, Green & Company.
In the fulness of his abundance he will be distressed;

Every hand of the miserable will come upon him.

1866 [Anonymous.] *The Book of Job*. Boston: Printed for the editor by G.C. Rand and Avery.

In the fulness of sufficiency, he shall be in straits:
No calamity of wretchedness shall he escape.

1866 Rev. Francis Bolton. *Biblical Commentary on the Book of Job*. Edinburgh: T. and T. Clark. [A translation of F. Delitsch.] Clark's Foreign Theological Library, Series 4. Vols 10,11.

In the fulness of his need it shall be strait with him,
Every hand of the needy shall come upon him.

1867 Joseph Smith, Jr. *The Holy Scriptures, Translated and Corrected by the Spirit of Revelation*. Plano, Illinois: Church of Jesus Christ of Latter-Day Saints. Joseph Smith, I. L. Rogers, E. Robinson, Publishing Committee.

In the fullness of his sufficiency he shall be in straits; every hand of the wicked shall come upon him.

1869 Rev. John Noble Coleman. *The Book of Job. Translated from the Hebrew*. London: James Nisbet.

In the fulness of his abundance he shall be distressed,
Every branch of misery shall come upon him.

1869 Henry John Marten. *A Metrical Study of the Book of Job*. London: Hodder and Staughton.

When most exalted, he shall be in straits;
Foreclosing misery shall weigh him down.

1869 William Meikle. *The Book of Job in Metre*. Falkirk: William Meikle.

He surely shall never have peace in his mind,
Nor save of the thing which he chiefly inclined.

1872 A. Elzas. *The Book of Job*. London: Trubner and Company.

In the fulness of his abundance he shall be in fear,
Lest misery come upon him from every side.

c. 1874 Tayler Lewis. *The Book of Job: A Rhythmical Version*. New York: Scribner, Armstrong & Company.

In the fullness of his wealth, his straits begin;
When every hand of toil against him comes.

1875 Oliver S[pencer] Halsted. *The Book Called Job. From the Hebrew*. Newark, New Jersey: Jennings & Hardham.

In fulness of redundance of him, it shall be narrow to him; every hand of wretched comes upon him.

1876 Julia Evelina Smith. *The Holy Bible . . . Translated Literally from the Original Tongues*. Hartford, Connecticut: American Publishing Company, 1876.

In the fulness of his abundance it shall be pressed to him: every laboring hand shall come to him.

1877 Henry Cowles. *The Book of Job*. New York: D. Appleton.

At the point of his full sufficiency, he is in straits:
every hand of the wretched comes down on him.

1878 Rossiter W. Raymond. *The Book of Job*. New York: D. Appleton.

His want amid his wealth shall grow
While victims' hands of long ago
Shall reach to strike him, blow on blow.

1879 William Kelly. *Notes on the Book of Job, with a New Version.* London: G. Morrish.
In the fulness of his superfluity he is straitened,
Every hand of a wretch shall be upon him.

1879 John [Medley], Bishop of Fredericton and Metropolitan of Canada. *The Book of Job.* St John, New Brunswick: J. & A. McMillan.
In the fulness of his abundance he shall be in straits,
All the power of trouble shall come upon him.

1880 Henry James Clarke. *The Book of Job: A Metrical Translation.* London: Hodder & Stoughton.
Amidst his overflowing affluence
He finds himself in straits; upon him comes
The hand of every wretched, toil-worn man.

1880 Samuel Cox. *A Commentary on the Book of Job with a Translation.* London: Kegan Paul and Company.
In the fulness of his abundance shall he be straitened;
Trouble of every kind shall come upon him.

1880 Rabbi Hermann Gollancz. *The Holy Bible, Containing the Pentateuch, the Hagiographa, and the Former and Latter Prophets; Translated out of the Original Tongues; and with the Former Translation Diligently Compared and Revised. For Jewish Families.* London: John G. Murdock & Company; L. Schaap.
In the fullness of his sufficiency he shall be in straits:
every hand of the wicked shall come upon him.

1880 Arthur Malet. *The Book of Job in Blank Verse.* Bridgwater: Ashcott.
Even in his fulness he shall be in straits,
Beset on every side by wicked men.

1880 G. Cecil White. *The Discipline of Suffering. Nine Short Readings on the History of Job.* Part II (The Conversation in Blank Verse). London: W. Skeffington & Son.
[No exact equivalence in White's highly abbreviated blank verse dialogues with the comforters, Elihu, and God. The closest would be these lines:
. . . wicked men soon lose prosperity,
And all their glory fadeth as a flower.]

1881 Rev. Cornelius Van Dyck. *Renderings of the Recent Arabic Version of the Book of Job Which Vary from the English Version.* New Haven, Connecticut.
the hand of every wicked one (miserable one) shall come upon him

1882 Henrietta Emily Benson. "Thoughts on the Book of Job." In *Life and Love: Records of the Lord's Gracious Dealings with Henrietta Emily Benson* . Second Edition. Hertford: Stephen Austin and Sons.
[No exact parallel.]

1882 J. Frederick Smith, trans. *Commentary on the Book of Job with Translation.* Theological Translation Fund Library, Vol. 28. [Translation of Dr.

Georg Heinrich August von Ewald.] London: Williams and Norgate.
in his richest abundance it is strait to him
every hand of the suffering overtaketh him

1883 G. H. Bateson Wright. *The Book of Job. A New . . . Revised Translation*. London: Williams and Norgate.
When his satisfaction is complete, he shall feel want,
Spite all the hands of the workmen bring him.

1885 [The Revised Version] *The Holy Bible . . . translated out of the original tongues: being the revised version set forth A.D. 1611 compared with the most ancient authorities and revised.*
Oxford: University Press.
In the fulness of his sufficiency he shall be in straits:
The hand of every one that is in misery shall come upon him.

1885 Helen Spurrell. *A Translation of the Old Testament Scriptures from the Original Hebrew*. London: James Nisbet.
In the fulness of his sufficiency shall he be in straits;
Every hand shall bring trouble.

1886 J[ohn] N[elson] Darby. *The "Holy Scriptures" Commonly Called The Old Testament. A New Translation from the Hebrew original. Part III. Job to Canticles.*
In the fulness of his sufficiency he shall be in straits; every hand of the wretched shall come upon him.

1889A. F. G. and W. M. T. [Henry Frederick Gibbons and William M. Thompson.] *The Book of Job*. [Translation of Ernest Renan.] London: W. M. Thomson.
In full prosperity he shall come to grief;
The blows of misfortune shall fall upon him.

1889 George H. Gilbert. *The Poetry of Job*. Chicago: A. C. McClurg.
While his riches are full, he is straightened;
Every sufferer's hand comes upon him.

1891 [James Davie.] *The Poetical Books of the Bible Rendered According to their Literary Structure*. Edinburgh.
Ay, midst his fulness straits hath come
And wicked's woes now him assail;

1891 John F. Genung. *The Epic of the Inner Life; Being the Book of Job Translated Anew*. London: James Clarke & Company.
In the fullness of his abundance shall he be straitened;
Upon him shall come every hand of the wretched.

1893 Talmid. *Poetical Parts of the Old Testament Translated into English Rhythm*. Edinburgh: James Thin.
Mid his full striking, trouble is for him;
Each hand of misery will come to him.

1894 Rev. Hiram Mason Sydenstricker. *The Epic of the Orient: An Original Poetical Rendering of the Book of Job*. Hartford, Connecticut: Student Publishing Company.
His richest stores shall bring him straits,

And every wicked hand shall scourge.

1895 Emile Joseph Dillon. *The Sceptics of the Old Testament (Job, Koheleth, Agur)*. London: Isbister and Company.

In the fulness of his abundance he shall be in straits,
Every hand of the wicked shall come upon him:

1897 Kaufmann Kohler. "*The Testament of Job*, an Essene Midrash on the Book of Job." In *Semitic Studies in Memory of Dr. Alexander Kohut*, ed. G[eorge] A[lexander] Kohut. Berlin: S. Calvary.

[The first English translation of the pseudipigraphic *Testament of Job*. Kohler translated Cardinal Mai's edition of the work in his *Scriptorum veterum nova collectio a Vaticanis codicibus edita* (Rome: Typis Vaticanis, 1833), an edition based on a twelfth century Vatican folio.]

1897 Ralph Sadler. *The Book of Ayub: Known in the West as Job*. London: Sheppard & St. John.

In the fulness of his redundancy he shall be in straits;
Every hand of toil shall come upon him.

1897 John Tattersall. *The Poem of Job, Rendered into English Metre*. London: Bernard Quaritch.

When he is full of goods he then shall fail,
The hate of wretched men shall make him quail;

1898 Otis Cary. *The Man Who Feared God for Nought, Being a Rhythmical Version of the Book of Job*. London: Elliot Stock and Printed at the Okayama Orphan Asylum, Okayama, Japan.

He shall be staitened e'en while full of wealth;
All kinds of trouble shall upon him come.

1898 Rev. George Hanbury Fielding. *The Book of Job*. London: Elliot Stock.

In the fulness of his sufficiency he shall be in straits;
The hand of everyone that is in misery shall come upon him.

1898 Ferrar Fenton [assisted by Henrik Borgstrom]. *The Book of Job. Translated Direct from the Hebrew Texts into English*. London: Elliot Stock.

He has fear in amassing his hoard
That the hand of distress may approach.

INDEX

A

Abbott, Geroge · 50·
Abbott, George· 51· 58· 119· 227
Achilles · 49· 71
Aelfric 2· 4· 27· 28· 120· 224
Aeschines · 32
Aeschylus 80· 112
Allen, William 31
American Standard Version 2· 3· 110· 119· 120
Aquinas, Thomas 12· 24· 26· 33· 34· 62· 63· 120
Arnold, Matthew 86· 112· 120· 234
Asher, David 99· 100· 233
Austen, Jane 92
Authorized Version 3· 6· 19· 20· 61· 92· 94· 99· 106· 116· 221· 226

B

Baker, Daniel 72· 119
Barker, Robert · 37· 226
Barnes, Barnes 233
Barnstone, Willis 4· 32· 34·
Batalion, Eli 1
Becke, Edmund · 30
Bellamy, Daniel 72· 91· 229· 232
Bellamy, John 238
Ben-Lakish, Simeon 12
Benisch, Abraham 92· 99· 100· 235
Benson, Henrietta Emily 98[8]
Beowulf 10
Beresford, Bruce 1· 128
Bernard, Valentine Lumley 89· · 239
Besserman, Lawrence · 33· 120
Beza, Theodore · 43· 45· 120· 222· 226
Bigger 2
Bildad 11· 13· 14· 56· 105· 141· 164· 178
Birch, Mrs. Walter 90· 94· 233
Bishops Bible · 141· 225
Blackmore, Richard 12· 68· 69· 70· 71· 72· 72· 82· 83· 106· 119· 120· 161· 222· 228
Bloch, Ariel and Chana 3· 120
Bolton, H. · 182· 222· 234· 236
Brenton, Lancelot 101· 233
Brett, Aurthur 12· 38· 53· 54· 55· 117· 118· 119· 121· 154· 228
Bristow, Richard · 30· 226
Broughton 4· 3, Hugh 7· 43· 44· 51· 54· 58· 119· 121· 131· 145· 226
Brown, John (Self Interpreting Bible) 65 86 130
Brown, John (Swan Song) 42 130
Browning, Robert 12· 26· 112
Budinger, M. 99· 233
Bunyan, John 5· 121

C

Calvin, John · 24· 33· 33· 38· 42· 43· 45· 57· 58· 121· 127
Carey, Carteret Priaulx 100· 234
Carlyle, Thomas 2· 9· 85· 86· 121
Carpenter, William 89· 231
Cartwright, Thomas · 43
Cary, Otis 109· 212· 239
Caxton, William · 28· 29· 224· 225·
Cecil White 108· 237
Challoner, Richard 5· 31· 35· 52· 77· 78· 131· 144· 226· 229
Challoner, Robert 5· 31· 77· 229
Chapman, George 5· 22· 23· 67· 121·
Chappelow, Leonard 229
Charles I · 38· 39· 52
Charles II · 38· 39· 41· 53· 117
Chaucer, Geoffrey 2· 27· 121
Cheke, John · 34· 113· 121
Chesterton, Gilbert Keith 118· 119· 121

Christopher Smart 85
Chubb 65
Cibber, Theophilus 82· 121
Cicero · 20· 23· 27· 32· 121
Clarke, Henry James 107· 108· 111· 129· 195· 222· 237· 238
Coleman, John Noble · 183· 236
Collier, Jeremy 69· 121
Complutum, Text · 35
Coverdale, Myles · 29· 30· 125· 135· 225
Cowles, Henry 236
Cowley, Abraham 66
Cranford, James · 51· 124
Cranmer, Tholmas · 30· 225
Croly, George · 25· 26· 122
Crump, Henry · 35
Crutwell, Richard 92· 231
Curll, Edmund 67

D

Dante 86· 127
Darby, John Nelson 238
Darlow, T.H. · 34· 122· 124
Davidson, A.B. 235
Davie, James 96· 238
Demosthenes · 32
Denham, John · 22· 23· 24· 66· 67· 68· 122
Derham, John 63· 81· 122
Devens, Richard 88· 89· 231
de Voragine · 29· 225
Dillon, Emile Joseph 117· 239
Dolet, Esienne 65· 122
Donne, John 2· 9· 91· 122
Douai (Doway) 3· 4· 5· 27· 30· 77· 84· 131· 142· 226
Dowglass, Thomas 12· 122
Dryden, John · 22· 23· 33· 46· 48· 49· 62· 65· 66· 67· 68· 69· 82· 83· 122· 123· 126· 127· 129
Du Bartas, Guillaume · 45· 128
Duvall, Robert 1

E

Earl of Winchilsea 4· 12· 113· 4· 12· 113· 179· 235· 179· 235
Edwards, John 10· 25· 122
Einstein, Albert 13
Elihu 11· 103· 14· 34· 48· 56· 97· 106· 191· 195· 197· 198· 229· 237
Eliphaz 13· 14· 40· 44· 45· 51· 113· 114· 157· 159· 173· 179
Elzas, A. 99· 236
Erasmus, Desiderius · 29· 90· 122· 129
Erskine, Ralph 78· 79· 113· 230
Eugenio 76· 229
Evans 4· 122
Ewald, Georg Heinrich august von 238
Ezekiel 11

F

Fagles, Robert 5
Fanshawe, Richard · 23· 24· 66· 122
Fenton, Farrar 3· 122· 215· 222· 239
Fielding, Henry 2· 65· 123· 239
Fitzgerald, Edward 86· 123
Fleming, Richard · 28· 35
Fox, Everett 3, 123
Fox, Sarah Hustler 101 245
Frost 1· 12· 33· 122· 123· 232
Fry, John · 169· 232

G

Garden, Charles 91· 124· 126· 159· 222· 231
Garnett, John 12· 65· 123
Gauden, John · 57· 123
Gell, Robert · 37· 123
Geneva Bible · 27· 30· 31· 34· 35· 37· 44· 35· 140· 222· 225
Genung, John F. 12· 112· 119· 238
George Hanbury Fielding 239
Gibbons · 200· 238
Gilbert, George H. 103· 104· 109· 118· 121· 210· 238
Gilby, Anothony · 30· 225
Golding, Arthur · 42· 121
Goldsmith, Oliver 62· 123
Goldstein,, Laurence 85· 123
Gollancz, Hermann 92· 100· 237
Good, John Mason 97 243

Goodspeed, Edgar 3· 123
Gotham, Hrvey 1
Gray, John Hamilton · 177· 222· 232
Gary, Richard 132
Great Bible · 30· 138· 222· 225· 226
Greenslade, S.L. · 34· 122· 123
Gregory the Great · 30· 226
Gregory VI · 28
Grove, Henry 69 131
Guarini, Baptista · 23
Gutiérrez, Gustavo 2· 123

H

Haak, Theodore 227
Halsted, Oliver Spencer 103· 111· 236
Handel 85· 124
Hannibal 122
Hardy, Nathaniel 42 133
Hare, Francis 13
Harriss, Charles · 40· 124
Heath, Thomas 6· 86· 90· 91· 92· 164· 230
Heinlein, Robert 2· 124
Henry Grove 65
Henry VIII · 29· 30
Herbert, A.S. 35 131
Hervey, James 75· 124
Hobbes, Thomas · 45· 63· 124
Hodge, Walter 229
Holden, Lawrence 87· 230
Homer 5· 10· 21· 22· 46· 49· 67· 86· 120· 121· 126· 128
Hooke, William · 40· 124
Horace · 20· 23· 27· 48· 58· 66· 124· 129
Hunt, George 91· 129· 175· 232· 234
Husbands, John 229
Hutcheson, George · 59· 124

I

Ibn Ezra, Abraham 9

J

Jackson, Arthur · 24· 124·
James I, 5· 31
James II · 19· 38· 41· 56· 62
Jameson, Fredrick 2
Jesus · 39· 51· 52· 98· 236
Johnson, Samuel 71 78 175
Jonson, Ben · 35
Judas · 20
Jung, Carl 2· 119· 124

K

Kallen, Horace Meyer 12· 124
Kelly, william · 193· 234· 237
Kenrick, Francis Patrick · 31· 77· 101· 234
King James Bible, 2
Kipling, Rudyard · 35· 124
Knox, John 3· 84· 124· 126
Kohler, Kaufmann 102· 239
Kokoschka, Oskar 2
Kushner, Harold 13

L

Lamb, Jonathan 82· 83· 125
Langhorne, William 88· 166· 230
Lee, Samuel · 47· 91· 101· 128· 233
Leeser, Issac 6· 92· 99· 178· 234
Lightfoot, John · 37· 125
Lillie, James 234
Lloyd, William 61· 125
Longfellow, Henry Wadsworth · 125
Lowth, Robert 62· 79· 80· 81· 82· 84· 86· 94· 125
Lucifer · 45
Luther, Martin 4· 22· 24· 26· 29· 33· 43· 54· 125

M

M'Even, William 232
Macaulay, Thomas Babington 62· 63· 81· 125
Macclesfield, Baron 83
MacGregor, Geddes · 34· 125
MacLeish, Archibald 1· 119· 125
Maimonides · 33
Malet, Arthur 107· 108· 111· 237
Mandeville, Bernard 63· 125
Manley, Thomas · 38· 52· 53· 54 125· 152·

227
Marsh, Richard 61· 125
Marten, Gregory 12· 117· 118· 119· 191· 236
Matthew, Thomas · 31· 34· 225
Medley, John 103· 237
Meikle, William 114· 117· 186· 236
Miller, William 97
Milton, John 2· 12· 2· 12· 42· 48· 57· 62· 73· 74· 125· 229· 42· 48· 57· 62· 73· 74· 125· 229
Moffatt, James · 126
More, Hannah 93 134
More, Thomas 29
Morris,William 86
Moses 3· 34· 64· 69· 102· 123· 129
Moule, J.F. · 34· 122· 124
Moulton, William F. · 34· 126

N

Nicholas of Hereford · 28
Nixon, Richard 2
Norton, David 4· 31· 34· 123· 126
Noyes, Georges 232

O

Odysseus 71
Origen · 21
Orton, Job 87· 231
Ovid · 49· 66· 122· 127

P

Pammachius · 20
Parker, Matthew · 30· 83· 123· 226· 231
Partridge, A.C. · 34· 122· 126
Patriarch of Alexandria 110
Patrick, Simon · 31· 38· 41· 55· 56· 61· 77· 101· 126· 157· 228· 234
Penchanskym, David 2· 126
Pety Job · 27· 28· 34· 224
Pindar 66
Pitt, Chistopher 231
Plato · 49
Pollard, A.W. · 34· 126
Prince Rupert · 50
Prometheus 5· 112· 113
Ptolemy Philadelphus · 35
Purver, Anthony 91· 167· 222· 230
Purvey, John · 27· 28· 126· 134· 224

Q

Quarles, Francis · 45· 46· 47· 48· 49· 87· 119· 58· 127· 149· 227
Queen Elizabeth · 31· 43
Queen Mary · 30
Quiller-Couch, Arthur 14· 127

R

R. H. · 48· 49· 227
R. P. 70· 72· 78· 228
Ray, John Mead 243
Raymond, Rossiter 117· 188· 236
Renan, Ernst · 200· 238
Revised Standard Version 3· 10· 126· 127
Revised Version 2· 10· 91· 109· 110· 111· 117· 119· 238
Richard of Hampole · 34· 224
Richardson, Samuel 62· 67· 127· 230
Richelieu, Cardinal · 51
Rider, Henry · 56· 57· 127
Rodwell, J.M. · 180· 235
Rogers, John · 29· 30· 127· 128· 136· 225· 236
Rosenberg, David 3· 127
Rossetti, Donie Gabriel 86· 127
Rowe, Elizabeth 80
Rowley, Abraham. 232

S

Sadler, Ralph 141 227 250
Safire, William 2· 127
Saibil, Jerome 1
Saintsbury, George · 33· 127
Sampson, Thomas · 30· 81· 124· 125· 225
Samuel W. 237

Sandys, George ·45·49·50·53·54·127·
150·227
Sarah Hustler Fox 95·233
Satan 11·13·33·41·48·50·64·65·87·89
Sawyer, Leicester Ambrose 235
Scattergood, Samuel ·40·127
Schleirmacher, Friedrich ·32·127
Schreiner, Susan ·33·57·58·127
Scott, Walter ·33·127·
Senault, Jean Francois ·51·222·227
Seneca
Shakespeare, William ·35·121
Sharpe, Samuel 98·235
Shaw, T.E 5
Shelley, Percy ·5·26·120·127
Sherlock, William 62·63·81·82·127
Socrates
Spark, Muriel 1·119·128
Spence, Joseph 13·61·128
Spurrell, Helen 97·98·238
St. Jerome 4·12·20·24·35
Stanton, Elizabeth Cady 97·128
Stather, W.C. 105·234
Steiner, George 5·5·32·33·128
Stillingfleet, Edward ·41·128
Stock, Joseph 91·92·93·123·231·239
Sumner, Charles
Sydenstricker, Hiram Mason 115·116·
117·238
Sylvester, Joshua ·45·46·49·128·148·
222·58·226

T

Talmid 111·238
Tanakh 3·128
Tattam, Henry 101·131·176·233
Tattersall, John 101·117·239
Tennyson, Alfred 5
Theodore of Mopsuestia 12
Thomson, William M. ·232·238
Thomson Charles 101·121·131·135
Thuesen, Peter 4·128
Tillotson, John 61·126·128
Tindal, Matthew 63·65·128
Trapp, John ·59·128
Tur Sinai, Naphali Henry 9
Tyndale, William ·19·28·29·30·34·129
Tytler, Alexander Fraser ·32·33·65·67·
85·129

U

Ussher, James ·47·58·61·129

V

Van Dyck, Cornelius 101·237
Venuti, Lawrence ·32
Vespasian ·47
Virgil ·23·49·66·122
von Nettesheim, Heinrich Cornelius
Agrippa ·58·120·58·120
von Schlegel, August Wilhelm 86

W

Walls, Alfred 108·129
Warburton, William 6·12·14·34·62·64·
65·79·80·82·86·90·123·129
Watson, John Selby 87·88·118·129·235
Watts, Issac 78·113·129
Webster, Noah 6·232
Weinbrot, Howard 85·129
Wellbeloved, Charles 233
Wells, Edward 1·72·129·229
Wemyss, Thomas 12·112·173·233
Wesley, John ·35
Weymouth, Richard Francis 3·129
Wheatly, Charles 81·129
Whittington, William ·30·225
Wiesel, Elie 2·129
William Allen ·30
William and Mary ·38·41·62
William Clark 228
Williams 7·235·238
William Thompson 74·78·131·213·229
Wolfers, David ·34·129
Wright, G.H. Bateson 1·105·123·129·
198·222·238
Wright, Richard 2 138
Wycliffe, John 6·19·27·28·34·224

Y

Young, Edward 67, 68, 73, 74, 75, 76, 83, 88,
Young, Robert 102, 104, 107, 111, 117, 119, 127, 129, 229, 235

Z

Zophar 11, 13, 14, 55, 94, 84, 148, 167, 169, 221